Character Education in America's Blue Ribbon Schools

Best Practices for Meeting the Challenge

Second Edition

Madonna M. Murphy

A SCARECROWEDUCATION BOOK

The Scarecrow Press, Inc.
Lanham, Maryland, and Oxford
2002

A SCARECROWEDUCATION BOOK

Published in the United States of America
by Scarecrow Press, Inc.
A Member of the Rowman & Littlefield Publishing Group
4720 Boston Way, Lanham, Maryland 20706
www.scarecrowpress.com

PO Box 317
Oxford
OX2 9RU, UK

British Library Cataloguing in Publication Information Available

Library of Congress Cataloging-in-Publication Data

Murphy, Madonna M.
    Character education in America's blue ribbon schools : best practices for meeting the challenge / Madonna M. Murphy.— 2nd ed.
        p. cm
"A ScarecrowEducation book."
Includes bibliographical references and index.
    ISBN 0-8108-4312-9 (alk. paper) —ISBN 0-8108-4313-7 (pbk. : alk. paper)
    1. Moral education—United States. 2. Character—Study and teaching—United States. 3. Values—Study and teaching—United States
I. Title.
    LC311 .M87 2002
    370.11'4—dc21
                                                          2002005560

♾™ The paper used in this publication meets the minimum requirements of American National Standard for Information Sciences—Permanence of Paper for Printed Library Materials, ANSI/NISO Z39.48-1992.
Manufactured in the United States of America.

To my mother, Dorothy Murphy,
the Blue Ribbon teacher in my life.

To Tom Lickona,
America's Blue Ribbon character educator.

To my brother, Bill Murphy,
Your courage and character as you fought cancer
inspired me as I wrote this second edition.

Contents

.

Figures

Tables

Foreword

Item: In a recent survey reported by the *Boston Globe,* more than half of the ninth-graders in an affluent suburb said they saw nothing wrong with stealing a compact disc or keeping money found in a lost wallet.

Item: 50 percent of U.S. high school seniors say they are currently sexually active; half of them say they have had four or more partners. The United States has the highest teen pregnancy rate and teen abortion rate in the industrialized world, according to the federal government's 1995 National Survey of Family Growth.

Item: Among leading industrialized nations, the United States has by far the highest murder rate for fifteen- to twenty-four-year-old males—seven times higher than Canada's and forty times higher than Japan's.

Reports like these give us pause. Children hold up a mirror to society: in it, we see ourselves. Disturbed by that image, increasing numbers of schools and their communities are coming together to return American schooling to its most important historical mission: the formation of good character.

The premise of character education is straightforward: Uncivil, irresponsible, and destructive youth behaviors such as disrespect, dishonesty, violence, drug abuse, sexual promiscuity, and a poor work ethic have a common core, namely, the absence of good character. Character education, unlike piecemeal reforms, offers the hope of improvement in all these areas. It reminds us that we shouldn't wait for kids to do something wrong before teaching them what is right. It invokes the wisdom expressed in Donald DeMarco's book, *The Heart of Virtue* "Trying to become virtuous merely by excluding vice is as unrealistic as trying to cultivate roses simply by excluding weeds."

In response to the moral crisis of our culture, character education has become what is perhaps the fastest growing educational movement in the country today. The 1990s saw a spate of books on the subject: the emergence of three national organizations—the Character Education Partnership, the Character Counts

Coalition, and the Communitarian Network—dedicated to promoting character education; federal funding of character education projects; four White House Conferences on Character-Building for a Democratic and Civil Society; state mandates requiring that schools spend time on character education projects, the creation of university-based centers and training programs in character education; and grassroots initiatives by schools that are reportedly having a positive impact on school climate and student behavior.

Madonna Murphy's book, *Character Education in America's Blue Ribbon Schools,* is a major contribution to the growing literature on character education. It will, I believe, be of great value to both college educators and school practitioners. I plan to use it in my own graduate course on character education and to recommend it to the schools working with our College's Center for the 4th and 5th Rs. Her book shows how character education was central to the mission of early American schools, why it declined in this century, and how its renewal has been spurred by the U.S. Department of Education's Blue Ribbon Awards program. It offers a rich compendium of character education practices drawn from more than 150 Blue Ribbon winners all across America—schools large and small, affluent and poor, homogeneous and diverse. It distills these many practices into seven that seem to represent the "best practice" of character-building schools. It provides conceptual criteria to help the reader understand why not every values-related practice in a Blue Ribbon School necessarily qualifies as true character education. Throughout the book, we are told where to get more information about the programs cited so we can judge them for ourselves. For all these reasons, Madonna Murphy's book provides, in my judgment, the most complete and detailed picture available of what is happening in character education today.

As character education has mushroomed into a movement, skeptics and critics have emerged to raise challenges. Does character education develop better people including people capable of critical moral judgment, or does it merely train students to do what they're told? Does it develop students' intrinsic motivation to be good or undermine it through reliance on external incentives? Is there research on the effectiveness of character education practices, and, if so, what does it show? Is character education something a school can evaluate? To questions like these, Dr. Murphy's book offers thoughtful answers that should elevate the level of national debate.

"The character education movement is a mile wide and an inch deep," said a skeptical middle school principal recently. "Everybody's talking about it, but nobody really knows what it is." *Character Education in America's Blue Ribbon Schools* makes it clear that "character education" is not one thing but many; that not all schools define it in the same way; and that not all approaches are equally sound. But contrary to what the middle school principal says, anyone interested in character education has a significant knowledge base to build on. And we are all indebted to Madonna Murphy's book for expanding that knowledge base in important ways.

Tom Lickona

Author, *Educating for Character*

Director, Center for the 4th & 5th Rs, State University of New York, Cortland

Preface

I was first introduced to Aristotle while in college at the University of Chicago. The study of his *Nicomachean Ethics* gave me the moral anchor I needed in order to realize that what my classmates were doing was not good nor right, even if they were of a different religion than my own. Aristotle reaffirmed what I learned from my parents. Moral values do exist and they transcend religious, cultural, and social differences.

I began to teach philosophy, ethics, and character education in the 1980s while at Lexington College. These students were preparing for careers in the business world and they came into my course imbued with relativism and very little background in the area of ethics and moral virtues. Through the course curriculum, I tried to teach the students key virtues that were desirable for them to develop in their chosen field while teaching them the philosophic principles required for ethical decision making and moral integrity in business endeavors.

Since 1990, I have been teaching philosophy of education, ethics, and character education to undergraduates and graduate students preparing to be teachers in public schools. These students also lack an understanding of the difference between personal values and moral values. However, in this situation, the challenge is not only to teach these students character education, but also to teach them in such a way that they will then be able to teach others. These future teachers need to be able to develop the character of young students through the elementary and secondary curriculum.

My experience in the 1970s as a Chicago public school teacher and my volunteer work at the Metro Achievement Center in Chicago in the 1980s put me in close contact with elementary school, middle school and high school students from inner-city schools. I saw that if the teacher has high expectations, students can be taught demanding academics and learn to develop their character by meeting these challenges. At Metro, girls from inner-city schools are taught academics and character education in an afternoon and weekend program. Graduates of Metro go on to college and then return to help change their inner-city neighborhoods. These experiences confirmed my convictions: character education can be taught to students and it does make a difference in their lives when they are taught about living a life of virtue.

My professional career took a significant turn in 1990. I graduated with my doctorate in education from Loyola University, met Tom Lickona at a pre-conference workshop of the Association for Moral Education's Annual Meeting, and began my post-doctoral work in values and character education by participating in the Hyde School Research Project.

The Hyde School Research Project was initiated by Lawrence Baer, the parent of a child in a small K–5 public school in Washington, D.C. The purpose of the Hyde School Research Project was to establish a national model of an elementary school based on a composite of the best examples from elementary schools that had been recognized through the U.S. Department of Education's School Recognition Program.

In July of 1990, Mr. Baer invited me to participate in the Hyde School Research Project with a group of eight other researchers from across the nation. The research group consisted of three Ph.D.'s, two doctoral candidates, three graduate students, and one college student. After five weeks of intensive work together and one year of correspondence from our respective cities, the research was completed. It soon became clear to the group that a "national model" of an elementary school was not emerging but that many models of different exemplary practices were emerging. This research was presented by the group at the American Educational Research Association's Annual Conference in San Francisco on April 18, 1992. In addition, individual members of the group have made presentations and published articles on the area(s) which they had researched (Kleitzen, 1993; Murphy 1991, 1995a, 1995b, 1995c, 1996, 1998a, 1998b, 1998c, 2001).

Although the original plan was to publish a book summarizing each of the researchers' findings in the areas they reviewed, the final decision was for each to publish their own area of investigation. I therefore returned to Washington, D.C., in 1994 to update my data, adding information from the applications of the 1991–1992 and 1993–1994 award winning schools. During 1995 and 1996, I visited a stratified sample of these schools. The first edition of this book, *Character Education in America's Blue Ribbon Schools* was the result of six years of research. It attempted to present a framework in which to understand the philosophic foundations of character education and to give a plethora of teaching ideas to help those who wish to teach character education in their classes. The book was well received and favorably reviewed (Cunningham, 1999).

In 1999, I returned to the U.S. Department of Education, to present my idea for a second edition of the book to Stephen O'Brien, the Team Leader of the Recognition Program. With his assistance, I was able to include the 1996–1997,

1998–1999 and 2000–2001 award-winning schools in the second edition. It is especially interesting to see that, in the past five years, character education has become a part of many schools' curricula. In fact, the 1998–1999 award year gave special honors for schools with impressive character education programs. It is my hope that this second edition will assist teachers, administrators, and teachers-in-training as they promote character education in schools of the twenty-first century.

Acknowledgments

I wish to thank Dr. Robert Hansen of National Professional Resources, Inc. for his enthusiastic support and promotion of the first edition of this book and for suggesting that I update it with the most recent award-winning schools for a second edition. The first edition owed its existence to Dr. Joseph Eckenrode at Technomic Publishing Company, who so positively responded to my first book proposal. The second edition owes its existence to Dr. Thomas Koerner, Cindy Tursman, and Kate Kelly at ScarecrowEducation/Rowman & Littlefield Publishing Group.

I would also like to thank the following people:

- J. Steven O'Brien, Kathryn Crossley, Louise Weber, Diane Jones, and Jean Narayanan from the U.S. Department of Education for facilitating the original and subsequent research on the U.S. Department of Education's Blue Ribbon School.
- Lawrence Baer for initiating the Hyde School Research Project and Sharon Kletzien for serving as the coordinator of the Hyde School Research Project.
- The Teaching and Professional Growth Committee at the University of St. Francis for the faculty scholarships in spring of 1996 and spring of 2001 and for the summer minigrant in 2001 which allowed me to work on the manuscript, the second edition, and the qualitative research conducted by visiting the schools.
- all my faculty colleagues at the University of St. Francis and Dorothy Murphy and Mary Ann Tyrny for their endless encouragement and support as I wrote the first and second editions of this book.
- Pat Joho, Debbie Davis, Casey Meeks, and Arlene Packley at the University of St. Francis for their assistance.
- Dorothy Murphy for typing the index.

- Richard Kloser and Joan Koran at the University of St. Francis and Eileen Sheu and Karen Bettinardi for their research assistance.
- Sharon Banas, Thomas Lickona, Joy Reiner, and Lori Wiley for their helpful comments and editing of the manuscript.

Finally, a very special thank you is extended to Tom Lickona for his very careful reading of this manuscript, his extensive editorial comments, and for his very insightful additions to this book.

Introduction

"I challenge all our schools to teach character education, to teach good values and to teach good citizenship" the president told the nation on January 23, 1996, during his State of the Union Address. He thus focused national attention on one of the fastest growing needs in public education. School principals might ask where they can find examples of schools that are teaching good values and good citizenship successfully to students. The president would refer these administrators to the Blue Ribbon Schools, the schools that have won the National Award for Excellence. For, in the words of the president, "The winners of the Blue Ribbon Awards . . . represent what is best in American education. These are schools producing world-class results by any rigorous measure. The challenge for us . . . is to figure out how to replicate them" (Clinton 1993). In the 1997 State of the Union Address this challenge was reiterated: "Character education must be taught in our schools. We must teach students to be good citizens . . ." (Clinton 1997).

Character Education in America's Blue Ribbon Schools is based on descriptive, documentary, and qualitative research conducted on the award-winning school applications in the U.S. Department of Education's Elementary School Recognition Program. William Bennett, secretary of education, began the "Blue Ribbon Award Program" in 1985. The program was modeled after its successful predecessor, the Secondary School Recognition Program that began three years previously as a positive response to the accusations made in the report "A Nation at Risk." Its purpose was to identify and give public recognition to outstanding public and private elementary schools across the United States. It focused national attention on schools that were doing an exceptional job with all of their students in developing a solid foundation of

1

basic skills and knowledge of subject matter and *fostering the development of character, values, and ethical judgement.*

Every other year, elementary and middle schools participate in the award program. The first edition of this book reported on the first decade of the Elementary School Recognition Program, from 1985 to 1994. The second edition adds the schools that have won the award from 1996 to 2001. The total number of elementary schools that have won the Blue Ribbon Award during this period is 2,017. Table 1 shows the number of schools recognized in each award year.

This book provides a historical and descriptive study of the Character Education programs found in the Blue Ribbon Schools from 1985 to 2001. A random sample of 500 applications was chosen from the total data base of 2,017 school reports that made up the eight years of the recognition program for elementary/middle schools, covering the sixteen year period from 1985 to 2001. The data were qualitatively validated through personal visits to these schools from 1994 to 1996 and again in 1999 to 2001. The programs mentioned in these "award-winning" schools that referred in any way to character development and fostering good behavior in students have been identified and categorized. Close attention was given in particular to the answers found in the section of the applications referring to "student environment," however the whole application form was studied.

Categories emerged through the analysis of the answers to these questions. These categories show the many different ways in which schools can promote character development. They showed that the majority of the schools use some kind of curricular program or unit of study to promote character development, however they also show the importance of a school-wide effort to promote character in all that the school does. An important consideration for national recognition is the school's success in furthering the intellectual, social, and *moral* growth of all its students. In fact, all schools selected as Blue Ribbon Schools must show evidence ". . . *that school policies, programs and practices foster the development of sound character, a sense of self-worth, democratic values, ethical judge-*

**Table 1.   Number of Blue Ribbon
Elementary Schools 1985–2001**

1985–86	212 Schools
1986–87	287 Schools
1989–90	221 Schools
1991–92	228 Schools
1993–94	276 Schools
1996–97	263 Schools
1998–99	266 Schools
2000–01	264 Schools
TOTAL	2017 SCHOOLS

ment, and self-discipline" in some way. This book reports on how these schools say that they do this, and also attempts to assess the effectiveness of the programs mentioned by these schools.

Percentages of responses quoted throughout the book will refer to the answers given by the schools to the questions asked on the application form. Quotes from schools are from direct conversations with the principal, teachers, and/or counselors when the school was visited and/or are taken directly from the school's application to the U.S. Department of Education School Recognition Program.

It should be noted however, that the existence of a particular program in a Blue Ribbon School does not necessarily mean that this is a "Blue Ribbon Character Education Program." Whenever research data was available, it has been presented in an attempt to evaluate the desirability and effectiveness of the programs in the particular Blue Ribbon Schools. As often as possible, complete information on the different programs and methods has been given so that the readers will have as much information as possible if they want to start a program.

The demographics of the random sample accurately represent the general Blue Ribbon School demographics. In particular, these schools are from all fifty states, including the District of Columbia, with the largest percentage of award-winning schools coming from the states of California (8%), Texas (8%), New York (6%), Ohio (5%), and Illinois (4%). With the exception of Ohio, this corresponds directly to the states with the largest population and therefore the greater number of schools. Public and private schools can participate in this award program and 84 percent of the winners in this sample were public schools, whereas 16 percent were private.

Fifteen percent of the schools were from large central cities, 14 percent from medium cities, 13 percent from towns, and 11 percent from rural areas with the majority (46%) of the award-winning schools coming from suburban locations. The socio-economic status of the students in the schools was measured by the number of the students in the school who qualified for free lunch. Eleven percent of the schools could be characterized as having more than half of their students from lower-income families, and 18 percent have 25–50 percent of their students from lower-income families. Racial and ethnic diversity of the Blue Ribbon School bodies was commonly a little more than 10 percent ethnically diverse; however, 25 percent of the schools had student bodies that were 20–60 percent ethnic minorities. In the descriptions of each school cited in the book, the former will be referred to as ethnically diverse, the latter will be referred to as a heterogeneous populations, an integrated school or a very diverse student body. Schools with less than 10 percent of the population from diverse backgrounds will be referred to as homogeneous student bodies.

The most common school organization in the Blue Ribbon Schools is K–5 found in 63 percent of the schools, with 15 percent of the schools having the common private-school K–8 organization. The organization of the schools cited in this book will be assumed to be K–5, unless otherwise noted. Variations of middle school configurations where found in 7% of the schools. A little under half (47%) of the schools had a student body of 500–750 students, and 37% of the schools had between 250 and 500 students. Schools falling in the first category will be referred to in the book as a large school, the latter as a small school and over 750 students will be referred to as a very large school. Seventy-seven percent of the schools had between 26 and 55 full-time staff members for their students. These statistics show that although almost half of the schools are suburban, middle- to upper-class, and not ethnically diverse; there are inner-city, poor-socio-economic status schools and ethnically-diverse schools among the Blue Ribbon Award-winning schools. Wherever possible, the success stories of these inner-city schools in teaching character education will be highlighted in this book.

For each of the Blue Ribbon Schools in the sample, the school application report and the U.S. Department of Education site visits report were read noting the programs mentioned in these applications that referred in any way to character development and fostering good behavior in students. The highlights of the notes were grouped into categories. Close attention was given in particular to the answers found in the applications referring to "student environment." (A sample application form can be found at www.ed.gov/offices/OERI/BlueRibbonSchools/materials. html.) Particular note was made of the answers to the following questions:

> *D2 What specific programs, procedures, or instructional strategies do you employ to develop students' interest in learning and to motivate them to study?*
> *D6 What is your school's discipline policy?*
> *D7 By what means does the school prevent the sale, possession, and use of drugs, including alcohol and tobacco, by it students on and off school premises?*
> *D9 How do school programs, practices, policies, and staff foster the development of sound character, democratic values, ethical judgment, good behavior, and the ability to work in a self-disciplined and purposeful manner?* In 1987–1988, this question became *"What are your schools' expectations in the area of character development, and how are these expectations communicated? What in the school contributes to the development of the attributes of sound character, such as a sense of fair play, a concern for others, a commitment to truthful and virtuous behavior, and the availability and willingness to assume responsibility for one's own behavior? How do school policies, programs, and practices foster the development of a child's self-discipline and self-confidence?"*

beginning in 1991–1992 this question was added.

> *D11 How is your school preparing students to live effectively in a society that is culturally and ethnically diverse, and in an economy that is globally competitive?*

Beginning in 1996–1997, the wording had changed on the application and the following questions were found:

B4 *Education serves a variety of important social, political, and economic functions. How does your curriculum foster your students' personal and intellectual growth, develop responsible citizens, and prepare them for further education and the world of work?*

D2 *How does the climate of your school reflect its mission, foster a sense of community and respect for diversity, and provide an atmosphere that is purposeful, conducive to learning, respectful of diversity and open to change?*

D3 *How does your school ensure order, safety, and develop a disciplined environment conducive to learning?*

D4 *"By what means does the school prevent the sale, possession, and use of drugs, including alcohol and tobacco, by its students on and off school premises and convey a clear "no-use" message?*

In 1989–1999, schools could apply for special honors in character education by answering the following questions in an addendum to the application. (Each year there is a different "special emphasis" category for honors, i.e. technology, arts education, special education, school safety, and professional development. In 1998–1999, it was character education.)

J2 *What is the school's philosophy on character education? How does the school incorporate and demonstrate the importance of family involvement in character education? What types of staff development are provided to encourage all staff to incorporate the core ethical values into school activities? How does the school assess the understanding and commitment to core ethical values of both staff and students?*

Responses given to these questions were noted, with significant quotes when appropriate. Frequencies of responses were tabulated using the computer program, "The Statistical Package for the Social Studies" (SPSS). Categories emerged through the statistical analysis of the answers to the questions that showed the many different ways in which schools can promote character development. A stratified sample of these schools was then visited in order to garner further information on their character education programs. Schools were chosen to be visited if their answers to the questions in section D were significant; some elaborated on specific programs that seemed to be effective in promoting character education and others proposed more creative, unique, or innovative ways of promoting character in their schools. In total, twenty schools were visited from nine different states (California, Illinois, Indiana, Maryland, Minnesota, Missouri, New York, Ohio, and Texas). The content of this book has been selected from the most interesting examples and programs found in the

Blue Ribbon School applications. In total, 150 schools have been cited. The Blue Ribbon Schools speak for themselves through direct quotes taken from the applications and from the teachers, administrators, and counselors visited at the schools.

The chapters of the book are organized around the categories that emerged from the statistical analysis of the responses given by schools to the different questions in the application which refer to student environment and address the various types of programs mentioned for promoting character, and ethical and moral development. The tables found in each chapter represent a tabulation of the methods and programs reported by the schools in their application form under the different question headings. These frequencies can be seen as indicators of promising practices (Isaac and Michael, 1984), but should not be considered as statistically significant nor rigorously valid, as they are the result of self-reporting by the applicants. Some applicants may have omitted some of the ways in which they promote character in their school because either: (1) they do these things on a school-wide basis as effective teaching and did not consider them as character education, or (2) they did not consider these activities as a valid answer to the question. For example, it will be seen that only a small percentage of the schools report that their Scouting program helps promote the formation of good character in their students; however, visits to the schools revealed that almost every school has a Scouting program. Principals interviewed explained that they did not include this as part of their answer, because the Scouting program is not *sponsored* by the school, but uses the school facilities for their meetings.

The backbone of the book is therefore the result of descriptive, documentary, and qualitative research of the award-winning school applications in the United States Department of Education's Elementary School Recognition Program and as such this can be considered a research report. The purpose of this research however, is practical and applied. It can be considered "action" research as it seeks to find out what the best schools in America are doing to teach character education in order to allow others to use this information and these ideas to start programs "that work" in their schools. Each chapter is thus written for two different audiences. It begins with a report of the research findings, it analyzes their validity, and it then synthesizes the best ideas for possible implementation by school practitioners. The premise is to use the emerging theoretical research findings on character education programs to inform practices. In addition, when available, research reports on the effectiveness these various programs have been cited in order to provide the reader with further criteria to weigh while deciding whether or not to implement a given program.

Chapter 1 provides an introduction to character education with a philosophic explanation of the terms which will be used throughout the book. Chapter 2 provides a brief historical background of character education. Chapter 3 presents the most common answers regarding the programs used found to promote character development. Chapter 4 examines teachers and teaching techniques that promote character development. Chapter 5 highlights the drug education programs used in these schools; chapter 6 focuses on motivation, self-esteem, and guidance programs; chapter 7 shows how discipline programs are used to promote character development; chapter 8 explains citizenship programs in the Blue Ribbon Schools; and chapter 9 focuses on the evaluation of character development programs. There is overlap among these programs; this categorization is not meant to be definitive, but of assistance to those looking for specific programs to meet their schools' needs in character education.

In appendix A, a thorough explanation of the Blue Ribbon Award program is given. The address, telephone number, and contact name for the Blue Ribbon Schools cited in this book can be found at the Blue Ribbon home page: www.ed.gov/offices/OERI/BlueRibbonSchools/sch_honor82.html.

This book attempts to show what the best schools in America are doing to train students in moral values and ethics. Using their own words, it documents the innovations in teaching and learning that they have implemented to foster the development of character. It can be seen as a compendium of programs found within schools that have been designated as among the best in the United States. It is a practical book that will guide school administrators, teachers, parents, board members and concerned citizens interested in having their school implement the president's challenge to teach character education in their schools. This challenge unites our country across political parties and was reiterated in the 2001 State of the Union Address:

> Every child must be taught these principles of what it means to be a citizen. If we do not turn the hearts of children toward knowledge and character, we will lose their faith and undermine their idealism . . . I ask you to be citizens, responsible citizens, building communities of service and a nation of character (Bush, 2001).

1

Can Good Character Be Taught?

Character is what we say and do when no one else is looking. It is not what we have done, but who we are.

—Anonymous

The final forming of a person's character lies in their own hands.

—Anne Frank

Character building begins in our infancy and continues until death.

—Eleanor Roosevelt

CAN VALUES AND VIRTUES BE TAUGHT?

"Can virtue be taught?" Meno asked Socrates over 2000 years ago in the *Meno* dialogue written by Plato. It is a question that is still of great interest today. Can we teach virtues, values, and character to students in today's schools? Some of these young people will be leaders in this twenty-first century. Will they be ethical, moral, and virtuous leaders who promote peace and justice, and show through their actions that they care for others? Or will they be hypocritical leaders who lie, steal, and cheat as long as no one catches them?

This first chapter tries to answer Meno's question regarding the teachability of virtue. The philosophic foundations of character education are explained. Some key terms such as virtues, values, and character are defined in order to clarify the subsequent use of this terminology throughout the book. This chapter concludes with a paradigm that summarizes the main ways in which character education is taught in America's best schools, the Blue Ribbon Schools. Chapter 1 seeks to answer the following questions:

- What are virtues and moral values, and can they be taught in the public schools of America's pluralistic society?
- What is a definition of good character? (Must a school have a character education program in order to be nominated as a Blue Ribbon School?)
- Why are a school's mission statement and school motto important for character development?
- What are the components of the "Blue Ribbon Schools' Comprehensive Model for Character Development"?

What is a Virtue?

Aristotle gives a helpful definition of "virtue" in his work *Nicomachean Ethics*: "Virtue is a state of character concerned with choice, lying in a mean between two vices, one involving excess, the other deficiency . . . with regard to what is best and right" (1107a1–7). He tells us that virtue is of two kinds, intellectual and moral. Intellectual virtue can be taught, while moral virtue comes about as a result of habit. Children need to be taught in order to *know* what virtue is, and then they need to be guided in order to reason well and choose the correct action in a given situation. It is no easy task to be good, according to Aristotle. This is because in everything we need to find the middle road of virtue: "to do this (the good) to the right person, the right extent, at the right time, with the right motive and in the right way is no easy task" (1109a27). According to Aristotle, we must also develop the *desire* and *love* for the good in able to be virtuous. Finally, we must have the opportunity for *action* in order to *live* virtuously. "The moral virtues we get by first exercising them . . . We become just by doing just acts, temperate by doing temperate acts, brave by doing brave acts" (1103b).

Character educators embrace Aristotle's definition of virtues as they define their own work. "Virtue is both the disposition to think, feel and act in morally excellent ways and the exercise of this disposition" (Ryan and Bohlin, 1999). "Virtues are objectively good human qualities . . . Virtues are grounded in human nature and experience; they provide a standard for defining good character" (Lickona, 1998).

Aristotle stresses the importance of developing moral habits from the earliest years. "It makes no small difference, then, whether we form habits of one kind or another from our very youth; it makes a very great difference, or rather all the difference" (1103b11–25). Character educators also agree with Aristotle on this point as they know that by the time children come to school, they are already well on their way in their moral education. Parents are the primary transmitters of virtue to children, and it is they who bear the major responsibility for teaching their child from their word and example what it means to be a moral person

(Devine, 1999; LeGette, 1999; DeRoche and Williams, 1998). Educators today might ask Aristotle, "What values and virtues should schools teach youth given America's pluralistic society?"

Moral Values

Thomas Lickona, author of *Educating for Character, How Our Schools Can Teach Respect and Responsibility* (1991) and director of The Center for the 4th & 5th Rs, defines moral values as "values that tell us what we ought or ought not to do." Among moral values there are two categories: 1) universal—those which have to do with fundamental human worth and dignity and which we have a duty to practice and enforce, and 2) non-universal—values that do not carry universal obligation but to which an individual may feel a serious personal obligation. Tony Devine, vice-president of the International Educational Foundation concurs, explaining that there are four widely recognized philosophic criteria for determining whether a moral value is universal—reversibility, generalizability, goodness, and conscience-compelling (Devine, 2000).

Larry Nucci, author of *Education in the Moral Domain* (2001) and director of The Center for the Study of Moral Development and Character Education, provides a helpful paradigm for understanding the difference between moral and non-moral values. In interviews with young children, he found that they were able to distinguish between those rules or values that are set up merely out of convention such as "not talking in line," and "not eating certain foods for religious reasons" and those values which are of a moral nature and should be followed whether or not there was a convention regarding them such as, "not deliberately hurting another," "not killing another," and "telling the truth" (Nucci, 2001). This distinction is nicely illustrated by an example taken from an interview with a four-year-old girl regarding her perceptions of spontaneously occurring transgressions at her preschool.

Moral Issue

Did you see what happened? *Yes. They were playing and John hit him too hard.* Is that something you are supposed to do or not supposed to do? *Not so hard to hurt.* Is there a rule about that? *Yes.* What if there were no rule about hitting, would it be all right to do then? *No.* Why not? *Because you could get hurt and start to cry.*

Conventional Issue

Did you see what just happened? *Yes. They were noisy.* Is that something you are supposed to or not supposed to do? *Not do.* Is there a rule about that? *Yes. We have to be quiet.* What if there were no rule, would it be all right to do then? *Yes.* Why? *Yes because there is no rule.*

(Nucci, 2001, p. 8)

CAN GOOD CHARACTER BE TAUGHT?

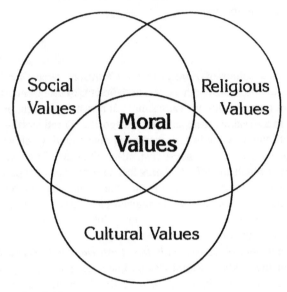

Figure 1.   Domain of Values.

A Venn diagram can perhaps illustrate these domains for us (see figure 1). Among social values, there are those that change—such as, what clothes or jewelry are proper to wear for a man or a woman—and those that never change, for instance, one's obligation to treat others with respect, civility and politeness.

There are cultural values that change, such as whether or not a woman changes her name upon marrying; and those values that do not change, for example, that the education and upbringing of children is primarily the responsibility of the parents.

Likewise, there are personal values that change, such as whether one prefers the color blue or the color yellow; and those that never change, such as ensuring one's word is always truthful.

In addition, there are religious values that change, for instance, whether one should go to church services on Wednesday, Saturday, or Sunday; and those that never change, such as the belief that one should respect the life of another.

Each of these domains intersects with the others in an area called the "moral values"- those values that all human beings should uphold no matter what their culture, society, or religion. These are the core values that define how human beings should or should not act toward themselves and others. These moral values can also be referred to as Aristotle's human virtues, for they are the qualities that define a person's character. Sanford McDonnell (1999), Chairman of the Board of the Character Education Partnership, asserts this: "Virtuous people, people of character, live by high ethical standards."

WHAT IS GOOD CHARACTER?

Character comes from the Greek word "*charakter,*" which means enduring mark. The "charakter" on a coin gave its worth. The "charakter" of a person is considered to be the distinguishing qualities or principles to which the person subscribes as a guide for his or her behavior. Character influences how someone makes decisions, or chooses to act or not to act; it summarizes the general way in which a person deals with others. Aristotle says, "Each man speaks and acts and lives in accordance with his character" (1127a27); the virtue of a man will be "the state of character which makes him good and makes him do his own work well" (1106a23). Aristotle tells us that there are three steps necessary in order to form one's character: "In the first place, he must have knowledge; secondly, he must choose the acts, and choose them for their own sake; and thirdly, his action must proceed from a firm and unchangeable character" (1105a31).

Character educators use Aristotle's tripartite domains as they define character. According to Kevin Ryan and Karen Bohlin (1999), from Boston University and the *Center for the Advancement of Ethics and Character*, "To have good character means to be a person who has the capacity to know the good, love the good and do the good" (p. 5). Gordon Vessels (1998), author of *Character and Community Development: A School Planning and Teacher Training Handbook* defines moral character as: "People with moral character have moral values and feelings (conscience), the ability to reason autonomously, fairly, and sensitively about moral issues (ethical reflection), and the habit of acting in a manner consistent with their moral reasoning and moral feelings (virtue)" (p. 3). Character therefore is a holistic term, concerning the whole person, cognitive, affective, and behavioral. It means to have a good head, good heart, and good hands. "In a person of mature character, the inner self, the heart and conscience, directs the outer person, the body and its behavior" (Devine, 2000).

"Good character," according to the traditional perspective, needs to be taught, modeled and developed in children by the significant adults in their lives. They are directly instructed in virtuous behavior and are given opportunities to live these virtues. The premise of character education is that there are virtues—objectively good human qualities—that should be taught to all. These virtues transcend religious and cultural differences (Traiger, 1995). "Character education" usually involves explicit teaching of what each of these different virtues is, how to distinguish "right" from "wrong," and the provision of examples of virtuous and morally correct behavior through the use of either literature or real-life models (Watson, et al. 1989). Virtues such as honesty, tolerance, respect, hard work, and kindness are taught, modeled, and reinforced by significant adults in children's lives. Students also need opportunities to practice virtuous actions, for as Aristotle pointed out, one becomes virtuous by practicing virtuous actions. In order to promote this aspect of character education, schools need to provide students with opportunities in which they can perform virtuous acts and acts of service for others.

For instance, schools might promote clubs or offer opportunities to volunteer. "Character education means helping students understand, through experience, that what they value matters, and that living these virtues lends meaning and richness to their own lives" (Berreth and Berman, 1997). "Far more important than knowing what is right is caring about what is right and desiring to do what is right" (Devine, 2000).

A Construct for Understanding Good Character

Lickona's model of character development, found in *Educating for Character*, defines good character as a combination of moral knowing, moral feeling, and moral action (Lickona, 1991). I have adapted this model so that good character is the point where all three of these aspects intersect (see figure 2). This is also a useful construct for organizing the many different ways that I found the Blue Ribbon Schools promote character development. First, schools must make an effort to teach specific values and virtues directly so students develop the "moral knowing" of what they should do. This can be done through a mission statement that identifies the virtues and values that a school professes to promote. It can also be accomplished through the use of curricular programs that teach what specific virtues and moral values mean, or by teachers who take advantage of specific "character moments," that is, incidents or situations in school or society that they use as content for a class on moral decision making. Second, through assemblies, school

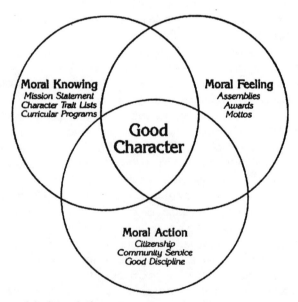

Figure 2. A Model of Good Character

mottoes, awards, and other special programs, schools can instill moral desire in students by encouraging students to *want* to live a life of good character values. This "moral feeling" aspect of character development is the way in which a school motivates students and guides them in the development of a sense of positive self-esteem based on human dignity. Third, schools wishing to foster character must encourage students' "moral actions" through high academic standards, good discipline, citizenship, and community service.

How do the Blue Ribbon Schools Foster the Development of Sound Character?

As stated in the introduction, this book is based on descriptive, documentary, and qualitative research conducted on the award winning school applications in the U.S. Department of Education's Elementary School Recognition Program, also known as the "Blue Ribbon Award Program." A total of 500 applications were chosen from the total database of 2,017 school reports submitted during the eight award years, from 1984 to 2001. Approximately 150 of the applications read had noteworthy character education programs or initiatives and these ideas were included in this book. Ten percent of these schools were personally visited in order to garner further information on their character education programs.

The programs mentioned in these "award winning" schools that referred in any way to character development and fostering good behavior in students were identified and categorized. As noted above in the introduction, close attention was given in particular to the answers found in the section of the applications referring to "student environment," especially the question that asked how the *school programs, practices, and policies foster the development of sound character, democratic values, ethical judgment, good behavior, and the ability to work in a self-disciplined and purposeful manner;* however, the whole application form was studied.

Categories emerged through the statistical analysis of the answers to these questions on the award winning applications (Table 2). These categories show the many different ways in which the schools promote character development. They show that the majority of the schools use some kind of curricular program or unit of study to promote character development; however, they also show the importance of a school-wide effort to promote character in all that the school does. The chapters of this book are organized around the main categories that emerged from the analysis of the responses given by schools to the different questions in the application. Percentages of responses quoted in each chapter refer to the percentage of schools who answered the question in a similar way. Quotes from schools are from direct conversations with the principal, teachers and/or counselors when the school was visited and/or are taken directly from the school's application to the U.S. Department of Education School Recognition Program.

Table 2.   Ways in which Character Education is Promoted in the Blue Ribbon Schools

Category Label	Count	Percentage of Cases
Assemblies, PA Announcements	55	12
Character List/Core values	82	18
Community Service	10	2
Curriculum Programs/Units	172	37
Discipline Plans	50	11
Integrated Throughout	87	19
School Awards, Mottoes	125	27
Staff Models Good Behavior	93	20

Schools may be counted on more than one category, so total percentage may total more than 100.
465 Valid Cases, 30 Missing Cases. This means that 30 of the schools did not report an answer that could be counted in this category.

Good Character As Defined By the Blue Ribbon Schools

Most interesting are the different ways in which the Blue Ribbon Schools defined "the development of sound character" as they sought to answer the questions (Table 3). The most common definition (31%) was "ethics, moral virtues, values, and character development." Recent research (this second edition) shows that more schools understand good character as being synonymous with "good citizenship" (24%). Good character is also understood to be exhibiting the key virtue of "respect"—for oneself and for others. This shows a decided growth in a common understanding of character as having to do with the development of moral virtues. In the first edition, there was more of an emphasis on "good discipline" and "good behavior," only one aspect of good character.

Above we presented a construct for understanding character as "moral knowing, moral feeling and moral doing." It can be seen from the three most common

Table 3.   How Do Blue Ribbon Schools Define "Character"?

Category	Count	Percent
Good Citizenship	85	24
Ethics, Morals, Values, Virtues	113	31
Good Decision Making	10	3
Having Good Discipline, Good Behavior	62	17
Leadership, Doing One's Best, Reach Potential	21	6
Respect for Others and Self	76	21
Responsibility for own actions	45	13
Service to Others	19	5

Total Valid Cases 360, Missing Cases 125

definitions of good character that the Blue Ribbon Schools also understand the three components necessary for good character: knowledge (virtues, ethics), attitude (respect) and action (good citizenship).

The Saddle Rock Elementary School in Great Neck, NewYork, is a school of 500 children with a growing ethnically and linguistically diverse student body. In addition, over 10 percent of the students are emotionally or physically challenged. Their staff tries to define good character succinctly: "Although such qualities as character, citizenship, and democratic values are intangibles, we make a united, concerted effort to make them meaningful for our students. Students learn to accept responsibility in student mediation groups. We help students build character by learning to derive satisfaction from intrinsic rewards."

The Barclay Brook School defines "character" as the "control center of a human life." They realized that in order for it to be developed, it must be consistently modeled and convincingly taught beginning in early childhood. Barclay is a midsize primary school (K–2) located in the small city of Jamesburg, New Jersey.

Good Character defined by a Private School

St. Luke's School, a private Catholic school (PK–8), in suburban Oak Park, Illinois, began its application with a definition of character, one of the two main goals of the school:

"Character" is defined as the inner strength of an individual that expresses itself in appropriate visible behavior. It is the sum of the attitudes and actions of a person that have become so ingrained through habit that they form part of his/her whole personality. The formation of good character in young people is primarily the responsibility of parents.

The principal, Dr. Judith Wynne, explained that St. Luke's School plays a supportive role in concert with parents in continuing the learning and development of Christian character in its students. St. Luke's students are expected to come to value and exhibit in their daily lives the virtues of respect, generosity, courtesy, integrity, and loyalty, which are manifestations of a person's inner strength.

IMPORTANCE OF THE SCHOOL'S MISSION STATEMENT

Character development, teaching values and virtues and promoting the ability to make ethical decisions, was specifically mentioned in the mission statement of many of these Blue Ribbon Schools (Table 4). According to Edward Wynne and Kevin Ryan (1993), authors of *Reclaiming Our Schools: A Handbook on Teaching Character, Academics and Discipline*, a school's mission statement is very important in making public the specific character-building goals that the administration, teachers, and staff are committed to fostering.

Table 4.   **Common Phrases Found in Blue Ribbon Schools'**
Mission Statements

Category	Count	Percent
Academics, Responsibility	27	6%
Collaborative Cooperation	5	1%
Create Positive Environment	51	12%
Develop Citizenship	148	33%
Have High Expectation of All	7	2%
Orderly Environment	19	4%
Student Centered, Develop Self-Esteem	40	9%
Teaching Decision Making, Problem Solving	76	17%
Teach Ethics, Character Development	114	26%
Whole Child Developed, Promote intellectual, social, physical, emotional, and moral development	155	35%

Total Response (Some schools included terms in more than one category) 642, Valid
Cases 443, Missing Cases 40

The most common mission of the Blue Ribbon Schools is to develop the "whole child." This is spelled out by phrases such as "promote the intellectual, social, physical, emotional, and ethical development" of students. Not all schools included the emotional and/or ethical/moral development of students as one of the components of developing the "whole child", however, this second edition finds more and more of the schools including these components. St. Rosalie School in Harvey, Louisiana, won the Blue Ribbon Award in 2001–2001 as well as in 1991–1992. The school added a pre-kindergarten to better serve its very large and ethnically diverse student body of PK–8 graders. They state that:

> As Christian Educators we view our education as a child-centered education helping each student to realize their potential—spiritually, morally, intellectually, emotionally, physically, culturally, socially, and aesthetically—thus enabling the student to become a fully integrated person.

Developing citizenship was the second most common mission, a well-accepted goal for schools, both private and public. St. Clement's Episcopal Parish School's mission is threefold: (a) to provide an academic environment in which each child's intellectual, emotional, social, aesthetic, and physical growth is accompanied by a corresponding spiritual and moral growth; (b) to nurture self-respect and a sense of fulfillment in each child; and (c) to cultivate in each child a sense of citizenship, moral responsibility, and genuine respect for others. St. Clement's is a PK–9 mid-size private school located in El Paso, Texas. The student body is heterogeneous with 40% of the students from Hispanic backgrounds.

The third most common mission was that of "developing character and teaching ethics." This character-building mission of the Blue Ribbon Schools is reflected in the comments made in many of the reports. For example, the Qualiwood Elementary School in the community-oriented suburb of Bakersfield, California, is committed to its mission to "develop students who have sound ethical values, a commitment to academic excellence, and a concern for the betterment of society." This vision is carried throughout the school's programs and in its monthly school-wide goal that focuses on developing positive student attitudes and behavior. Qualiwood has almost five hundred students, 15 percent of whom are racially and ethnically diverse.

A comprehensive mission statement was found in the McKinley Elementary School, located in Elkins Park, Pennsylvania, that seemed to include all of the major areas cited above: "We believe in educating the whole child so as to develop caring and cooperative individuals who accept responsibility, respect themselves and others, strive for excellence in their academic performance and social behavior and contribute to a safe and non-violent environment for living and learning in an ever changing and multicultural world."

CHARACTER EDUCATION IN PRIVATE SCHOOLS

It is interesting to note that character or moral development was not necessarily evident in all of the mission statements of the private, religiously based Blue Ribbon Schools in the first edition sample, but was seen more often in this subsequent research. Years ago, one could assume that schools with a religious focus, also promoted character development in their students. Nevertheless, the long-term decline in the conduct of young Americans outlined in chapter 2 has affected all our youth, those in private as well as public schools. Today both types of schools need to have specific instruction dealing with ethical issues, moral values, and character qualities. Religious schools develop students "spiritually and doctrinally," but specific efforts also need to be made to develop their character so that they do the good moral actions that their religious training tells them they should do. When a religion-based school also teaches character development to its students, there is a clear focus on growing in human virtues as a goal of the school.

Specific virtues are clearly a goal at the Katherine and Jacob Greenfield Hebrew Academy of Atlanta, a private K–8 Jewish Day School located in a suburb of Atlanta. "We nurture within our students respect for the individual, a commitment to Jewish religious observance, devotion to Israel, passion for learning, appreciation of American ideals of democracy, and dedication to the Jewish community." The values inherent in this statement are integrated into all phases of school life and abundant opportunities are provided for moral action to help students develop good character, and a strong commitment to uphold the core values. In as much as the Academy is a Hebrew day school, religious studies are an integral part of the school curriculum. The children learn daily from the rich primary sources and traditions of the Jewish religion. The ideals of "tzedakah" (charity), "chesed" (acts of loving kindness), "ben adam l'chavero" (responsibility for others), "yedidut" (friendship) and "kavod habriot" (respect) are imparted to the children to impress upon them the joy and satisfaction that comes from caring and doing for others, and "tikkun olam" (healing the world) through their "derech eretz" (personal conduct) of service towards others.

The Bible becomes the textbook for religious-based schools and it is replete with character messages. The Greenfield Hebrew Academy uses wise and ethical sayings from the Bible for the topic of religion lessons taught in each class at every grade level. The Grace School in Houston, Texas, also uses the Bible as its character education curriculum. The curriculum for grades K–5 is a three-year thematic series based on stories from the Bible. As the students advance through the grades, a different theme is taught that emphasizes the relevancy of God's Word in students' lives. Students learn to apply the inherent moral and ethical principles to their everyday lives.

THE BLUE RIBBON SCHOOLS' COMPREHENSIVE MODEL OF CHARACTER EDUCATION

Many character educators (Lickona, 1991; Huffman, 1994; Wiley, 1998; DeRoche and Williams, 1998; and Ryan and Bohlin, 1999) and the Character Education Partnership propose that character education must be comprehensive and involve the entire school if it is to be effective. Several of the Blue Ribbon Schools mentioned in their applications how important it is to have a comprehensive program. St. Gregory the Great School is a very large, middle class, homogeneous parochial school in a suburb of Cleveland, Ohio, that reports on its school-wide effort.

> Character and moral development are integrated throughout the learning environment at St. Gregory's in order to prepare students to embrace the new millennium as informed and participating citizens and as future leaders. Character education is more than just a learned set of skills or acquired habits. It is a commitment to the core social values of justice, tolerance, and concern for others.

Analysis of the categories of programs that Blue Ribbon Schools use to develop character (Table 5) also presents a comprehensive model for promoting character education. The "Blue Ribbon Schools' Comprehensive Model for Character Education" gives importance to all three aspects of character formation: developing moral knowing, moral feeling and moral action. All areas of the curriculum, the formal, informal and hidden curriculum, are important for developing these three aspects. The formal curriculum is the intended or explicit curricu-

Table 5.   What Programs in the Blue Ribbon Schools Promote
Character Development?

Category	Count	Percent of Responses
Character Education Program	92	25
Citizenship	41	11
Conflict Management	27	7
Discipline Program	58	16
Drug Education Program	83	23
Guidance Program	67	18
Motivation Program	18	5
School Developed Program	54	15
Self-Esteem Program	50	14
Social Skills	28	8
Other	33	9

Valid Cases 363, Missing Cases 122

lum, that is, the stated objectives, content, and organization of instruction as approved by the state and local boards. It is instituted through the formal adoption of character education programs and/or school-wide character traits. The informal curriculum deals with the interactions among students and teachers, that is how they should behave and act towards one another. It is found in the discipline codes and the citizenship programs that help to develop moral action in the character of students. The hidden curriculum is taught implicitly by the school experience, for example the effect of the architecture and environment, the use of time during school, and ways students are rewarded both in and outside of the classroom (Ornstein and Hunkin, 1988; Schubert, 1986). It is expressed by school award programs, and by the presence of—or absence of—drug education and sex education programs.

The Blue Ribbon Schools' model for character education provides a research validation of Lickona's twelve-point comprehensive model developed in *Education for Character (1991)*. Both models give students opportunities for developing all the areas of their character: moral knowing, moral feeling, and moral action. This is visually shown by the inner core of the model. The Blue Ribbon model emphasizes the important role parents, teachers, counselors and principals play when working together to promote character in youth. This is shown by the outer core. The model also shows how each subject in the curriculum can be used to promote character and how extracurricular activities can give students opportunities to manifest good character qualities and do good actions. The model recognizes that students should be helped to develop their character in such a way that they naturally do good deeds out in their neighborhood and community, on the playground, on the sports field, and in their family, showing an authentic and comprehensive development of their character. Evaluation is conducted that documents the effectiveness of this comprehensive, school-wide effort to promote character development in students. The Blue Ribbon Schools' model for character education is comprehensive because it gives students opportunities for developing all areas of their character: moral knowing, moral feeling, and moral action through the total moral life of the school.

The best way to understand the "Blue Ribbon Comprehensive Model for Character Education" is to visit one of the five Blue Ribbon Schools that also received Special Honors in Character Education. These five schools are: Belmont Elementary School in Belmont, Michigan; McCoy Elementary School in Carrolton, Texas; Patterson Road School in Santa Maria, California; Walnut Hill Elementary School in Dallas, Texas; and West View Elementary School in Spartanburg, South Carolina.

CAN GOOD CHARACTER BE TAUGHT?

Figure 3.   Blue Ribbon Schools' Comprehensive Model for Character Education (adapted from Lickona, 1991)

I visited each of these five schools in preparing this second edition. These schools, and others mentioned in this book, are models of what a comprehensive approach to character education is all about because at these schools, the administration, faculty, staff, parents, and students are working together to promote character. All school activities, classes, and events are opportunities for learning about, caring for, and demonstrating good character. The school is committed to character education and it is evident in every aspect of the school. I will give examples from two of the schools. Each school will be described in more detail in later chapters.

From the moment you call on the phone or come in the door at West View Elementary in Spartanburg, South Carolina, you are kindly greeted and helped. I was tired when I entered West View School for I had been visiting Blue Ribbon Schools for four consecutive days during my fall break. I stopped in the ladies room before I met Mr. Sam Bingham, the principal. There in the restroom were all sorts of inspirational character-promoting messages about having a positive attitude. I left the room smiling and renewed. I met the custodial staff as well as teachers, counselors, and administrators during the visit. All of them were proud of their school, the students, and their character education program.

Walnut Hill in Dallas, Texas, is a very busy school, with parents coming and going, but principal JoAnn Hughes is always available for whoever needs her. The hall walls are decorated with all sorts of character building bulletin boards and each teacher integrates character into his or her daily lesson plans. As I toured the school with Ms. Hughes, she proudly pointed out the different additions made to the school by the community and the parents, including the different gardens planted by community members, students, and teachers. The school celebrates the diversity of its students who speak six different languages and represent twelve nationalities. Everyone I met wanted to tell me about their school, including the librarians who were on their lunch break. Ms. Hughes showed me the new playground the fathers built. A map of the United States was stenciled on it. This is part of Peaceful Playground, a program of stencils to put on the playground that gives students things to do at recess. I was treated to lunch with the principal and her staff in the principal's office, a daily sharing time for these professionals. At this school everyone is working on developing character, striving to develop their own and that of the students.

The Blue Ribbon Schools' responses to the question: "How do school programs foster the development of sound character?" is used as the organizing framework for the chapters in this book on character development, teaching techniques, drug education, motivation, guidance and self-esteem programs, discipline programs, citizenship development, and evaluation. The purpose of this book is to present the "best practices" in character and moral education programs as found in the Blue Ribbon Schools. It can be seen as a compendium of programs found within schools that have been designated as the best in the United States. However, as stated in the introduction, the existence of a particular program in a Blue Ribbon School does not necessarily mean that this is a "Blue Ribbon Character Education

Program," so data is presented, wherever it is available, that will assist the reader in evaluating the desirability of implementing a particular program found in the Blue Ribbon Schools.

One could ask, are Blue Ribbon Schools more likely to have a character education program than other schools? To answer this conclusively, data from other schools, not nominated as Blue Ribbon Schools, would have to be compared to the data of our sample. Nevertheless, an analysis of the findings in this research, which will be elaborated in each subsequent chapter, show that although each school had to answer this question, many of the Blue Ribbon Schools cited in the first edition of this book did *not* have a character education program *per se* in place. Schools included in their answers to this question a large range of other types of programs. These different programs are mentioned in Table 5, but will be discussed in subsequent chapters. Some schools said that they foster the development of character in their students through their drug education program or their discipline program. Although these are important components of a moral education program, they are not sufficient in themselves. I concluded in the first edition that character education and moral education in schools is an emerging area that needs to be further developed. This second edition reports on positive progress in the past six years. Forty percent of the schools now have a character education program in place, whether school developed or adopted from a curriculum. This book, by highlighting the ethics, moral development, and character education programs found in America's best schools, provides much needed guidance as schools seek to meet the challenge of promoting character education.

SUMMARY

This chapter provides the rationale behind the book. The philosophic foundations of character education are outlined. Terms are defined as they are presented in order to provide readers with a common conceptual basis. The importance of a school mission statement that addresses character education is highlighted. The National Award Winning Elementary Schools, the Blue Ribbon Schools, were chosen to show the reader what the best schools in America are doing to promote character education. The information found in these schools was categorized in order to construct a comprehensive model for character education. These categories form the basis upon which this book is organized.

2

A Brief History of Character Education in U.S. Schools

America is great because she is good; but if America ever ceases to be good, she will cease to be great.

—Alexis de Tocqueville

People of character are the conscience of society.

—Ralph Waldo Emerson

To educate a person in mind and not in morals is to educate a menace to society.

—Theodore Roosevelt

SHOULD OUR PUBLIC SCHOOLS TEACH VIRTUES AND VALUES?

Just a decade ago, some people still debated whether our public schools *should* teach virtues or values. In 1985, the *New York Times* quoted educators who said that "they deliberately avoid telling students what is ethically right or wrong" (Bennett, 1988). However, today people are debating *what* values to teach and *how* to teach them in a more effective way. In 1995, the same *New York Times* quoted educators as saying, "A whole generation has grown up in a moral vacuum . . . Character education is a great hope for our future" (Rosenblatt, 1995).

This chapter highlights the main historical events that have precipitated this dramatic change in attitude. It presents a short history of character education as taught in our nation's schools from the colonial times to the current day. It shows how a national movement has begun promoting the vital importance of once again teaching character education in our schools. It shows the reader what the best schools in America, the National Award Winning Elementary Schools, the Blue Ribbon Schools, are doing to promote character education.

Chapter 2 seeks to answer the following questions:

- Why was character education an aim of American schools in the colonial times?
- Why did the teaching of character education decline and values clarification and cognitive moral development approaches take its place?
- What events have led to the renewed national interest in character education?
- Why will this book, *Character Education in Our Nation's Blue Ribbon Schools* make an important contribution to the character education movement?

A NATION AT RISK

Although the reform document *A Nation at Risk* (National Commission on Excellence in Education, 1983) focused mostly on academics, it did catch the public's attention through its statement that our nation was at risk and it went beyond matters such as industry and commerce. "It (our concern) also includes the intellectual, moral, and spiritual strengths of our people, which knit together the very fabric of our society." The public did not need a national document to tell them what they already knew. There had been a substantial long-term decline in the conduct of young Americans (e.g., rising youth homicides, suicides, teenage pregnancies, and school vandalism) along with declining academic performance in school. In addition to these indicators were statistics that showed the effect that the breakdown of the traditional family and the lack of traditional socialization for the youth had had on school performance (Wynne and Ryan, 1993; Kilpatrick, 1992; Lickona, 1991).

These societal problems have fueled the re-evaluation of moral education in America. The school reform movements that followed upon the release of *A Nation at Risk* looked at the important role character development in schools played in promoting academic excellence. Students in schools that promoted character and moral values had better test scores and had lower incidents of vandalism, absenteeism, and dishonesty on tests (Wynee and Walberg, 1985).

The most broad-based efforts to revitalize moral education came from a variety of individuals who favored traditional, virtue-centered approaches that sought to cultivate good conduct, now labeled "character education." The most articulate of the group was William J. Bennett, director of the National Endowment for the Humanities in the early Reagan years, then secretary of the U.S. Department of Education and initiator of the National School Recognition Program, also known as the Blue Ribbon School Award program (McClellan, 1992). The research data for this second edition is based on fifteen years of Blue Ribbon Award Winning Schools.

Currently, politicians from both parties, concerned citizens, business leaders, educational researchers, and parents are urging the schools to return to a deeper and more conscientious involvement in the moral life of their students. The recognition that schools inevitably teach values has become widespread through a realization that the very act of educating another is a moral act (Goodland, et al., 1990; and Tom, 1984). Possibilities for moral education lie in every part of the curriculum. There is a general consensus that we need a comprehensive approach for teaching character education and moral values, one that begins in the early grades and continues through the college years. Teachers and schools, like parents and families, cannot avoid teaching values. In fact, one might ask, why did American schools ever stop teaching students about good character, human virtues, and moral values?

Character Education in the Colonial Schools

Historically, character education was one of the missions of the American public schools from the first formation of the New England Town School in Boston during the Colonial period. Using the *Hornbook*, and *The New England Primer,* students learned the close relationship among reading, religion, and character education; the integration of these was the hallmark of elementary education in this period (Gutek, 1970). The child learned "An Alphabet of Lessons for Youth," "The Dutiful Child's Promises," and "The Duty of Children toward their Parents."

The Dutiful Child's Promises

> I will fear GOD and honour the King
> I will honour my Father & Mother
> I will obey my Superiours
> I will submit to my Elders
> I will love my friends
> I will hate no man.
> I will forgive my enemies and pray to God for
> the will as much as in me lies to keep all God's
> Holy Commandments

Gutek, 1970, p. 251

The Founding Fathers, especially Thomas Jefferson, were advocates of character education for all in order to train students in democratic citizenship. The Declaration of Independence and the Preamble to the Constitution are clear statements of the moral values and virtues we hold sacred in our democracy. "We hold these truths to be self-evident, that all men are created equal, that they are endowed by their Creator with certain unalienable Rights, that among these are Life, Liberty and the pursuit of Happiness."

Educators continued to foster these values in the nineteenth century. For instance, the McGuffey Readers (Vail, 1909) were the primary character education curricula in the 1800s. Students read stories about children their own age who successfully learned to live good virtues in their every day life.

Mc Guffey's Primer—Lesson XIV

This old man cannot see. He is blind
Mary holds him by the hand.
She is kind to the old blind man

Vail, 1909, p. 20

Character Education at the Turn of the Century

During the opening decades of the twentieth century, interest in character education and citizenship training flourished (Pietig, 1977). There were national contests for the best morality codes and the best methodologies for teaching character education. They were sponsored by the Character Education Association, a private organization created in 1911 and headed by Milton Fairchild. The "Children's Morality Code" outlined "ten laws of right living": self-control, good health, kindness, sportsmanship, self-reliance, duty, reliability, truth, good workmanship, and teamwork (McClellan, 1992). Youth organizations that promoted moral education were founded. The character education movement identified a body of activities and principles by which moral education could be transmitted in a secular institution (ASCD Panel, 1988a).

Character education programs then, as now, used either the direct or the indirect method of moral instruction. The direct method viewed character development as the acquisition of desirable traits or virtues. This method centered on learning creeds, slogans and pledges, and reading classical texts with heroes and noteworthy actions. The indirect method, by contrast, did not explicitly teach the desirable virtues but created the situations in which these virtues could be developed and practiced. All the processes of school life—classroom activities, disciplinary procedures, personal contacts, and extracurricular functions—were scrutinized for their character-training potential. Each of these methods was explained in detail in the classic textbook of the era, *Character Education*, written by Harry McKown (1935), which was used by all teachers-in-training who wanted to know how to teach character education.

John Dewey's Criticism of Character Education

John Dewey, America's chief philosopher of education at the turn of the twentieth century, could be considered to be singularly responsible for the dramatic change in the character-promoting mission of American education. On the surface, it may seem that Dewey was merely a proponent of indirect instead of direct moral instruction, because he focused on the moral organization of the schools rather than instruction in virtue formation (Dewey, 1909). However, Dewey based his educational ideas on his pragmatic, philosophic ideas, that is, an instrumentalist's view of truth: something was true "if it worked" as a solution to a practical problem. Dewey therefore was a moral relativist who believed that values arose as outcomes of human responses to varying environmental situations (Gutek, 1988). To ask if something was of value, was for Dewey to ask whether it was "something to be prized and cherished, to be enjoyed" (Dewey, 1929). He wrote, "A moral agent is one who proposes for himself an end to be achieved by action and does what is necessary to obtain that end" (Dewey, 1891; cited in Copleston, 1967).

According to Dewey, moral education was not a matter of teaching students what to do or not to do, but it was to be a method to help them decide what to do. "Moral education in school is practically hopeless when we set up the development of character as its supreme end" (Dewey, 1916). Dewey articulated a theory of moral development that emphasized reflective thinking rather than moral lessons (ASCD Panel, 1988a). His writings focused moral education, for the next fifty years, on a process-oriented approach rather than the content-oriented approach of character education. Dewey promoted logical positivism and pragmatism. His philosophy formed the basis for values clarification and Kohlberg's developmental approach to moral education (Carlin, 1981; Harrison, 1980; Kolhlberg, 1975). Dewey's ideas on education and his philosophy still influence American thinking and schooling today.

Character Education Under Fire

The research of Hartshorne and May in 1930 added support to Dewey's contention that character education was ineffective. Hartshorne and May assessed the character-related behavior of almost 11,000 youths in grades five through eight by administering thirty-three different behavioral tests of altruism (service), self-control, and honesty versus deceit. Analysis of the results of each individual test showed that there was little evidence that classrooms that had character education produced a lower incidence of deceit or a higher incidence of service behavior in their students. The researchers concluded that the character education techniques then in use in the schools bore little or no significant relationship to pupils' general patterns of moral conduct (Leming, 1993a). These findings resulted in a general decline in interest in character education research and/or policy proposals. (It should be noted that recent and more sophisticated research has used the principle of aggregation to combine the multiple test measures into aggregate sets. These batteries of scores have thus revealed a much higher correlation between participation in the character education class and the students' likelihood to continue to practice these virtues in other contexts [Rushton, et al., 1983; Wynne, 1989]). McClellan suggests that character education did not really decline after Hartshorne and May's research but transformed its focus. Instead of teaching character education using the traditional direct method, indirect methods, that is, school practices such as homeroom, clubs, and grades in citizenship on report cards were begun which were to help "build character." During and after World War II the importance of good character and citizenship was emphasized (Leming, 1997).

The Value Free Society

The protests of the 1960s led to the fall of many established American values such as respect for authority and rules, hard work, sexual restraint, and patriotism. Educational institutions were told to become value-free. The values clarification movement of the 1970s taught students that the process of valuing is value-free, that is, there are no better or worse answers. Values clarification helps students to "clarify their own values, choose their beliefs, and then be willing to act on their beliefs" (Raths, *et al.*, 1966). As a natural application of Dewey's value theory, values clarification does not stress true and right behavior. It is a relativistic approach. Today, many one-time proponents of this approach have admitted that they made a mistake in devaluing and taking for granted traditional values (Harmin, 1988; Kirschenbaum, 1995). However, many teachers in the field today are still trying to teach in a value-free way using values clarification activities, since this is the way that they were taught to teach when they were in college.

The Cognitive Moral Development Approach

In the 1970s, Lawrence Kohlberg proposed a cognitive-developmental approach to moral education based on the work of Dewey and Piaget (Kohlberg, 1978, 1984; ASCD Panel 1988a). His doctoral dissertation findings led to a resurgence of research interest in moral education in the United States. Kohlberg's research validated the Dewey-Piaget levels and added to their model; his theory asserted that a person developmentally progresses through a series of moral stages; or, more specifically, three levels with two stages in each level (Kohlberg, 1975).

Kohlberg's Stages of Moral Development

I. Preconventional level
- Stage 1: The punishment-and-obedience orientation.
- Stage 2: The instrumental-relativist orientation.
II. Conventional level
- Stage 3: The interpersonal concordance or "good boy-nice girl" orientation.
- Stage 4: The "law and order" orientation.

III. Postconventional, autonomous, or principled level
- Stage 5: The social contract, legalistic orientation.
- Stage 6: The universal-ethical-principle orientation.

Kohlberg asserted that cognitive development was important for moral development; that is, logical reasoning is necessary for moral judgment, and moral judgment is necessary for moral action, but neither is sufficient in itself. Kohlberg found, similar to the research of Hartshorne and May, that there are additional factors necessary for principled moral reasoning to be translated into moral action. Kohlberg emphasized the development of moral reasoning toward increasingly complex concepts of justice (Kohlberg, 1975).

Research has been supportive of the teacher's ability to foster the development of higher cognitive levels of moral reasoning through the use of dilemma discussions in the classroom (Nucci, 1987). The "just community" approach to moral education evolved out of a practical application of Kohlberg's theory in prisons and then in schools. In the just community, students develop the basic elements of morality by democratically deciding all of the rules and norms of their school by the application of certain "master virtues of the community," such as caring, trust, collective responsibility, concern for fairness, and community (Power, et al., 1989).

Although values clarification and moral reasoning classroom methods are different in many ways, the theoretical premises upon which they are based are similar. They both avoid the virtue-centered approaches to character education, emphasizing instead the *process* of moral decision making and the importance of individual freedom and autonomy. Both believed that their open-ended approaches offered a moral education consistent with contemporary American lifestyles. In both of these systems, teachers are not to moralize; teachers are facilitators of student-generated discussion, creators of cognitive conflict and/or stimulators of social perspective taking in students (Reimer, et al. 1983; McClellan, 1992). Research on the effectiveness of these two approaches has shown that the moral discussion approach is effective, that is, one can measure increases in cognitive reasoning levels through the use of moral dilemma discussions; but values clarification research findings are inconclusive; it does not seem "to work." However, it is also hard to define exactly what it would do effectively if it did work (Leming, 1993b). Values clarification and moral reasoning can be classified as process-oriented approaches to moral education that lack a contextual base.

AS WE BEGIN THE TWENTY-FIRST CENTURY

Today, the escalating problems in society, such as crimes of violence by young people, make it imperative that schools once again directly address the subject of values and character (Traiger, 1995). Research cited above, and to be cited throughout this book, helps us to understand that it is difficult, no matter what method is used, to shape moral conduct, because the process of moral shaping is enormously incremental, cumulative, and complex (Wynne, 1989). However, it is possible. We can answer Socrates' question, "Can virtue be taught?" affirmatively.

The teaching of human virtues and the subsequent shaping of "good character" needs to be restored to its historical place as the central desirable outcome of the school's moral enterprise (Lickona, 1993a). The school reform movement precip-itated by the report *A Nation at Risk* has engendered many reports on what makes for excellence in education; included within these reports are many discussions of the need to return to the moral purpose of teaching (Fernstermacher, 1990).

In 1988, the Association for Supervision, Curriculum and Development (ASCD) brought together eleven experts in moral education to form a panel. The panel drafted the document *Moral Education in the Life of the School* (1988b) in which they listed the six characteristics of a "morally mature person." The morally mature person habitually:

1. Respects human dignity
2. Cares about the welfare of others
3. Integrates individual interest and social responsibilities
4. Demonstrates integrity
5. Reflects on moral choices
6. Seeks peaceful resolution of conflict

The panel also gave eight recommendations for moral education.

Four years later, in March of 1992, the ASCD, the Princeton Project 55, and the Johnson Foundation convened a Wingspread Conference in Racine, Wiscon-sin, around the question, "How to provide effective K–12 character education?" "The goal of the conference was to encourage leaders of national education asso-ciations to give greater attention and priority to character education. The confer-ence participants recommended the formation of a new national coalition to sup-port and facilitate efforts to disseminate information about the need for K–12 character education and to provide assistance to schools and communities across the country as they became interested in initiating character education activities" (Character Education Partnership, 1996).

In July of that same year, twenty-eight leaders of diverse backgrounds met for four days in Aspen, Colorado, at a summit hosted by the Josephson Institute. The con-ference was entitled "Teaching Ethics and Character: What Should be Done? What Can Be Done? What Will Be Done?" It looked at ways in which character and val-ues could be instilled in young people in all areas of their lives. After hours of de-bate and discussion, the twenty-eight participants signed a declaration that defined six core ethical values that "form the foundation of democratic society" and called for character education programs to implement them. "People do not automatically develop good moral character; therefore, conscientious efforts must be made to help young people develop the values and abilities necessary for moral decision making and conduct" (Aspen Declaration, 1992). The Character Counts Coalition was founded as a result of this conference. It is "a national partnership of organizations and individuals involved in the education, training or care of youth, joined together in a collaborative effort to improve the character of America's young people based on six core ethical values, the Six Pillars of Character: trustworthiness, respect, responsibility, fairness, caring and citizenship" (Josephson Institute, 1993).

The Character Education Partnership was founded on February 5, 1993, by a number of individuals and organizations, many of whom had actively participated in the Wingspread and/or the Aspen meeting. The group defines itself as "a national, non-profit, non-partisan coalition dedicated to developing good character and civic virtue in young people as one way of promoting a more compassionate and responsible society" (Character Education Partnership, 1996b).

The Character Education Partnership with the assistance of the Association for Supervision and Curriculum Development has worked on getting character education endorsed by the major educational associations, such as, the National School Board Association, the National Association of Elementary School Principals, the National Association of Secondary School Principals, the National Association for the Education of Young Children, the National Education Association, the National Society for the Study of Education, and by state departments of education. According to a report from Andrea Grenadier (2001) at the Character Education Partnership, eleven states mandate character education through legislation, thirteen states encourage character education through legislation, and twenty-five states support character education but have no current legislation. Vessels' (1998) research revealed that twenty-five state constitutions mandate moral or character education and Nielsen (1998) reports that forty-eight of the fifty states have completed or are in the process of completing state educational standards that address character education either directly or indirectly through state standards (usually defined in terms of general democratic values). Some of these state legislatures have passed bills requiring the development of a character curriculum based on a list of core values (Milson, 2000). Several of the Blue Ribbon Schools mention in their report that they are meeting specific state goals for character education and several show how their program also meets state standards.

Through the joint work of the Character Education Partnership and the Character Counts Coalition, bipartisan support for character education was garnered from the federal government. In 1994, both the House and Senate unanimously adopted a joint resolution (Public Law 101–301) supporting character education and designating October 11–22, as National Character Counts Week. In July of 1994, Congress re-authorized the Improving America's Schools Act (Public Law 101–382) of the Elementary and Secondary Education Act (ESEA) and added to the statute two sources of funding for character education (See ESEA: Section 10103 "Partnerships in Character Education Pilot Project"). This addition allows schools, public and private, to use "federal drug education funds" to initiate or support their character education programs. It also provides awards of large character education grants to states that apply to the U.S. Department of Education. To date, forty-eight states, plus the District of Columbia have received these grants. Character education was selected as a special emphasis option for the 1998–1999 (elementary and middle schools) and 1999–2000 (middle school and high schools) Blue Ribbon School Program to provide model schools that exhibit best practice in character education. Ideas from the 1998–1999 award winning school are included in this second edition. It is my hope to include the 1999–2000 schools in a second book for this series, entitled *Character Education in America's Blue Ribbon High Schools.*

The White House sponsored conferences on Character Building for a Civil and Democratic Society, from 1994–1998. These conferences brought together educators, community leaders, and representatives of national organizations to exchange ideas on how character education can be provided most effectively and how it can be spread to more U.S. school districts (Character Education Partnership, 1996b). All of the senators, representatives, and political leaders who addressed this group reiterated that character education was a national priority. Character education was mentioned in the 1996, 1997, and 2001 State of the Union Addresses by two different presidents.

It is with this historical momentum that this book is presented to parents, teachers, school administrators, and concerned citizens. It outlines what the Blue Ribbon Schools, the best schools in America, are doing to promote character education and train students in ethics and moral values. It provides a plethora of ideas that can be analyzed, assessed, and perhaps adopted in particular schools and school districts that are interested in joining the national movement by integrating character education into their school curriculum and programs.

SUMMARY

As this chapter shows, character education was one of the original purposes of the colonial and American schools until the beginning of the twentieth century. John Dewey's instrumental, relativistic philosophy promoted a decline in the direct teaching of character education in the schools and inspired values clarification and cognitive moral development approaches. As these methods did not prove effective in teaching moral content to students, a renewed national interest has grown in character education. The Blue Ribbon Schools provide examples of what the best schools in America are doing to promote character education.

3

Character Education Programs in the Blue Ribbon Schools

Education worthy of its name is essentially education of character.
—Martin Buber

We must remember that intelligence is not enough. Intelligence plus character— that is the goal of true education.
—Martin Luther King, Jr.

In matters of opinion, swim with the fish; but in matters of principle, stand firm like a rock.
—Mark Twain

MORAL EDUCATION REQUIRED FOR NOMINATION AS A BLUE RIBBON SCHOOL

Even today some people still debate whether public schools should teach values or virtues. However, judging by the application form for the Elementary School Recognition program, this question is not an issue for the Department of Education. In order to be recognized for Blue Ribbon achievement, a school must already be successfully furthering the intellectual, social, and *moral* growth of all its students. One of the purposes of the recognition program is to "identify and give public recognition to outstanding public and private elementary schools across the United States . . . that are doing an exceptional job in this area of values education and character development." Specifically, the application asks, "How do school programs, practices, and policies foster the development of sound character, democratic

values, ethical judgment and the ability to work in a self-disciplined and purposeful manner?" In fact, in order to clarify even more what was meant by
character education, in 1987–1988 the question was: "What are your
schools' expectations in the area of character development, and how are
these expectations communicated? What in the school contributes to the development of the attributes of sound character, such as a sense of fair play, a
concern for others, a commitment to truthful and virtuous behavior, and the
availability and willingness to assume responsibility for one's own behavior? How do school policies, programs, and practices foster the development
of a child's self-discipline and self-confidence?" In 1998–1999 schools
could apply for special honors in character education by answering the following questions in an addendum to the application. "What is the school's
philosophy on character education?" "How does the school incorporate and
demonstrate the importance of family involvement in character education?"
"What types of staff development are provided to encourage all staff to incorporate the core ethical values into school activities?" "How does the
school assess the understanding and commitment to core ethical values of
both staff and students?"

This chapter reports on the different character education programs found in the
Blue Ribbon Schools (Table 2). Specifically, it seeks to answer the following
questions:

- What value do school-wide, district-wide, or state-wide character traits have
  for promoting character in students?
- What are some programs Blue Ribbon Schools have developed to teach char-
  acter education?
- Should character education be a separate class, or is it possible to integrate it
  into the academic curriculum?
- What are some of the commercial character education curricula used by the
  Blue Ribbon Schools?

This chapter presents those programs mentioned by the Blue Ribbon
Schools that explicitly attempt to teach character education in the school; thus
reflecting the more traditional "direct approach" to teaching virtue discussed
in chapter 2. Programs were selected for this chapter if they specifically referred to character development and/or made reference to other programs that
were specifically designed to teach students moral values or virtues. Schools
also included a large range of other types of programs as they sought to answer this question. These different programs will be mentioned in the tables
that summarize the results, but will each be dealt with in an appropriate later
chapter.

IDENTIFYING CORE VALUES AND KEY HUMAN VIRTUES

The identification of the moral values and human virtues that particular schools or districts intend to promote is the first step to be undertaken before character education can begin in the school. Each school or district needs to clarify what its community understands by "good character" and what core values it feels each student should learn.

Character education was studied in the 25th, the 26th, and the 31st Annual Phi Delta Kappa/Gallup Poll of the Public's Attitudes toward the Public Schools. The 25th Gallup Poll (Eliam, 1993) asked if the respondent thought it would be possible for local communities to agree on a set of basic values to be taught in the public schools. A solid majority (69%) said yes and went on to approve strongly the teaching of eight values: honesty, democracy, patriotism, caring for others, moral courage, the golden rule, acceptance of people of different races, and religious tolerance. The 26th Gallup Poll (Eliam, 1994) registered strong approval for yet another set of personal traits or virtues that could be taught in the public schools. These virtues included respect, industry or hard work, persistence, fairness, compassion, civility or politeness, self-esteem, and high expectations for oneself. The 31st Gallup Poll (Rose and Gallup, 1999) showed strong approval for a slightly different set of values. They included honesty, democracy, acceptance of others, caring, moral courage, and patriotism.

Phi Delta Kappa conducted research on core values by collecting data from 10,000 persons in over 150 communities across the country in 1994. It found high levels of agreement about values young people should learn. Democratic values such as civility, honesty, equality, freedom, nonviolence, responsibility, and respect should be taught by the family, the church, and the school. They found agreement on the understanding of a "person of character" as one who is honest, responsible, dependable, loyal, and having integrity. Their report concluded that schools are not teaching these values as well as most educators think that they should (Frymier, et al., 1995).

Many of the Blue Ribbon Schools stated that they had developed their own character education curriculum and that the essential organizing framework for their curriculum was a set of core values chosen. This was especially true of schools researched for the second edition (42% of the total sample of 150 schools mentioned this as their primary method for promoting character). The collegial work of teachers, parents, and administrators in drawing up the list of core values and virtues was central to their curricular success. All involved had a sense of ownership for the virtues chosen. Henry Huffman states that at the heart of a district's character education program is the process for deciding the set of core values that the school will promote.

In one sense, it really does not matter which virtues are chosen; even learning to live one virtue alone will help to build a student's character. The words of

Josemaria Escriva de Balaguer (1973), the founder of Opus Dei and a person responsible for the foundation of many schools internationally that focus on character development, are particularly helpful in this area:

> I don't know if I could say which is the most important human virtue. It depends on the point of view from which they are considered. In any case, this question doesn't really get us anywhere, for it is not a matter of practicing one or even a number of virtues. We have to try to acquire and practice all of them. Each individual virtue is interwoven with the others and thus, our effort to be sincere will also make us upright, cheerful, prudent and composed. (pp. 6–7)

William Kilpatrick (1992), professor of education at Boston College and author of *Why Johnny Can't Tell Right from Wrong,* agrees with this idea that the virtues form a unity, and that in order to be a person of character you must have several virtues working together. He and most other character education scholars (Vincent, 1994; Ryan and Bohlin, 1999) agree that, as a bare minimum, every list of character traits ought to contain the four cardinal virtues that have come down to us from the Greeks: prudence, justice, courage and temperance. They are called cardinal because they are the axis (cardo) on which the moral life turns. A comparison of the Blue Ribbon Schools' lists of character traits finds these four virtues are usually included, although may use more modern terminology for them: For example, prudence is "good decision making skills," fortitude is "courage," temperance is "self-discipline," and justice is "fairness."

BLUE RIBBON SCHOOLS' LISTS OF KEY CHARACTER TRAITS

The Blue Ribbon Schools have developed their lists of character traits in different ways. Some have chosen their own schoolwide traits, others have district wide core values, some have state legislated character traits, and others have chosen to adopt the federal list of core values.

School-Wide Character Traits

Fredon Township School, in Newton, New Jersey, has developed its character list using the letters of its school name: Fair, Responsible, Enthusiastic, Distinguished, Optimistic, Noble. It emphasizes a different character trait each month that focuses on helping the students make good decisions, develop caring attitudes towards others, and practice good manners. Fredon is a K–6 homogeneous school of 250, in a rural area.

Monthly Character Traits

Washington Township Elementary School in Valparaiso, Indiana, had a Character Committee composed of staff and parents solicit input from all staff and parents through a survey they developed. They then came up with their list of eight Core Values that the school would teach, emphasize, reinforce, and celebrate throughout the curriculum: Honesty, Integrity, Respect, Responsibility, Kindness, Citizenship, Cooperation, and Courteousness. The Character Committee then researched and gathered material to support instruction in each of the eight Core Values and they assembled these ideas into a curriculum binder for each grade level. The goal was to focus on a value each month, and to integrate each of the Core Values into the whole school day and every subject, supplying the teacher with supplementary materials that would help them focus on each value. Each teacher could then "find" the core values in every subject he/she were teaching, focusing on the "teachable moment" when it occurs. The Core Values are incorporated into Washington Township's school discipline program, Student-of-the-Week recognition, peer mediation program, service learning, cooperative learning, and cross-age activities. During my visit to the school, I was able to attend their monthly assembly focusing on the value for that month—citizenship; I could see how the core values are an integral part of the school. Washington's mission statement directly addresses its commitment to the core values: "Our School Community educates children in a positive learning climate emphasizing core values within a solid academic foundation." The motto of the school is "What you are is more important than what you know." Even the school stationery states that it is "A Core Value School."

Word of the Week

Guntersville Elementary School uses the "Word of the Week" program to guide its character education initiative. Some of the words are caring, attentive, cooperation, fairness, responsibility, and respect. Parents are asked for their help in teaching students the "Word." The "Word of the Week" is also emphasized throughout the community. Each week it is published in the local newspaper, announced on local radio stations, and printed in church bulletins. It is also shown on cable television and it is displayed in store windows and in every classroom. The "Word" is incorporated as a vocabulary word and used in actual situations in the classrooms to enhance the understanding and meaning for students. Guntersville Elementary School is a large, ethnically diverse primary-level school on a six-acre campus located in northeastern Alabama in a small town nestled between mountains, almost completely surrounded by water. Almost half of the student body qualifies for free lunch, for parents have a variety of jobs working as fishermen, poultry processors, and government employees.

Character Traits in a Scope and Sequence

West View was one of the five schools to receive Special Honors in Character Education in 1998–1999 and was selected as a Blue Ribbon School. Its comprehensive character education program involves both the home and school working together. West View has been on the cutting edge of the character education movement in South Carolina. West View is a K–5 integrated school located in a suburb of Spartanburg, South Carolina.

West View began with seven character traits—respect, honesty, responsibility, courage, loyalty, justice, and patriotism—as the core of its program along with an emphasis on the Golden Rule: Treat others the way you would want them to treat you. As some schools have found, when you have a set group of traits to be taught each year, some students lose interest saying that "We learned that last year." So West View teachers decided to adopt the *Core Essentials Curriculum* developed by the Georgia Department of Education Center for Character Education with its U.S. Department of Education Character Education Grant. This three-year curriculum is based on teaching twenty-seven different character traits (nine each year) broken into two levels K–2 and 3–5. The program consists of a teacher guide, parent guide, value reward cards, and posters for each character trait. For more information on this curriculum contact: www.coreessentials.org.

Students are initially introduced to the character traits and the Golden Rule through classroom guidance lessons incorporating books, videos, role-plays, and other learning strategies. All teachers are trained in the Character Education Program so they reinforce and connect the traits to real life through daily activities in their classrooms. Teachers use the traits as they work with students to develop classroom rules. The traits are posted in every classroom and referred to as the rules are reinforced. The teachers give examples of how they teach these attributes by naturally integrating them into lessons, stories, and activities.

"In studying Abraham Lincoln, students are asked to identify his character traits in relation to West View's core traits." "First graders are asked which character traits they are demonstrating as they work together in cooperative groups." "Fifth grade classes each take one of the monthly character traits and develop a presentation, such as a skit or commercial, to be included on our weekly in-house television program, Paws 4 News." "The students publish books on traits for others to read." During my visit to the school, students sang different songs for me that they had learned that focused on their character traits. One song was "Check It Out! (It's About Respect)" written by John Higgins and John Jacobson and available from Cherry Lane Magazines. Another song was Clifford's Manner Song:

Clifford the B-I-G red dog is here to say, Do you H-E-L-P someone every day?
Do you cover a sneeze, say thank you and please? Do you wait your turn in line?
It's always right to be polite. Hooray you're doing,
Hooray you're doing, Hooray you're doing fine.

As students understand the meaning of these traits, they are able to recognize the traits in themselves and in others. Every six weeks, the students in each classroom choose one boy and one girl who has consistently demonstrated good character traits as a "Good School Citizen." The selection is used as another opportunity to teach and reinforce the traits. Good School Citizens are recognized in the school newspaper and in announcements. They also receive certificates and pencils and their pictures are displayed in the school.

District-Wide Programs of Character Development

Plano School District in Texas

Whole school districts have adopted sets of core values that the particular Blue Ribbon Schools also support. For example, the Plano School District in Texas has adopted a set of citizenship/character traits for its schools. These traits are: courtesy, courage, discipline, honesty, human worth and dignity, justice, patriotism, personal obligation for the public good, respect for self and others, respect for authority, tolerance, and responsibility. At the Huffman School in suburban, middle-class Plano, the staff and teachers model these twelve traits of good citizenship and sound character. Each week teachers emphasize a school-wide specified character trait at teachable moments. This trait is taught through lessons involving discussion, identifying examples and non-examples, and modeling. The teachers expect all of the students to develop each of these character traits over time. The school shares the targeted weekly citizenship trait with parents through newsletters, monthly calendars, and the marquee. These twelve traits are posted in every classroom.

At Hedgcoxe School, also in Plano, the twelve district-wide character traits appear on the screen whenever a school computer is turned on. The teachers use these traits as a foundation for their discipline program and for their enrichment activities. They seek to develop a sense of social responsibility and citizenship in the students. Hedgcoxe has experienced large increases in student enrollment and has had to divide into two schools. Hedgcoxe's student body is 15% ethnically diverse and over 10% with some physical/learning handicap. By emphasizing the trait of respect for others and tolerance, students have learned to get along well with all of their different schoolmates.

Character education permeates every aspect of academic and extracurricular practice at Wells School, a large school also in Plano, with a more homogenous school body. The entire staff participates in community service. Custodians, food servers, coaches, teachers, and the principal are mindful of the image they portray—as children are forever watching. The school also uses, in every classroom, the district posters that identify the good character traits, and they have also programmed this list onto their computer screens. One of the teachers concurs on the importance of these posters, "The character posters in the classrooms remind you to try to make a connection between the character topics and whatever you are teaching." Each month one trait is spotlighted, taught, and recognized schoolwide.

When visiting the Plano school district, I received a Plano "Character Traits Poster" and I learned that these character traits have been in the Plano district for over fifteen years. They were developed by teams of teachers, counselors, and administrators and have been well accepted by the total community. They have been successfully incorporated in each new district curriculum revision. Plano Schools have used them as objectives in district grade-level and subject-level curriculum guides, in cooperative groups, as a basis for thematic instruction, for the development of their outcomes, goals and assessment plans and most recently, as standards. According to the counselor at Wells, "Promoting life-long learning traits is where the district is heading now and these character traits fit right into the life-long learning traits as well."

Princeton School District in Ohio

The Princeton City School District in Cincinnati, Ohio, has the motto: "Respect yourself and others." It has also adopted a set of character education values for the entire school district. Dr. Richard Denoyer, superintendent at that time, began a district-wide, yearlong process in 1987 to identify these core values. Dr. Denoyer believes that Princeton was one of the first public school districts in the country to attempt to integrate a system of values into the curriculum beginning with kindergarten. Its goal was to coordinate the establishment of the character education program with the celebration of the Bicentennial of the U.S. Constitution. He invited all interested instructional leaders, principals, faculty, parents, and students to district-wide discussions to identify these core values. The group then forwarded its ideas on important values to the character education committee. The committee finally came up with its list of twelve values, which consisted of the following:

1. Honesty and Integrity—Be truthful and sincere to others and yourself.
2. Trustworthiness—Be true to your own word.
3. Civility and Compassion—Be polite and caring to others.
4. Loyalty—Be faithful to lawful ideals and beliefs of country, school, and friends.
5. Wisdom—Search for knowledge and truth: the ultimate realities of life.
6. Freedom—Express yourself responsibly in making choices.
7. Justice—Be fair to others and accept consequences for your own actions.
8. Equality—Support free choice and opportunities for all.
9. Diversity and Tolerance—Appreciate differences and variety in people and nature.
10. Responsibility—Maintain personal accountability, exercise rights and exert influence as a citizen in a democratic society.

11. Unity—Support family and group cohesiveness through appropriate inter-personal relationships.
12. Self-discipline and Courage—Demonstrate self-control and be true to your convictions.

The principals and staff were then asked to develop a plan to incorporate these values into all phases of the day-to-day school activities. The twelve values were included in the district curriculum guides, the annual report and each school's annual goals and objectives. The process, program, and its results were reported in many newspaper articles.

Visits to the schools in the district show that their effort has been successful. For instance, these values are prominently displayed in each classroom of the Stewart School in the Princeton School District. Stewart School is a racially and socio-economically diverse school. It has experienced large enrollment increases over the past five years with minority enrollment increasing by almost 200%. Personal responsibility is stressed at Stewart. Students are expected to be prompt and prepared, and they are asked to perform regular jobs within the school environment. Older students model good behavior when reading with kindergarteners and first-graders. Students work cooperatively in their classrooms and together on committees and special interest groups.

The Everdale School is a K–6 school, also in the Princeton School District, that is about 10% racially/ethnically diverse. At Everdale, teachers systematically and sequentially teach these twelve character traits as they teach any other part of the curriculum. The principal explains the school's philosophy: "Students are taught attributes of sound character in much the same way as any other subject is taught." By all working together on the district core set of values, they showed that they accepted as a tenet that public schools were to teach values. "We believe that the teaching of values has a place in the classroom."

State Legislated Core Values

As mentioned in chapter 2, eleven states have mandated character education instruction through legislation. Some states' laws mandate that character education be taught so many minutes a day, others actually specify the character development traits to be taught.

Georgia Schools

The County Line Elementary School is a beautiful, renovated, well-landscaped school in Widner, Georgia. It adheres to the Georgia State list of twenty-seven core values and character education concepts adopted by the State Board of Education in August, 1997, and tries to integrate both implicit and explicit values instruction throughout the curriculum. These values are included in the curriculum manuals and must be included in each teacher's daily lesson plans. The school provides opportunities for practicing these values through such activities as student organizations, team sports, assembly programs, and community service. Good manners, consideration for others, freedom from prejudice, and high ethical and moral values are modeled by faculty and staff. These practices encourage students while they strive to fulfill the school motto, "Learn Today to Lead Tomorrow."

In line with the renewed interest in values education, both nationally and at the state-level, teachers at Elm Street School in Newman, Georgia, incorporate "mini lessons" that they have developed on character development, as opportunities arise. For example, a discussion about accepting difference in others evolved naturally when a kindergarten class observed a wheelchair-bound student's arrival at school. Elm Street's population is one of social and economic extremes. Of the 572 students, approximately one-half are transported from low-socioeconomic, inner-city areas. In sharp contrast, the other 50 percent of the population reside in middle to upper-income neighborhoods due to system-wide redistricting. Forty percent of the students are from an African American heritage, and over 25 percent of the student body are handicapped. Teachers have had extensive staff development training on multiculturalism and seek to integrate intercultural experiences into all areas of the curriculum. For example, a first grade whole-language unit on "Christmas Around the World" now includes a study of African customs, music, art, and literature. To better understand world cultures, the school participates in the International Internship Program and currently hosts a Japanese intern who teaches the students about the culture, food, art, and customs of her country.

Federal Support for Pillars of Character

Walnut Hill Elementary School is one of the five schools to receive Special Honors in Character Education in 1998–1999 as well as be selected as a Blue Ribbon School. Walnut Hill is a school in Dallas, Texas, with 418 unique three to twelve-year-old children. The school is very diverse with 50 percent of their student body Hispanic and 21 percent limited English. There are twelve nationalities and six primary languages spoken at the school. The school building is also diverse and unique. It is of Spanish mission architecture with an arched doorway, a red tile roof, and a central courtyard with plants.

In 1997, the principal, JoAnne Hughes, and the faculty decided to go with the Character Counts Pillars in order to implement their character education program. The Character Counts Pillars are found in Public Law 103–301 that was unanimously based in July 1994. The resolution states that it supports the Aspen Declaration (see chapter 2) which stated that there are universal moral truths, and adopts the six values they identified as defining the essence of character—the Character Counts Pillars—and proclaims that the third week of October will be "Character Counts Week" each year in all schools. These six character pillars are respect, responsibility, trustworthiness, fairness, caring, and citizenship.

Each six weeks, Walnut Hill focuses on one pillar while continuing the infusion of the other five. School-wide music, hallway bulletin boards and character pillars greet students as they enter the building and set a positive atmosphere. Students practice responsibility and citizenship as they manage the school store, make morning announcements, or take turns cleaning the cafeteria tables. Children creatively incorporate the pillars of respect and responsibility into their talent show performances.

Once the six pillars were chosen, the teachers, counselors and principal reviewed curricular materials available. They chose to use *Lessons in Character* from the Young People's Press. The character education curriculum became an integral part of the atmosphere of the school, not merely another subject to teach. JoAnn Hughes, the principal, regularly shares character proverbs on an office communication board and each month she reads a character book to the faculty during their monthly meeting, encouraging them to use it with their classes. In October, the book was *Chrysanthemum*.

I observed a fourth-grade science class during my visit to Walnut Hill School. The book was used in a unit on flowers, studying the chrysanthemum and other types of flowers. Then in order to emphasize that students should use nice words to one another and not use "put downs" students completed an art project. They were to write a negative word on construction paper folded down the middle. Then they traced around each letter of the word and cut it out. When opened up, they now had a flower—like the *Chrysanthemum* story, they had changed a negative word to a pretty flower. This class had also just finished a writing assignment in which they wrote about why you should not tease someone because of the way they look—because it is not kind and our body is a result of the science of how we are made. Gabie Torres shared her essay with me:

> My brother picked on me because he says I don't have a bone in my nose. Whenever I push my nose it goes flat. I told him nobody has bone in their nose but they have cartilage. Other people just have a little more cartilage in their nose than I have. I don't take it personally because I know that I'm not the only one who lacks cartilage.

LIFE SKILLS

In the last five years, more and more of the Blue Ribbon Schools are calling their character qualities "Life Skills." Some schools have adopted Susan Kovalik's *Life Skills* with the *Life Long Guidelines*. Others are developing their own list of qualities that they call "Life Skills." Belmont Elementary School in Belmont, Michigan, is also one of the five Blue Ribbon Schools to receive Special Honors in Character Education in 1998–1999. The Respect Committee at Belmont spearheaded the character education program and implemented *Life Skills,* a program that identifies appropriate behaviors and provides models for teaching them. *Life*

Skills includes the following behaviors: 1) Caring; 2) Common sense; 3) Cooperation; 4) Courage; 5) Curiosity; 6) Effort; 7) Flexibility; 8) Friendship; 9) Initiative; 10) Integrity; 11) Problem solving; 12) Patience; 13) Perseverance; 14) Responsibility; and 15) Sense of humor. Each grade level is responsible for teaching two to three specific skills, which the committee chose based on the age appropriateness of the skill. By the time the students graduate from Belmont, they will have had instruction in all of the *Life Skills*. A *Life Skills* video helps introduce the terminology and explain appropriate behaviors. Songs and rhymes help students remember terms as well. *Life Skills* posters are put in each room as visual aids. As part of the instructional process, teachers explain each *Life Skill* strategy. For example, a teacher might say, "I like how Johnny persevered when he continued to work on his report, even though it was difficult." In the lunchroom students hear, "I like how all of you were active listeners paying attention to the announcements." The staff uses *Life Skills* terminology in their classes and the teacher newsletters includes the terms. *Life Skills* terminology is a part of the language spoken at Belmont. Students learn the importance of appropriate behavior from other students, teachers, and parents.

The Patterson School (another of the five schools to receive Special Honors in Character Education in 1998–1999), uses another set of Life Skills as its character education program. The Life Skills addressed in its program include honesty, good judgement, compassion, respect, cooperation, building self-esteem, responsibility, motivation, being a hard worker, initiative, perseverance, and critical thinking. One of its teachers, Annette Taul, co-authored a book *Developing Character: A Classroom Approach* which is a curriculum guide for each grade level giving ideas on how teachers can teach that month's life skill. The curriculum was designed to be implemented within the structure of instruction in science, language arts, and social studies. There are four lessons written for each skill, a total of forty-four lessons per grade level.

For example, activities on responsibility from the *Developing Character* program include kindergarten students proudly charting the things they do independently at home that are responsible, and first-grade students discussing and drawing pictures of what would happen if the garbage collectors did not pick up the garbage. Second-grade students learn the difference between reporting, which is being responsible, and tattling, which is just to get someone in trouble. In third grade, children ask their parents to teach them a new skill, such as ironing or sewing on a button. Fourth-grade students read about Angelina and Sarah Grimke, abolitionists and social reformers. In fifth grade, students brainstorm ways the class can help those less fortunate in the community, and sixth grade students develop a Decision Tree to see how their decisions affect those around them.

In addition to these activities, each month's Life Skill is emphasized on an ongoing basis throughout the school. Teachers compliment students displaying the Life Skill by saying, "That was very responsible of you." or "You're using good judgement," or " I'm proud of your perseverance." Citizens of the Month are chosen based upon Life Skills for special school-wide recognition. Individual classrooms have special ways of recognizing students who display Life Skills throughout the year. The Patterson School is a large, ethnically and socio-economically diverse, K–6 school in California.

CHARACTER EDUCATION INTEGRATED
THROUGHOUT THE CURRICULUM

As shown in Table 2, approximately one-fifth of the Blue Ribbon Schools reviewed stated that they integrate character development throughout their curriculum. Some school districts have developed curriculum guides that incorporate character education qualities such as honesty, kindness, truthfulness, fairness, responsibility, appreciating differences, and valuing friendships into the social studies, English, and guidance program objectives. Other schools focus on a "Virtue-of-the-Month" or "Virtue-of-the-Week" and include family participation in the character development program by sending home notes outlining the virtue under study and asking parents to encourage specific virtuous actions at home.

For example, character development goals are incorporated into the daily learning activity at the Governor Bent Elementary School in Albuquerque, New Mexico, whenever appropriate. Governor Bent serves a large and diverse population from distinctly different geographic and socioeconomic areas. The population includes middle-income homeowners, professionally educated families and lower-income families who live in government-subsidized housing. Almost 40 percent of the student body are of Hispanic ethnicity. According to Marilyn Davenport, the principal, the school makes a conscious effort to communicate its expectations of children.

> All the adults in the school strive to model an appreciation and respect for others and for children, which we feel is reciprocated by the student body. The students are expected to actively contribute to the overall environment. They are given leadership roles in organizations such as the student council and are helped to be sensitive toward the needs of others through food and clothing drives. We feel children should develop the positive attributes of patriotism, honesty, and empathy for others to become strong citizens of the community. Character development goals are incorporated into all daily activity in the school. We make a conscious effort to communicate our expectations for children.

The students at the Volker Applied Learning Magnet School in Kansas City, Missouri, would be characterized by others as an "at risk" student body. More than half of the student body of this middle school of fourth- and fifth-graders are of African American origin and are from lower-income families. One-quarter of the students qualify for special education services. According to Dr. Rayna Levine, the principal:

> Knowing right from wrong is taught and reinforced at the school. Honesty is appreciated and commended. We use students' sense of fairness, equality, and justice when discussing incidents. In this way, personal responsibility is built. Our goal is for students to assume personal responsibility for their actions and not blame others when things do not go as envisioned.

Some schools reported a variety of methods used to integrate character education in the curriculum. At the Harrison Elementary School in Harrison, Ohio, core values include honesty, respect, acceptance, and justice. Staff teach these values in classroom activities involving role-playing and discussion as well as through the use of literature, films, and other media. Harrison is a very large K–6 suburban school with a middle class, white student body. Harrison has also instituted a P.R.I.D.E. Program (Positive Recognition for Individual Discipline and Enthusiasm) that strives to build students' self-esteem and to recognize students who display good conduct and work habits.

Puppets with a Purpose

A unique curricular program designed to develop ethical judgment, manners, and values was found in the Irwin School, a K–5 school in suburban East Brunswick, New Jersey. In this program, Puppets with a Purpose, students supply ideas for the topics of the plays. The puppets act out the situations suggested by the students. Then students in the class comment on the actions of the puppets: "Rudie's being Rude . . . Betsy is Bossy." Post-play discussions are lively and help students to verbalize their feelings about situations similar to those they personally have experienced. The puppets are able to bridge cultural and linguistic differences and bring their message to the large group of Asian students as well as to the Caucasian students.

CURRICULAR PROGRAMS

Almost 40% of the schools answered the question "How do school programs, practices, policies, and staff foster the development of good character. . . ." by stating that they promote character development through a specific curricular program or units in the curriculum. In the first edition, the majority of the curricular programs identified by schools were drug education curricula more than "character education" curricula. These will be described in chapter 4 on Drug Education. Due to the growth in the importance of character education in the past few years, this second edition is happy to report that the majority of the schools are now using a character education program that is either a commercial program or a school developed program, rather than using a drug education curricula as their primary vehicle for character development.

Most of the school-developed programs are based around deciding on school-wide values, virtues, character qualities, or life-skills, as described above, and then having teachers integrate these qualities into their lesson plans. Some schools have done this so effectively that they have written their own curriculum.

Some of the commercial programs used by the Blue Ribbon Schools are the Character Education Institute curriculum, the Jefferson Center for Character Education, the Child Development Project, the Giraffes Program, the Heartwood curriculum, and the Wise Quotes curriculum.

Character Education Institute

The Del Cerro Elementary School, a magnet school in suburban, middle class Mission Viejo, California, uses the Character Education Institute curriculum for its character education program. Del Cerro has designed its school program so that staff promote the teaching of positive attitudes and behavior on a regular basis. A word is highlighted each month in every classroom and the teacher is provided with opportunities in the curriculum to reinforce and use the concept. Words such as friendship, kindness, cooperation, responsibility, honesty, sportsmanship, respect, courage, self-control, and freedom are presented schoolwide. Numerous suggestions are given to the teachers for using written language, literature, science, social studies, reading, art, and oral language classes to promote further understanding of the target values. Each teacher encourages discussions regarding ways in which to apply the values that have been introduced. Cooperative learning groups further help children learn to work together and be more accepting of others' opinions. In addition to assemblies and awards, a banner displays the "Word of the Month," bulletin boards portray the word, and cards and certificates are given during the month by adults when they notice someone exemplifying the month's word.

The Character Education curriculum focuses on instilling universal values, refining critical thinking skills, clearly teaching right from wrong, and building good self-esteem. Though most of the values taught through the curriculum are overt, additional objectives are reinforced through topic lessons. These include responsibility, self-esteem, conflict resolution, respecting the rights of others, obeying rules and the law, service learning, and cooperative learning. Some of the ancillary concepts taught that further aid in building good character include setting goals, planning ahead, sharing, cliques, patience, perseverance, using time wisely, managing money, and table manners. More information on the curriculum can be obtained by contacting Jay Mulkey at the Character Education Institute, 8919 Tesoro Drive, Suite 220, San Antonio, TX 78217-6253, Telephone (210) 829-1727, www.charactereducation.org/.

The Giraffe Project

Henry W. Allen Fundamental Elementary School in New Orleans, Louisiana, uses the Giraffe Project, *Standing Tall* with their fifth grades. This curriculum intro-duces students to "Giraffes" real-life heroes, men, women, and children who have stuck their necks out for others. *Standing Tall* helps students distinguish media celebrities from every day heroes worthy of admiration, one time acts of heroism from the perseverance necessary to achieve long term results, selfishness from selflessness, and the generosity to work for the common good. The project helps students see service to others and to their communities as an integral part of their plans for a meaningful life. By the end of the curriculum, the kids are in action, doing a service project they design to address public problems that concern them. The Allen Elementary School, is a PK–6 grade school with a student body that is 98 percent African American, and 85 percent at poverty level. Coming from a violence-ridden neighborhood, the Giraffe Program challenges the children to cre-ate a better future. For more information contact: The Giraffe Project, P.O. Box 759, Langley, WA 98260, Telephone (360) 221-7989, www.giraffe.org/giraffe/.

Jefferson Center for Character Education Curriculum

The Bellerive School, with a culturally diverse population of over 500 students in suburban Creve Coeur, Missouri, uses the Jefferson Center for Character Educa-tion Curriculum with the STAR system. This curriculum focuses on the system-atic teaching of common values that cut across ethnic, cultural, and religious lines. These values include honesty, respect, responsibility, integrity, courage, tol-erance, justice, and politeness. According to Dr. David Brooks, the program di-rector of the Jefferson Center, the Character Education curriculum is used in about six thousand schools and approximately fifty thousand classrooms. The curriculum teaches students the four step decision-making model to solve prob-lems and resolve conflicts. The model is known as STAR or "Stop, Think, Act, Review." It also teaches them to accept the consequences of their actions; develop and improve self-confidence, self-esteem, and positive attitudes; set and achieve realistic goals; and accept that attendance, punctuality, and reliability are part of being personally responsible. STAR also stands for Success Through Accepting Responsibility, a school-wide systematic program for improving school climate, attendance, achievement, and self-discipline.

The curriculum includes short and easy-to-follow weekly lessons that can be infused into the regular curriculum. It encourages the use of monthly themes that are featured on classroom posters.

For example, at Bellerive the October theme was "Be a Goal Setter." Other monthly themes are: "Be Responsible," "Be Polite," "Be on Time," "Be a Lis-tener," "Be a Risk Taker," and "Be a Tough Worker." The personal values of ac-countability, honesty, integrity, responsibility, and self-esteem are taught through the Bellerive Cadet Helper Program. The Cadet Program provides students with the opportunity for providing service to the school. Teachers ask for assistance in the classroom in such areas as reading aloud to a student or helping with math facts. Cadets pick the teacher, job, and time they will be able to assist. In this way, they are given actual opportunities in which they can live the monthly themes.

More information on the STAR curriculum can be obtained from Dr. David Brooks at the Jefferson Center for Character Education, P.O. Box 1283, Monrovia, CA 91017-1283, Telephone (626)-301-0403, www.jeffersoncenter.org/. Information on the Multicultural Literature, which the Jefferson Center has developed around the STAR process, can be obtained from the Young People's Press, Inc., 1731 Kettner Blvd., San Diego, CA 92101, Telephone (800) 231-9774.

Child Development Program

Recognized schools from California's San Ramon County were members of the Child Development Project Program (CDP), which has been implemented in eight schools in the district. This project has now become nationally known as the only character education program included in the National Diffusion Network of "Educational Programs that Work." The Country Club Elementary School is a model school of the Child Development Project (CDP). The families in the Country Club attendance area have the lowest average income in the district and the greatest number of students whose native language is not English. The CDP program was conceived after a review of the literature on promoting caring and responsible behavior in students suggested that a long-term, comprehensive school intervention program, delivered primarily by classroom teachers but with considerable parental involvement was likely to produce widespread and long-lasting changes in children's pro-social attitudes, motives, and behaviors (Kohn, 1990, Watson et al., 1989). The major components of the project include: (1) direct teaching of prosocial values through the use of a literature-based reading program, (2) developmental discipline as an approach to classroom management, which involves creating a warm, caring classroom where children help to solve problems through classroom meetings, (3) cooperative learning, which fosters children working together and practicing pro-social values, and (4) mutual understanding, promoted by allowing students to help one another. The program is designed to increase childrens' responsibility, helpfulness, cooperation, and social skills. Ongoing evaluation of the project has indicated that it is successful and effective (Developmental Studies Center, 1994). This evaluation model will be described in more detail in chapter 9.

A visit to the school confirms the positive effect of the program. Although the official funding for the program at Country Club Hills ended more than eight years ago, principal Carol Rowley and the faculty who participated in the original program continue to pass on the CDP philosophy to new faculty. A caring environment truly exists in the school. An effort is made to give the students many examples of the character qualities of respect, responsibility, problem solving and caring throughout the curriculum.

For more information on the Child Development Program and the Literature-Based Curriculum that they use, contact Eric Schaps at the Developmental Studies Center, 2000 Embarcadero, Suite 305, Oakland, CA 94606, www.devstu.org/. Telephone, (800) 666-7270, or (510) 533-0213.

The Heartwood Curriculum

The Hartwood Elementary School in Pittsburgh, Pennsylvania, uses the Heartwood Curriculum. Hartwood is a midsize K–5 school with a diverse group of children whose families come from mining and farming communities. Once a blue-collar community, the school is now socio-economically diverse with 13% of its students qualifying for free lunch and 20 percent qualifying for special education services. Heartwood is a multicultural curriculum that uses stories that convey basic ethical concepts directly and effectively. The stories, from award-winning children's literature, exemplify the concepts of courage, justice, hope, love, loyalty, respect, and honesty. The Heartwood curriculum is a comprehensive program that includes varied materials for teachers such as exercises that encourage student writing, storymaking, and group interaction. The process stimulates the children to grapple thoughtfully with profound concepts, share their own experiences, and make personal connections with ideas. The children apply the concepts in their daily lives and carry home activities to involve their families in the teaching and learning process as well. The manual is organized for classroom use. It outlines the best sequence for teaching the books: a preview, reading, discussion, activities, interdisciplinary ideas, wrap-up, resources, and strategies for achieving the objectives of the lessons.

An evaluation conducted by the Research for Better Schools reported that the Heartwood materials were highly commended by the field test teachers. Almost all of the teachers emphasized the importance and need for this type of program in their schools. Teachers felt strongly that students were lacking in their ethical development and that this program provided a constructive strategy for initiating discussion with students in this critical area. The Heartwood curriculum is one of the best character development programs that I have found. It teaches the direct instruction of specific virtues; it uses classical literature to provide models of character who have lived these virtues; and it includes comprehensive, interdisciplinary lesson plans that allow teachers to integrate character education into literature, social studies, art, and music. The most recent evaluation of the Heartwood curriculum will be summarized in chapter 9.

Information on the Heartwood curriculum can be obtained by contacting Eleanor Childs at The Heartwood Institute, 425 North Craig Street, Suite 302,

Pittsburgh, PA 15213, Telephone (412) 688-8570 or (800) 432-7810, www. enviroweb.org/heartwood/.

Wise Quotes

The Daisy Ingraham School in Westbrook, Connecticut, formed a character development steering committee with parents, teachers, the principal, the school psychologist, the public librarians, and the YMCA children's programming director. As a group they chose to adopt "Wise Quotes," a program for third to fifth graders, which features an exemplary character trait each month, including honesty, respect, and responsibility. Every week a quote is highlighted that illustrates the monthly trait. The quotes are read over the Kids' News in the morning, and discussed in the classrooms. The cafeteria's bulletin board has become a character trait showplace. Each month, a different grade level creates a display using students' work to represent that month's virtue. Upon the launching of this program, every staff member received a notebook containing the program's mission, the monthly traits, and the weekly quotes. This gave them a shared vocabulary, so the children found consistent expectations throughout the school.

A strong aspect of the program is the level of commitment on the part of the faculty. Several teachers introduced their lessons with a brief comment about the trait of the month. The teachers model courtesy, politeness, and kindness in the manner in which they treat students and colleagues. Several parents and faculty members stated that the Character Education program has had a positive influence on the school. According to the principal, this program has improved the atmosphere of the school and the behavior of the students. The commitment to character is clearly evident in the daily lives of the students. Their weekly classroom meetings focus on becoming a community whose members treat each other with kindness and respect. Every classroom displays the teacher's expectations, along with the classroom rules the children help compose. Lessons are drawn from literature as well as from life. Books that exemplify positive values, such as biographies of inspiring people, are read and discussed. Students who exemplify the monthly character traits are recognized by the principal on the Kids' News program. The Superintendent's Award is given each year to the student who serves as a model leader to his or her peers. The Daisy Ingraham School is a mid-size, homogeneous school located in the small shoreline town of Westbrook, Connecticut. The school is built upon traditional New England values: dedication, hard work, and a strong sense of community.

Wise Quotes is one part of the comprehensive Wise Skills program—a school-wide, multicultural and interdisciplinary character building and drug and violence prevention program written by Seth Schapiro, the founder. For more information on the Wise Skills program contact: Wise Skills Resources, P.O. Box 491, Santa Cruz, CA 95061-0491, Telephone (888) WISESKILLS (888) 947-3754, www.wiseskills.com.

TEACHING CHARACTER
DEVELOPMENT THROUGH LITERATURE

In addition to these curriculum materials, many of the Blue Ribbon Schools mentioned that they use good literature for character education. Many character education experts (Estes, 2001; Ryan and Bohlin, 1999; Wiley, 1998; Vincent, 1994) would concur that literature is always concerned with questions of value and confronts the reader with moral and ethical questions. Teachers at Guntersville Elementary School in Alabama select stories from William Bennett's book, *Children's Book of Virtues* for their story time or circle time with children. The stories are chosen as an avenue for discussions regarding the essentials of good character: Courage, Self-discipline, Honesty, Friendship, and Loyalty. Their teachers share their favorite books: "*Charlotte's Web* by E. B. White and *Ira Sleeps Over* by Bernard Waber are used as a springboard to discuss friendship and self-esteem." "*The Boxcar Children* by Gertrude Chandler Warner presents another opportunity for a study of self-esteem since the children in the book are portrayed as resourceful, and self-sufficient." "Another favorite book at the school is *The Rainbow Fish* by Marcus Pfister, about a fish who is proud and vain, and none of the other fishes want to be his friend until he learns to give away some of his most prized possessions." These books and others provide an opportunity to study ways to build character.

Another strategy used at Guntersville to teach good character is "bibliotherapy." A book or story is chosen which has characters that have the same problems as those that exist in the classroom. As the book characters are discussed, all students feel free to participate in the discussion and help the class come to a conclusion about what would be the appropriate behavior. A popular book that provides an avenue for such a discussion is *The Hundred Dresses* by Eleanor Estes. This timeless story is used to teach kindness because its theme is peer group acceptance. A character in the story is shunned and teased as an outsider until she wins a contest with her drawing of one hundred dresses, but by then she has moved away. Teachers ask questions, such as, "What were some things that could have been done differently by the classmates?"

Many of the Blue Ribbon Schools have prepared lists of books to use when teaching specific virtues. Their school libraries also have collections of books on character development relating to honesty, fairness, character, responsibility, dedication, and other virtues. Teachers can use these books in various classes. The schools also make a conscious effort to choose textbooks that foster traditional American values and tradition; many of them use the Open Court Series for reading; the Joy Wilt books, the Ann Johnson biographies, and the Capstone Press books were cited as excellent character building books to include in the library.

Joy Wilt Berry has written over two hundred self-help books for children from birth through age twelve. Her goal is to help children become competent, responsible, and happy individuals. There are several series of books that are produced by Living Skills Press, Sebastopol, California, and published by Children's

Press, Chicago, that can be purchased for school libraries. One series, called the Living Skills, includes titles such as *Every Kids' Guide to Manners, . . . to Making Friends . . . to Handling Arguments . . . to Family Rules and Responsibility*. Another series includes such titles as: *About Divorce, About Change and Moving About Death*. Finally, for pre-schoolers there is another series: *Teach Me About Looking . . . about Smelling . . . about Pretending . . . Tasting*.

Ann Donegan Johnson has written a series of biographies that emphasize specific character qualities. Called the ValueTale Series, they are published by Value Communications, Inc., P.O. Box 101, La Jolla, CA 92038. They include such titles as *The Value of Determination: The Story of Helen Keller, The Value of Courage: The Story of Jackie Robinson, The Value of Respect: The Story of Abraham Lincoln,* and *The Value of Honesty: The Story of Confucius*.

Capstone Press features a series of books on character education written by Lucia Raatma. I served as the character education consultant for this series. Each easy-reading text focuses on a different character quality (twenty in all): caring, consideration, courage, friendliness, honesty, patriotism. . . respect, responsibility, and tolerance. Written according to the paradigm of character education presented above, each book helps students explore what the value is, gives them everyday examples of how to live the virtue, and hands-on activities that help them to want to live the value at home, in school, and in their family. For more information contact Capstone Press, 151 Good Counsel Drive, P.O. Box 6609, Mankato, MN 56002-0669, Telephone (800) 747-4992, www.capstone-press.com.

Several schools also noted that the *Weekly Reader* has actual lessons on character development. Robbie the Raccoon is the section in which these citizenship and moral situations are discussed in the primary editions. For example, in the January 1997 Grade Three *Weekly Reader* the students are given the following situation to discuss:

Hi Girls and Boys!

It snowed yesterday. My friends and I . . . made some snowballs, and we started tossing them around. I tried to throw one up on the roof of Mrs. Perkin's house. But it didn't make it. The snowball smashed one of the house's upstairs windows. Now what should I do? Have you ever broken something that didn't belong to you? What did you do?

Your friend,

Robbie Raccoon

The *Weekly Reader* is one of the most widely read newspapers for children, reaching 40 percent of the elementary school children in this country. It is published by The

Weekly Reader Corporation, 245 Long Hill Road, P.O. Box 2791, Middletown, CT 06457-9291, www.weeklyreader.com.

Finally, there is a growing trend, especially noted in the research for this second edition, to use films and videos to promote character education. In a visit to the Coronodo Village Elementary School in San Diego County, the visitor observed an intriguing literature lesson in which the students had to just watch a video of Anne Frank. They were doing a comparison and a contrast of behaviors:

- Hatred and intolerance versus kindness and acceptance
- Bully and opponents versus shared conflict
- Enemies versus friends
- Win/lose versus win/win

For each area, the students discussed the video and also related it to real life experiences on how they have handled situations. Students were totally engrossed in this class discussion. Coronado is a very large, ethnically diverse school in the small, island resort community off the coast of San Diego and ten miles from the Mexican boarder.

The Belmont School in Michigan has "film nights" in which children and parents watch specific films and discuss them. They use quality films with an underlying message of family, friendship, truth, trust, and responsibility as being the most important thing in life, rather than money or fame. The idea behind the Family Feature Films is that a child will learn appropriate ideas and behaviors through modeling. The following are the grade level films chosen by the Pride Committee:

Grade Level	Film Title
Pre and Kindergarten	Willy the Sparrow
1st	On Our Own
2nd	Secret of Treasure Mountain
3rd	The Buttercream Gang
4th	The Rogue Stallion
5th	Split Infinity

The character education holdings of the Plano school libraries include the Joy Wilt and Johnson biographies as well as many other value-rich books.

SUMMARY

This chapter shows the many ways in which the Blue Ribbon Schools teach moral education and values, using deliberate school-wide efforts to integrate character development throughout the curriculum and school community. All members of the school community are important players in the realization of this goal. Parents, teachers, principals, and students are involved in the writing of mission statements, and the identification of core values for schools and school districts. Every subject matter lends itself to providing opportunities for teaching character education. In order to use these opportunities effectively, teachers need training. Some curricular programs are available that provide this guidance through their teacher materials and guides, but in this area, much growth is in need.

This chapter shows that character education is alive and is working well in many of the Blue Ribbon Schools today. There are many different ways in which a school defines its core character qualities and tries to develop character in its students. Indeed, there are different levels towards which a school can strive to become a value-conscious community. As explained by the Regnart Elementary School, a very culturally diverse K–6 school in suburban Cupertino, California:

The stages of character development can be compared to that of a flower. It begins with a tightly folded bud and then with the nurturing of sun, water, and soil, it blossoms into a cluster of petals. Each petal of that flower represents a different aspect of a child's character development: honesty, integrity, responsibility, consideration of others, respect for self.

4

Teachers of Character

Work while it is called today, for you know not how much you will be hindered tomorrow. One today is worth two tomorrows; never leave that till tomorrow that you can do today.

—Benjamin Franklin

Whatever I have tried to do in life, I have tried with all my heart to do well.

—Charles Dickens

Teach your students to use what talents they have; the woods would be silent if no bird sang except those that sing best.

—Anonymous

Meno tells Socrates that if virtue is knowledge, there can be no doubt that virtue is taught. Socrates replies that if it is taught, there must be teachers of virtue. Socrates was not able to find any "teachers of virtue" in Athens before the end of the dialogue, but Aristotle in his writings described such teachers of virtue. He said that teachers help students to become good when they teach in such a way that they help students to cultivate good habits, or virtues. For "with regard to virtue, it is not enough to know, but we must also try to have and use it, and in this way become good" (1179a).

The Blue Ribbon Schools have found teachers of virtue. The first teachers of character are the student's parents. Then the school's teacher, principal and counselor each play an important role. Teachers promote character in students by capturing the teachable moment and addressing moral and ethical issues. They challenge their students to develop good study habits in order to be the best students that they can be. Teachers have high academic standards for all their students, but they also have high standards for themselves, seeking to do their best as teachers. Blue Ribbon teachers implement the latest pedagogical methodologies that enable students to have academic success while helping them develop their character through the effort to do their work as a student well. In order to be nominated as a Blue Ribbon School, applicants had to show that they were doing an exceptional job with all of their students in developing a solid foundation of basic skills and knowledge of subject matter in addition to promoting the development of their character. The bulk of the application form concerns the former. It asks for evidence that the students are developing a solid foundation of skills in reading, writing, and mathematics; and the schools must include separate documentation on each of these areas. For a complete review of these academic areas, the reader should refer to other books that have been written about the Blue Ribbon Schools: *The Nation's Best Schools: Blueprints for Excellence, Volume 1: Elementary and Middle Schools* (Ogden and Germinarion, 1994), *Best Ideas from America's Blue Ribbon Schools, Vol. 1 and Vol. 2* (National Association of Elementary School Principals, 1994, 1995).

This chapter reports on teachers, principals, counselors, and parents who promote character in students. It also reports on the teaching techniques, methods, or programs that the schools specifically mentioned in the section on "promoting the development of sound character, a sense of self-worth, democratic values, ethical judgment, and self-discipline in students." This chapter looks at teachers and their important role in teaching character education in the Blue Ribbon Schools and it identifies teaching techniques that promote character found in the Blue Ribbon Schools. It shows how these schools develop the academic ability of students, and, in so doing, help them to actually live good character traits. It reports on a few of the instructional programs mentioned by the Blue Ribbon Schools as important for the development of character; it makes connections between these pedagogical methodologies and the development of character, and cites research that documents the effectiveness of these techniques in promoting learning. The chapter tries to answer the following questions:

- How are the teachers, principal, counselors, and parents involved in promoting character development in young people?
- Why is it important for a school to stress academics in order to promote character development in students?
- Why must the value of work be understood if a student is to become a person of character?
- What are some instructional strategies that contribute to the character development of students?
- Why is it key to develop thinking skills in students through whole language, thematic instruction, or other methods in order to develop their character?

THE TEACHER'S ROLE IN CHARACTER DEVELOPMENT

The role of the teacher was found to be very important especially in schools that do not have specific character education curricular programs for the character development of students. The teacher has to model character and thus encourages students to want to develop their own character. As the anonymous sage tells us: "A mediocre teacher tells, a good teacher explains, a superior teacher demonstrates, but a great teacher inspires." Inspiration is moving students to want to become better and this is the key to character growth (Ryan and Bohlin, 1999). Great teachers find the "teachable moments" in which to show the intersection of moral issues in the curriculum under study. The Teacher Handbook at the Barclay Brook School, a moderate-sized primary school in the town of Jamesburg, New York, expresses these expectations of its teachers clearly:

> The children in our school are very special. We are charged with the profound responsibility of educating children in a manner that will enable them to develop into caring and productive citizens. Our habits and manners are quickly observed by the children and impact on their personal development. As leaders in our school, we are expected to interact with students in a caring and courteous manner at all times. We set the example.

Other Blue Ribbon Schools report that their "teachers try to incorporate a strong sense of values in all that they teach." The teachers and staff are expected to be character models for the students. "Each teacher fosters good character and democratic values in the classroom and on the playground. Ethical judgments are fostered by modeling appropriate behaviors through classroom management techniques." "We believe that students must be taught by word and example the moral principles upon which our nation was founded. Each teacher is expected to teach character education." According to Gary Fenstermacher (1990), the teacher is a key player in promoting character education in the schools. He states: "There are three different ways in which teachers serve as both moral agents and moral educators. They can be quite directive, teaching morality outright—a form of instruction called didactic instruction. . . . Second, teachers can teach about morality. A third way is to act morally, holding oneself up as a possible model for the students, a model of honesty, fairplay, consideration of others, tolerance, and sharing" (p. 134). William Bennett (1991) expands upon this last point:

> To put students in the presence of a morally mature adult who speaks honestly and candidly to them is essential to their moral growth. It seems to me that this is why many teachers entered the profession in the first place–because they thought they could make a positive difference in the lives of students, in the development of their character, i.e., to make them better men and women. (p. 134)

The Lugoff Elementary School in Lugoff, South Carolina, is a large, ethnically diverse primary building with one-third of its children from a low socioeconomic background as most of its parents are employees of the local manufacturing companies. Its report expresses the high expectations for its teachers:

> We believe each teacher has a responsibility to perform in a professional manner and engage in continuous study and self-analysis. We believe each teacher should possess the kind of moral character, educational philosophy and professional attitude that has a positive influence on learning and attitude development of the students.

The teachers in the Blue Ribbon Schools try, in the words of one school, to "offer experiences throughout the program which teach the values of character, ethics, and democracy." Examples in these schools include English classes that use Aesop's fables and other stories to foster character development and exemplify values which lead to writing assignments such as "How to settle a disagreement" or "How to avoid a fight." Social studies classes teach the values and ideals of famous Americans, and teachers make special efforts to emphasize some of the virtuous qualities of national heroes. Fair play is often developed in physical education classes.

In order to do this effectively, one needs a strong background in character education content and methods. How did these teachers get this preparation and training?

TEACHING CHARACTER EDUCATION TO TEACHERS

Schools and districts wishing to begin a character education program need to provide for staff development. As noted by Henry Huffman (1994) in his book on the development of a character education program in the Mt. Lebanon School district, "Most teachers have not received any formal preparation at the undergraduate or graduate level for their role as character educators" (p. 45). In fact, according to Wynne and Ryan (1993), many teachers lack "moral literacy," that is, a framework regarding concepts of character, values, and moral behavior; they lack the psychological principles of how humans develop morally and they have not learned methodologies appropriate for developing character. A doctoral dissertation by Alice Lancton (cited in Wynne and Ryan, 1993), found that in a sample of thirty middle school and junior high teachers not a single teacher recalled being told in college or in a district in-service about the teacher's role or responsibility as a moral educator or developer of good character. A survey of forty-three heads of teacher education from denominational, state, and private higher education institutions from four distinct regions in the United States (east, west, midwest, and south) was conducted by Dara Vernon Wakefield (1996) of Baylor University.

She found that although the heads of these teacher education programs supported the notion of instruction in moral education methods, more than half of the programs indicated that these methods are not directly taught to any significant extent. This is true today, even though a survey in 1991 by the American Association of School Administrators indicated that moral education programs were a part of the curriculum in more than ten thousand schools nationwide (Wakefield, 1996). In the fall of 1997, the Center for the Advancement of Ethics and Character at the Boston University School of Education and the Character Education Partnership surveyed six hundred teacher education institutions across the country in order to discern the current preparation of teachers in character education. They found that although there is overwhelming support for the concept of character education, it is not a high priority in the curriculum of teacher education and there is little philosophic consensus about what character education is or how it should be taught (Nielsen Jones, 1998).

Ryan and Bohlin (1999) list seven particular competencies teachers need to become character educators: Teachers must: (1) be able to model good character and character building themselves, (2) make the development of their students' moral life and character a professional responsibility and a priority, (3) be able to engage students in moral discourse, and be able to talk about what is right and what is wrong in life, (4) be able to articulate clearly their own positions on a range of ethical issues, (5) be able to help children empathize with the experience of others, (6) be able to establish a positive moral ethos in their classrooms, (7) be able to provide activities . . . that will give students experience and practice in behaving ethically and altruistically.

As Lickona (1993) explains, "Character education is far more complex than teaching math or reading; it requires personal growth as well as skills development. Yet teachers typically receive almost no pre-service or in-service training in the moral aspects of their craft" (p.7).

The author is a professor at a teacher preparation institution and teaches character education to her students. Character education principles and the specific moral education methodology mentioned above could fit well in the following teacher certification courses: History and Philosophy of Education, Educational Psychology, Methods of Teaching Reading/English, Methods of Teaching Social Studies/History, and Classroom Management and Discipline. It can also find its way into other teacher preparation courses with a little initiative and creativity on the part of the professor. We have the ideal set-up at the University of St. Francis because our students are able to do their clinical experiences in schools with teachers who have taken my graduate course in character education and are teaching in schools that have adopted character education. Our student teachers are actually able to practice teaching character education under the guidance of a mentor teacher.

I also teach graduate courses on character education to practicing teachers. Titles can vary, such as Character Education for Teachers, Teaching Respect and

Responsibility in the Classroom, Moral Development, Values Education and/or Issues in Education.

Associations of teacher educators, school administrators, and curriculum directors are aware of the challenge and have begun to speak out about the need for teaching ethics and character education to pre-teachers and teachers in-service. Entire journal issues have been dedicated to this topic. The reader is referred to the *Bulletin of the National Association of Secondary School Principals*, Vol. 83, No. 609, 1999; the *Journal of the Association of Teacher Educators,* Vol. XX, No. 4, winter 1998; *Phi Delta Kappan*, Vol. 78, No. 6, February 1997; *Journal of Education*, Vol. 179, No. 2, 1997 and Vol. 175, No. 2, 1993; *Journal of Staff Development*, Spring, 1996; *The School Administrator*, Vol. 52, No. 8, Sept. 1995; *Educational Leadership*, Vol. 51, No.3, Nov. 1993; and the *Journal of Teacher Education*, Vol. 42, No. 3, May-June, 1991.

As noted in chapter 2, any educator who has learned about teaching values in schools was probably taught the values clarification philosophy prevalent in the 1970s—a philosophy which purports that the teacher should use morally neutral methods—or the moral dilemma discussion method of Kohlberg that was prevalent in the 1980s. Both methods focus on process, not on moral content. Training in these process approaches does not prepare teachers for their role as character educators, which includes teaching–directly and indirectly–the virtues (moral content) that make up good character.

There is a real need for teachers in schools today to learn how they can foster and develop good character through their teaching. Hopefully, teachers reading this book will find some valuable ideas on how to promote character while teaching their subject area. In the theoretical comments included in each chapter, I am trying to give the reader an intellectual framework for understanding character education and for evaluating the curricular programs that are found in the schools. I also suggest that teachers read *Educating for Character: How Our Schools Can Teach Respect and Responsibility* by Thomas Lickona. This book provides an excellent foundation for understanding character education. One can then continue one's formation as a character educator by reading the other books cited by name in the text of this book (Devine et al., 2000; Ryan and Bohlin, 1999; DeRoche and Williams, 1998; Wiley, 1998; Goleman, 1995; Kilpatrick, 1992; Benniga, 1991). The involvement of teachers in the formulation of a district/school's core values and as key players in the development of the curriculum also provides an invaluable faculty development experience.

Teachers can receive valuable in-service training on how to promote character if their district adopts a set curriculum. The Character Counts Curriculum, the Heartwood Foundation, the Quest Foundation, and the Thomas Jefferson Center all offer initial in-service training upon adoption of the curriculum. Teachers can augment their knowledge of character education by taking one of the graduate courses listed above at their local teacher training university, by attending a summer institute or by attending a national conference on character education.

Summer institutes for teachers have begun across the nation. Tom Lickona sponsors a summer institute through the Center for the 4th & 5th Rs at the State University College in Cortland, New York. Contact the Center for the 4th & 5th Rs, P.O. Box 2000, Cortland, NY 13045, Telephone (607) 753-2455, www.cortland. edu/www/c4n5rs. Karen Bohlin and Kevin Ryan, from the Center for the Advancement of Ethics and Character, offer a one-week summer institute for school districts on site. Contact the Center for the Advancement of Ethics and Character at 605 Commonwealth Avenue, Boston, MA 02215, Telephone (617) 343-3262. These "teacher academies" emphasize the use of the curriculum as the primary vehicle for transmitting moral values to the young. Edward DeRoche and Mary Williams offer an annual international summer workshop for teachers and administrators at the International Center for Character Education at the University of San Diego, Telephone (619) 260-5980, www.teachvalues.org/icce. The author offers workshops and in-services for teachers and a one week summer graduate course on Character Education at the Center for Character Education at the University of St. Francis, 500 Wilcox, Joliet, IL 60431, Telephone (815) 740-3212, email: mmurphy@stfrancis.edu, www.stfrancis.edu/ed/murphy/chared.

Additionally, there are three national conferences on character education and moral development that can provide valuable faculty development in character education. The Character Education Partnership sponsors the Character Education Forum in October of each year. Contact Character Education Partnership, 1025 Connecticut Ave., N.W., Suite 1011, Washington, DC 20036. Telephone (202) 296-7743, www.character.org. The National Character Education Conference is in July each year in St. Louis, Missouri. Contact Linda McKay at the CHARACTER plus-Prep, 8225 Florissant Rd., St. Louis, MO 63121, email: character@info.csd.org, Telephone (800) 478-5684. Finally, the Association for Moral Education sponsors a conference in November.

ROLE OF THE PRINCIPAL AS MORAL LEADER

The principal also plays an important part in creating a climate for character development in the schools. Gordon Vessels (1998) defines school climate as "the readily perceptible personality or atmosphere within a classroom or school that is created by its unique combination of organizational characteristics" (p 172). According to Lickona (1991), whenever you find a school with a healthy moral environment, you will find a principal—or another person with responsibility delegated from the principal—who is leading the way. How do principals lead? Recurring leadership methods cited in almost half of the Blue Ribbon Schools include character building assemblies, plays, school mottos or slogans, bulletin board messages, posters, and public address (P.A.) announcements. In some schools, the Pledge of Allegiance is followed by an inspirational thought or quote from the principal. *Project Wisdom* is a program many principals use to help them in this endeavor. This centerpiece of this program is a collection of thought-provoking message designed to be read over the P.A. or in-house television set. Each message highlights a quote from a famous person which helps students to reflect on their personal values and moral principles and apply them to their daily life. For more information contact: Project Wisdom, Inc., 4747 Bellaire Boulevard, Suite 210, Bellaire, Texas 77401, Telephone (800) 884-4974, www.projectswisdom.com. Through these means, principals try to foster individual self-discipline, values, and new understandings of behavior.

For example, at the Crest Hill Elementary School, in Casper, Wyoming, the biweekly American Heritage assemblies give students the opportunity to practice good behavior, democratic values, and sound ethical judgement. Assembly programs present such topics as respect, courtesy, getting along with others, friendship, self-reliance, sportsmanship, and sharing. Crest Hill is a K–6 school with a homogeneous student body of five hundred. Students are highly motivated to learn and participate in school activities. A very large proportion has qualified for special education services, from gifted education to instruction tailored to physical and emotional disabilities. Getting along with others and understanding others are key character development goals at Crest Hill.

At the Como Park Elementary School in Lancaster, New York, the sign on the office door of Andrea Stein, the principal, reads: "The answer is "yes" unless there is a compelling reason to say 'no.' In this way, she conveys confidence in her staff and students. There is a sense of pride that permeates the entire building. Como Park is a large school in a suburban district with two diverse economic groups. Most of the students are white, however, 17% of them come from lower-income families.

Miriam Remar, the principal at the Howard Reiche Community School in Portland, Maine, has a "Principal's Corner." In this section of the office, she displays the students' quality work and also lists the students who have achieved awards or honors. She tries to send the message that positive attitudes, respect, and quality work go hand-in-hand. Classrooms at Reiche have a unique blend of student backgrounds, cultures, and aspirations. Many students are considered "high risk," while many others are at-risk of not reaching their potential due to low motivation and the multiple consequences of poverty and family substance abuse. Expectations are consistently high for each and every child. By giving recognition to students who exhibit good character qualities, the school encourages them to do their best.

James Kolb, the principal at Brumfield Elementary School in Princeton, Indiana, helps build character by talking to students personally about morally significant events. One Brumfield parent who had a very positive regard for Mr. Kolb recounted a key incident: "My son lied in school. Mr. Kolb, the principal, talked to him about responsibility and honesty. He has never had a problem since." Brumfield is a large rural school with almost all Caucasian students.

However, the Brumfield student body has diverse economic and linguistic backgrounds. Almost 10 percent of the students are limited English speakers, over 15 percent are from low-income families, and another 15 percent qualify for special education services.

THE SCHOOL COUNSELOR AS CHARACTER DEVELOPER

The counselor is mentioned in several schools as also playing a very important role. The Kilgour Elementary School in Cincinnati, Ohio, explains: "The counselor plays an important role in the development of sound character. Class presentations and discussions are used to explore social responsibility, values, and ethical judgement. The classroom teacher then integrates these discussions appropriately."

Visits to the Blue Ribbon Schools helped me to realize how important the counselor is to a school's character development program. According to Lori Wiley, author of *Comprehensive Character-Building Classroom* (1998) and a teacher educator who specializes in early childhood education, guidance counselors realize a key role as character educators:

> Their primary responsibility is helping students who have problems functioning in a school environment. Through individual counseling, small group work, teaching in the regular classroom, and other techniques, they work with needy students. They also teach regular students how to make good choices so as to function well in society. Developing character is the essence of the guidance counselor's work.

The counselors at Locke Hill School play an essential role in the school–wide goal of character education. They make bimonthly visits to the classroom with good character lessons on such topics as loyalty, tattling versus reporting, sportsmanship, respect, kindness, citizenship, justice, name-calling, cheating, and conflict resolution. They use literature, puppet stories, filmstrips, videos, anecdotes, and role-playing activities that explain and illustrate desired behaviors or responses in a developmentally appropriate way. Students often make appointments with the counselors to talk through a problem. Their counselors are know as the "lady bugs" because students can talk to them about what's bugging them and the counselors will still love them.

In subsequent chapters we look at the different programs schools use in the areas of motivation, drug education, and self-esteem building. Many times these programs originate from and/or are supported by the counselor's office. A good principal knows how important a good counselor is for the school. In a small school, many times the counselor acts as an assistant to the principal. One Blue Ribbon principal told me that when she was offered the principalship of the school where she was currently employed, she said that she would take the job if she could also bring with her the counselor from her previous school. The important role of the counselor in character development will be seen in more detail in chapter 5 on guidance and self-esteem programs.

ADVISOR/ADVISEE PROGRAMS

Several schools reported having an advisor/advisee program for character development that is organized by the school counselor. Each student picks a faculty member to be his or her advisor. Typically, advisors and advisees meet each day for five minutes and once a week for forty-five minutes. In most of the schools reporting an advisory system, the advisors use a character development curriculum during this period to discuss social and emotional concerns important to children at this age. The goal is that the students learn to respect themselves and others. The advisor makes a special effort to maintain contact, greet them, and ask about their progress. The advisor/advisee program helps develop students' self worth, cooperation, and teamwork.

Another method reported by several schools is to sponsor activities and clubs through the counselor's office. Students can participate in these if they demonstrate appropriate character qualities. For instance, students might need to get "letters of recommendation" from teachers and other adults who have noted their character qualities in these areas. Some of these activities include CLASS–"Community Leadership Activities for Students;" Peer Tutor Program, Safety Patrol, Scouts, and Leadership Conferences in which selected student leaders meet with leadership groups from other district schools. Research for this second edition found more and more schools providing students with opportunities to attend leadership conferences. These activities are reported in more detail in chapter 8.

Long Hill Elementary School in Fayetteville, North Carolina, is a racially integrated intermediate school near the Fort Bragg Army Military Base. They have a Leadership Service Club that was established to encourage effort, reward merit and promote those qualities of character that make for good citizenship, that is, worthy character, good mentality, creditable achievement, and commendable attitude. Members are nominated by their teachers and meet monthly with the teacher.

THE KEY ROLE OF PARENTS IN CHARACTER EDUCATION

Parents are the primary educators of their children and their key character educators as well. Helen LeGette has character education experience as a teacher, counselor, and administrator. She states that "The family lies at the heart of any effort to re-focus on character development" (LeGette, 1999). Her research has lead her to see that a good family life not only lays the foundation for good moral development, but it also increases the likelihood that young people will exhibit great character and be able to resist strong peer influence.

At the Monte Garden School in Concord, California, the teachers, principal, and parents cooperate to ensure that students achieve academically, while also developing personal values of self-esteem, honesty, and responsibility. As stated by the principal in a letter home to the parents, "You , as parents, are the primary educators of your children. You know your children differently than the school does. It is important that you communicate with the school what you know about your children. Your input can make a difference." Monte Garden is a large school (over 500 students) in suburban Concord, with a diverse student body that is 10 percent Asian American and 9 percent Mexican American.

Tony Devine, vice-president of the International Educational Foundation, is committed to promoting holistic character education. The international research of the foundation has also led them to advocate for the important role parents play in the moral education of their children. "By the time they come to school, children are already well on their way in their moral education. Family interaction invariably teaches moral lessons that have repercussions in growing childrens' futures. Indeed the family is a melting pot of the emotional and moral learning— the crucible of character" (Devine, 2000). He suggests that the most promising character education practices are those that focus on creating a family-like atmosphere in school, thus reinforcing in a school setting the competencies that should naturally be fostered in a good home.

West View School in Spartanburg, South Carolina, also believes that parents are the most important moral educators and that their involvement in the school is vital to its success. Parents are involved in their School Improvement Council and the PTO board. They have parent workshops at least once a month throughout the school year. Parents share concerns and preview ideas and materials before they are implemented. Parents are kept informed of the character education goals through letters containing specific skills and ideas for home use. By using the same vocabulary and skills at home and at school, they are able to make a tremendous impact on their children. Updates on the program are given in the school newsletter every six weeks, and in classroom newsletters weekly. Core values are also promoted through school-wide family activities. Information on character education is also available for parents in a parent resource library.

Hundreds of parents volunteer at the Blue Ribbon Schools. They are actively involving themselves in their children's learning. Yet, it is true that family life and the basic structure of the family are changing, and schools are asked to do more. Statistics show that approximately one-third of the children in school today come from single-parent families. The presence of other parents in the schools can help those students who only have one parent at home.

At the Flanders Elementary School in Connecticut, the parents show that they are interested in learning, and their children understand the importance of school particularly because of their parents' physical presence. Parents are everywhere: the media center, classroom, publishing center, playground and anywhere else their help is needed. Flanders is a large K–5 school, a "microcosm of society" in which students find themselves in heterogeneously grouped classrooms where they learn to work with different kinds of people. Parents are active and frequent participants in the school as visitors and volunteers.

The dads at the Walnut Hill Elementary School in Dallas, Texas, have started the "Do Dads Club." This caring group meets regularly to find ways to make a difference in the school. Every other month they hold a workday to hang curtains, build shelves, repair furniture, plant trees, lay walkways, and offer a strong back or a helping hand. All of the things they do demonstrate and model a sense of responsibility and caring. Each Wednesday the school enjoys inspirational messages from one of the "Do Dads" reinforcing the curriculum's character pillars. Of course, dads take great pride in mentioning the name of their child when making these announcements.

According to the research of Robert Chaskin (1995), the family is the most common context in which a human being learns about care and nurturing. Not enough research studies have sought to examine the links between family characteristics and pro-social moral development. Those that have report a positive correlation between an adult family member's involvement in volunteer work and a young adolescent's involvement in the same or like works of caring for others. In addition, special attention should be given to the role that parents, (as well as the media and private associations) play in helping children develop into informed and effective citizens who understand and appreciate the fundamental values and principles of American democracy. According to former Secretary of Education, Richard Riley (1995), "We know that all families can make a difference in their children's learning, and we also know that linked to academic achievement is the development of standards of character: hard work, discipline, respect for others and good citizenship" (ix–x).

THE ROLE OF ACADEMICS IN
PROMOTING CHARACTER DEVELOPMENT

The actual role of students places them in a key environment for developing their characters. Their job is to be the best student that they can be (Lickona, 1991). If we understand good character as the intersection of moral knowing, moral feeling, and moral action, we can see that studying and learning give students key opportunities to show their character through their actions.

Although learning can be very exciting and fulfilling, it is hard work. As Wynne and Ryan (1993) note, profound learning is difficult and uncomfortable. Profound learning is learning about important things, and this knowledge brings about important changes in students' conduct or way of looking at things. Profound learning includes learning about the basic events and features of Western culture, and developing an understanding of other cultures. It helps students to develop both a cultural and a moral literacy, that is, a knowledge of culture's moral wisdom and those enduring habits or traits needed for good character.

Learning and studying these demanding subjects not only is the heart of students' liberal education, but also helps develop their characters. For example, children develop self-discipline and responsibility if they devote the necessary time to studying and doing their homework instead of watching television. They develop the courage to attack difficult assignments and the perseverance to keep at the assignments until they have completed them. They acquire diligence, if they do this day after day (Kilpatrick, 1992). Studying and learning also help to develop intellectual virtues in students such as a love of learning, valuing the opportunity to learn, respect for the truth, objectivity, prudence to think critically, understanding, humility to accept limitations, and a concern for excellence.

THE VALUE OF WORK AND OF A STUDENT'S WORK

Given a challenging curriculum, excellent instruction, and high expectations, students come to recognize that they need to work in school if they are to learn. Students need to do their schoolwork the best that they can: neatly, with care for details, expending appropriate effort and time. Finally, students learn to check and evaluate their work before they turn it in or call it finished, to be sure that it is done well and meets standards of excellence. Lickona (1991) states that it is important for students to learn the value of work done well, as this is a fundamental source of their dignity and sense of worth as human beings. One could summarize all of the problems in our society today as resulting from a lack of care in work. Many people work for money alone and fail to see that work is the way in which they can fulfill themselves and develop their character, affect the lives of others, and contribute to the betterment of society.

In the words of Josemaria Escriva de Balaguer (1973):

> A complete range of virtues is called into play when we set about our work with the purpose of doing it well: fortitude, to persevere in our work despite the difficulties that might arise and to ensure that we never let ourselves be overwhelmed by anxiety; temperance, in order to spend ourselves unsparingly and to overcome our love of comfort and our selfishness; justice, so as to fulfill our duties toward God, society, our family, and our fellow workers; prudence to know in each case what course to take, and then to set abut it without hesitation. (p. 62)

According to Donna Barton, principal of the St. Joseph Montessori School in Columbus, Ohio, work is often discussed in terms of being the student's "job" for that is the Montessori philosophy. School is their workplace. Pride in work, completion, and content knowledge are expected. The curriculum used stresses knowledge in the content areas and is enhanced with daily discussions and tasks necessary to survive in the world of work.

Several Blue Ribbon Schools encourage the Junior Achievement program in their school as they see that the curriculum helps to develop productive, reliant citizens, and good character by emphasizing the importance of good business and economic principles. At the Zelma Jutsell Elementary School in Katy, Texas, local business leaders teach the Junior Achievement curriculum about the free enterprise system and communities in general to students in grades K–5. Zelma Jutsell is a very large suburban school with a very large (1,000+) diverse student body that is racially, economically, and linguistically diverse. Junior Achievement provides an authentic educational experience that is a common career and work experience for all students. For instance, the fourth grade Junior Achievement lessons teach students how to establish a business plan, implement the plan, and decide its profitability. Students extend these concepts by participating in a *Trade Fair* during the economic unit of the social studies curriculum. Students make a product at home and then barter and trade with students at the fair to obtain desired items. In addition, local businessmen and women visit the Zelma Jutsell students to discuss their careers and answer any questions students may have about the community businesses. For more information on implementing a Junior Achievement program in your school contact: Junior Achievement, Inc., One Education Way, Colorado Springs, CO, Telephone (719) 540-8000, www.ja.org.

In order to emphasize the value of work well done, the Daisy Ingraham School's report card includes a section on work habits that rates students in the following areas:

- Concern for quality and accuracy in school work
- Positive response to guidance
- Responsibility for actions
- Practice of self-discipline and control
- Respect for peers and adults
- Observation of the rules of school and classroom

Daisy Ingraham is a homogeneous PK–5 school of 486 students located in the small city of Westbrook, Connecticut.

ACADEMIC WORK IN THE BLUE RIBBON SCHOOLS

Schools need to help students to take their work seriously, perform it to the best of their ability, and thereby develop the qualities of character inherent in the capacity to work well. The Blue Ribbon Schools do this by setting high expectations for all students and finding ways to challenge gifted, average, and at-risk students. They realize that in order for students to be productive citizens and workers in this twenty-first century, they need a strong foundation in literature, history, geography, science, economics, the arts, and other subjects. Therefore, high-quality instruction appropriate to each child's age, grade, and learning style needs to be provided. Alternative modes of assessment help children to show what they have learned and thereby develop a positive self-imaging regarding their work as students.

Table 6 lists the instructional innovations mentioned by the Blue Ribbon Schools as key in their effort to develop the character of their students through schoolwork well done.

Table 6. Instructional Methodologies Cited by
Blue-Ribbon Schools

Category	Count	Percent
Brain-Compatible Instruction	14	5%
Cooperative Learning	75	26%
Cross Grade Groups	6	2%
Dimensions of Learning	6	2%
Engaged Learning	6	2%
Higher Order Thinking Skills	16	6%
Interdisciplinary/Thematic	17	6%
Junior Achievement	20	7%
Junior Great Books	12	4%
Learning Styles	49	17%
Multiple Intelligences	31	11%
Portfolio Assessment	11	4%
Technology	7	2%
Whole Language	14	9%

Total N=392, 113 missing cases

LEARNING THAT PROMOTES
"ACHIEVEMENT SELF-ESTEEM"

Historically, one can see the different instructional emphases in different Blue Ribbon Award groups. Cooperative learning was in vogue in 1985–1986. Then consideration of learning styles theory led to brain-related instruction and modality instruction in 1988–1989. Whole language and thematic instruction dominated the early 1990s. The latest years of award winning schools tell about the value of teaching to multiple intelligences, using multiple forms of assessment, and implementing technology-enhanced instruction. Why do the Blue Ribbon Schools cite these instructional methodologies as important contributions to the development of character? They are methodologies that help students to succeed at the work of learning. Academic success promotes a student's feeling of self-worth and accomplishment—"achievement self-esteem."

The Red Bank Elementary School in California is "dedicated to preparing students for the twenty-first century by providing an academically rigorous and emotionally supportive program that promotes positive self-esteem, values, and personal growth for the leaders of tomorrow." Red Bank is a very large K–6 school with a population of 883 students, 21 percent of whom are ethnically and racially diverse. Students come from families that are middle- to upper- middle class, well-educated semi-professionals who have a high regard for schools and education. In order to provide this environment, teachers target learning modalities, using both whole-class and small-group instruction. They use portfolios, journals, and new assessment techniques, hands-on science and field trips, and a relevant "real-life curriculum" that is developmentally appropriate while seeking to develop higher-order thinking processes. They seek to integrate technology into the curriculum as a tool for the students to access in the learning process.

The Junior Great Books program is in 5 percent of the Blue Ribbon Schools including the Randolph Elementary School in Universal City, Texas. The program brings the joy of independent reading to children in grades two through five through a shared- inquiry process. Junior Great Books is a program that uses excellent, classical works of children's literature to teach analysis of reading through a process of interpretive reading. The books read expose the students to rich character messages and the method used to discuss these literary pieces allows the students to develop the habits of mind of a self-reliant thinker, reader, and learner. Teachers do this through a method of open-ended questions that help students to generate their own insights and perspectives, based on the text, while appreciating the perspectives of other students in the class. Holy Family is a large K–8 school of 457, with a very diverse and integrated student body with Caucasian, Asian, Hispanic, and African American students all studying together. The Junior Great Books method helps develop this appreciation for others. In order to implement Junior Great Books in your school contact The Great Books Foundation, 35 East Wacker Drive, Suite 2300, Chicago, IL 60601-2298, Telephone: (800) 222-5870, thecommonreview.org/gbf/about/contacts.html.

COOPERATIVE LEARNING

In cooperative learning, students work together to achieve shared learning goals and complete specific tasks and assignments. Students seek outcomes that are beneficial to all those in the cooperative learning group. A criteria-referenced evaluation system is used. Cooperative learning is different from traditional small-group work in the sense that there is individual accountability along with group or team rewards. Students need to develop interpersonal and small-group skills because there is a positive interdependence as members of the group. "We sink or swim together" is a common cooperative learning motto (Johnson and Johnson, 1986a, 1986b).

There are many different cooperative learning methods in use in schools that are applicable to a wide range of grade levels, subjects, and classrooms: Learning Together, Group Investigation, Jigsaw, Students Teams-Achievement Divisions, and Teams-Games-Tournaments. For a complete description of these methods the reader is referred to *Learning Together and Alone, 2nd ed.* (1986) by David and Roger Johnson, and *Cooperative Learning* (1990) by Robert Slavin. Cooperative groups are particularly helpful in promoting high academic performance and the ·value of a student's work well done because the process of working together helps students to improve academic skills and thus helps them to develop their character. Curriculum materials for cooperative learning methods are available from: The Johns Hopkins Team Learning Project, Johns Hopkins University, 3505 N. Charles Street, Baltimore, MD 21218, Telephone (301) 338-8249.

One of the goals of the Spring Glen Elementary School in the state of Washington is to "encourage students to engage in cooperative strategies and team building techniques." Its staff believes that cooperative learning helps students practice proactive social skills by working together. Leadership, social skills development, and democratic values are fostered in cooperative group learning activities. Spring Glen Elementary School tries to build a positive, nurturing environment where each individual is valued and enriched by providing students with:

1. An integrated curriculum that uses conceptual themes for the entire school, thus creating greater opportunity for meaning-driven learning to occur at all levels;
2. Learning modalities/styles instruction that teaches to the auditory, visual, tactual, or kinesthetic strengths of the students, thus increasing learning success;
3. Cooperative learning groups that emphasize team-building and communications skills for students to peer-tutor, problem-solve, and make decisions.

Research has consistently found that students in cooperative learning classes have significantly greater achievement than do students in control group classes not using cooperative learning (Slavin, 1991). Several researchers working on cooperative learning techniques have found that in addition, these methods increase students' self-esteem due to the sense of accomplishment engendered. Cooperative group work can help students of low academic and peer status gain acceptance into classroom groups when their intellectual contribution to the group is recognized (Cohen, 1998).

Most importantly, cooperative learning leads to other benefits that are more directly related to character development. A 1990 study by Solomon and others found that students who had been taught cooperatively ranked significantly higher

than control students when measured for supportive, friendly, and pro-social behavior, and they were better at resolving conflicts and supporting democratic values (Slavin, 1991). Johnson and Johnson (1986a) acknowledge that to achieve mutual goals, students must develop skills in working together that include: (1)
getting to know and trust one another, (2) learning to communicate accurately, (3)
accepting and supporting one another, and (4) resolving conflicts constructively.
Lickona (1991) states that the character development benefits of using the cooperative learning instructional process include growth in interpersonal moral skills
such as increased perspective-taking, appreciation of those who are different, and
valuing cooperation. Philip Fitch Vincent (1994), author of *Developing Character
in Students*, agrees that cooperative learning is a valuable tool in the development
of character. He has found that this process helps students to develop good character traits such as being responsible for their work, being respectful of the abilities of others, and caring for others and for the finished product.

The O.C. Taylor Elementary School in Coleville, Texas, also cites cooperative
learning as an integral component of its character education program. Mr. Odle
the principal explains that:

> the use of cooperative learning in the classroom develops interpersonal skills needed
> in the work place. Our students learn how to listen attentively and constructively crit-
> icize ideas, praise the work of others, and compromise willingly in the quest for co-
> operation. These qualities, as well as many others developed in group work situa-
> tions, serve our students well as they move into secondary and higher education and
> on to the world of work and to success in life.

He describes his school as a suburban school of 600 enthusiastic, highly motivated learners from middle- to upper-income families with a dedicated, caring
faculty.

LEARNING STYLES

"Learning style" is conceptualized as a biologically and developmentally determined set of personal characteristics that influence the way students perceive,
process, and learn. The Blue Ribbon Schools are well versed in the different theories of "characterizing" learning styles instructional strategies. Some use right-
and left-brain instruction; some use McCarthy's 4MAT or Gardner's "Multiple
Intelligences;" others use a combination of teaching for learning styles and learning modalities.

The entire faculty at Rice Creek Elementary School in Columbia, South Carolina, decided through consensus to adopt the 4MAT Model of Bernice McCarthy
(1983) as outlined in her manual *4-MAT in Action* (Excel, Inc.). All of the teachers were trained and the principal, a certified trainer, continues training the new

teachers. Teachers use the model as an overlay for lesson planning, assuring that lessons have varying activities that address the four major categories/quadrants of learning styles: (1) feelers, (2) thinkers, (3) sensors, and (4) intuitors. Instruction provides "comfort time" for each learner with his own style, but also demands "stretching" within the other styles. For example, a child who learns best and more easily through hands-on manipulation will have the opportunity to *perform* a puppet show but will also be required to *write* a description of each puppet. The teachers feel that the school-wide use of 4-MAT, through a common language and understanding, provides a balance to keep student needs in the forefront and helps to accommodate the unique learning styles of their diverse learners. Rice Creek is a school of 815 with a well-integrated student body, half white, and half African-American, one fifth of whom are from a low economic background and 14 percent who have special learning needs.

Howard Garnder's theory of multiple intelligences, as outlined in *Frames of Mind: The Theory of Multiple Intelligence (1983),* helps students to develop their unique talents by assisting them in the identification of their strengths, that is, their intelligences. Teachers can then guide them towards fields of work in which they will be competent and satisfied because their talents will fit these jobs well. As Gardner (1995) points out, "there are hundreds and hundreds of ways to succeed and many different abilities that get you there." The teachers at the Adairville School in Adairville, Kentucky, apply the theory of Howard Garnder's *Different Ways of Knowing (DWoK)* in order to give their students choices about the instructional pathways they follow. Their philosophy is that "learners learn what matters to them," and they use the modules of *DWoK* as a framework to construct a meaningful, arts-infused learning environment. Adairville School is in a farm community and almost half of its students qualify for free lunch and one third qualify for special education service. All teachers have been trained and collaborate to ensure that at-risk students receive the opportunities to access multiple modalities and learn at their own developmental pace. One of their teachers explains the change:

> Since implementing *DWoK,* it is not necessary to have a pull out program for gifted and talented students because we see all students expressing their artistic, social, verbal, and logical-mathematical intelligences. We recognize and accept the responsibility to create environments within our classroom that set the stage for continuous progress not based on arbitrary standards, but rather based on individual student progress. It was through our training with Different Ways of Knowing that we are now able to meet the needs of a multi-aged, multi-ability group, in a heterogeneous environment. It is our belief that all students can learn at high levels.

Knowledge of learning styles helps students appreciate their own uniqueness as a person and to understand the different needs of others. It gives them knowledge of their intellectual strengths and awareness of areas in which they will be more challenged. It helps them to make informed choices that will help them to study and learn better. Learning styles helps students to learn about their personality and character. All of us are unique, with certain strengths and certain areas of concern. People of character seek to capitalize on their positive qualities while learning to change or compensate for their weaknesses.

Nadine Mouse, principal at St. Thomas More School in Houston, Texas, explains how learning styles instruction also helps students to develop their character:

> Taking responsibility for one's own learning is an important goal at our school. To help students achieve this, we all completed learning style inventories during orientation at the beginning of the school year. The following week, an afternoon was devoted to acquainting each student with his or her special style—visual, auditory, or bodily-kinesthetic. Students formed groups with others of their preferred style. Teachers then shared research data and personal learning experience concerning the most effective ways of receiving, processing, and giving back information for each style.

In order to actualize their philosophy that "All Children Can Learn," the staff at the Quail Creek Elementary School in Oklahoma use instructional strategies geared towards learning styles and "hands-on" techniques.

> Children at Quail Creek are allowed to experience the educational process in the style most conducive to their individual modes of learning. Teachers develop strategies around visual, tactile, auditory, and manipulative modalities, within the learning process. Children have the opportunity to excel in their learning mode. This is important as all children have different abilities and talents. Our desire is to see that all children are comfortable in the learning process.

Quail Creek is a K–5 school in Oklahoma City with a heterogeneous student body of 350, 10 percent of whom are African American, and 5 percent Asian; with almost 10 percent from low-income families.

Dr. Cherry Jones, the principal at Flanders Elementary School in Connecticut, explains that her teachers are aware of the many different types of intelligences and the different learning styles:

> We approach our students as individuals who all have special gifts and talents. Each teacher plans lessons that address the various types of learning styles of individual students and stimulates them through both individual and group activities. All children have gifts and talents and we attempt to let every child shine.

Research has found that student achievement is significantly higher whenever students are taught through approaches that allow them to learn through their preferred style. In addition, the research shows that when students are permitted to learn difficult academic information or skills through their identified preferences, they tend to achieve significantly higher test and attitude scores than when instruction is dissonant with their preferences (Dunn, et al., 1989). This success at the "work of learning" helps students to realize the high expectations for learning that the Blue Ribbon Schools hold for all students. "High expectations for student achievement" has been found to be "what works" in schools; that is, it is one of the characteristics of effective schools and a mark of a high standard of excellence in the school (United States Department of Education, 1987).

INTEGRATED LANGUAGE ARTS
OR "WHOLE LANGUAGE" INSTRUCTION

Years of research in linguistics, psycho-linguistics, sociology, anthropology, philosophy, child development, curriculum, composition and literary theory, semiotics, and other fields have contributed to the development of the concept of whole language. Whole language seeks to connect skills, concepts, and content through integrated, theme-based learning activities (Robbins, 1990). Instead of using short selections of stories in a basal text, this methodology has students reading whole books starting in kindergarten. The story in the book leads to major theme-related projects. A comprehensive and extensive array of classical literature should form the backbone of an integrated language arts program. Although one of the criticisms of whole language instruction was its failure to teach phonics, most of the Blue Ribbon Schools have integrated phonics and spelling instruction within this reading program (Ogden and Germinario, 1994). They also use "Daily Oral Language" (DOL) in order to improve writing skills. Of particular interest is the DOL program used by the Heatherstone Elementary School in Kansas. They use sentences with character education and drug awareness messages. As students improve their written language skills they are building their character. For more information on *Daily Oral Language with Character* contact The Young People's Press, 3033 Fifth Avenue, Suite 200, San Diego, CA 92103.

The use of a whole language program at Burruss Elementary School in Marietta, Georgia, has greatly helped to motivate students who now see a clearer purpose for reading and writing, according to Jerry Locke, the principal. Burruss is a school of 570 culturally diverse students: 24 percent African American, 20 percent from low-income families, and 11 percent who qualify for special education services. The principal, Jerry Locke showed me the school and explained, "Other instructional strategies that our teachers use to motivate students are extensive use of cooperative learning . . . integrated content areas, hands-on math activities, and a continually changing assortment of interesting learning activities. The school motto, "Burruss Beavers are Real Achievers," reflects a commitment to motivation and learning."

Research evaluating the effectiveness of whole language instructional techniques has found that "student achievement is strongly affected when reading and writing are taught as integral and connected processes" (Robbins, 1990).

Why do the Blue Ribbon Schools consider whole language instruction relevant to the development of the character of their students? First, whole language instruction helps students to see the unity of knowledge; instead of seeing academics as discrete subjects that have no connection to one another; students read, write, and speak about topics that naturally flow from the content of the book they have read. Second, a good whole language program has students reading classical literature. According to Vincent (1994), "Great readings illuminate human struggles, successes, strengths, weaknesses, virtues, and vices. A study of great ideas allows us to gain greater understanding of ourselves" (p. 111). Third, whole language engages students in reading for the sake and excitement of reading. There is no better way to discover the joy in working hard to learn than to discover the joy inherent in learning to read.

THEMATIC INSTRUCTION

When teachers are able to apply whole-language principles that link reading and writing activities to other subject matters, students are able to make interdisciplinary connections. At the Whittier Elementary School in Lawton, Oklahoma, teachers use *Expressions*, a cross-discipline curriculum that utilizes the interrelationships of the physical, mental, and creative processes.

> The purpose of *Expressions* is to organize the students' experience in art, music, language, drama, and movement into a curriculum rich with multi-sensory experiences. It also provides for the students' growth in attitude, conduct, and self-esteem. A strand of values runs through *Expressions*: truth, beauty, justice, love, and faith. These values give their students an understanding of humanity.

Whittier is a K–6 school of 287 racially/ethnically diverse students living in a small town, 20 percent of whom come from low-income families.

Interdisciplinary, or thematic instruction, while maintaining the centrality of content-based knowledge, integrates social studies, science, mathematics, and literature to foster the pursuit of knowledge and understanding of a particular theme or the resolution of a specific problem (Hiebert and Fisher, 1990). At the Washington Township School in Valparaiso, Indiana, teachers use *Breakthroughs* a unique series combining science, social studies, and language arts to work at finding solutions to current problems our society faces. Problems discussed include: "Are we killing our lakes?" and "Forest Fires: Disaster or not?" Washington Township is a K–5 building in a rural area.

At Centennial Elementary School in Tucson, Arizona, higher-level thinking skills, curricular, and technological areas are integrated into thematic units. These units often have differentiated assignments and a variety of activities so that students of different academic levels are challenged and enriched.

An example is the fourth-grade unit on Native Americans. Students use reading, writing, and spelling to prepare a research report and oral presentation on authentic Indian weapons, tools, games, homes, artwork, and handcrafts. They learn the science of firing pots and the importance of math as the kachina maker teaches them about proportions. Through art, students use authentic colors and materials to make corn jewelry, sand paintings, and story turtles. Higher level thinking becomes a natural part of the unit as students compare and contrast different cultures and draw conclusions about environmental adaptations tribes have had to make.

When students are presented with a real problem that needs to be studied and solved, they are presented with an authentic task that has tangible consequences for them. Participation in these authentic activities allows them to develop a real sense of purpose and motivation as they seek to present "action-oriented" solutions to real social problems. One of the most popular themes mentioned in the Blue Ribbon Schools was the study of the environment, which often would lead students to set up recycling programs in their schools and even in their communities.

Thematic instruction shares many of the character-building advantages of whole language instruction mentioned above. In addition, it gives students opportunities to further investigate areas of interest to them that are related to the unit. Letting students' interest be the subject of their investigation maximizes their involvement in learning and often liberates astonishing energies for work. This gives students the opportunity to make a commitment to develop a real expertise in a given subject or skill. When students achieve this expertise, competence becomes part of their self-images, and they are more motivated to do quality work in other areas as well (Lickona, 1991).

Roguewood teachers use integrated thematic instruction as a strategy for making content meaningful. Students learn useful information and develop a positive emotional bridge as content and skill are taught with enthusiasm by the teacher. Thematic instruction incorporates programs and strategies that challenge the gifted as well as the special needs students. Roguewood Elementary School in Rockford, Michigan, is a PK–5 school in a small town with a heterogeneous school body. Because Roguewood teachers understand that all learners have unique needs, students are offered choices as to how they select, organize, and experience new content to build independence as learners in an enriched learning environment incorporating real-life experiences. An example of a real-life experience includes taking students on meaningful field trips: Kindergarteners visit a local apple orchard when they study plants, while fourth graders studying Michigan government visit the capitol in Lansing. Another example includes bringing in many resource people to present a real life experience for the students. One of the third grade units is entitled "Free to be You and Me" a unit that has to do with handicap awareness; students have an opportunity to meet and interview a blind person and his dog from "Paws With a Cause." Roguewood's enriched learning environment includes using multiple resources in the classrooms, such as simulations, literature studies, technology, math manipulatives, scientific observations and experiments, community service projects, and parent involvement.

TEACHING THINKING SKILLS

Thematic instruction helps students to develop their thinking skills and strategies. Students develop higher order thinking skills as they compare and contrast two characters in a story and analyze and evaluate characters' choices and authors' purposes. Developing thinking skills is key to developing character, as students need to be able to reason, make decisions and take the perspective of others in order to develop moral knowing, an essential element of good character (Lickona, 1991).

At Saigling School in Plano, Texas, the emphasis on critical, evaluative, and creative thinking seen in the rigorous, content-rich academic program extends into the citizenship program. Students express their social responsibility by regular community service projects that address areas of concern that the students with their teachers have identified. Philip Vincent (1994) states that one of the major functions of education is to develop in students the ability to think clearly and consistently. Only by becoming adept at thinking can we know the good and therefore pursue it.

Many Blue Ribbon Schools, including the Locke Hill School in Texas, use Bloom's Taxonomy of Higher Order Thinking Skills as the measuring stick by which teachers and students evaluate the level of thinking required to accomplish a learning task. Teachers strive to incorporate opportunities for all students to use thinking skills from the application, synthesis, and evaluation levels, the "higher-level" thinking.

Odyssey of the Mind (OM) is a national program in which many of the Blue Ribbon Schools participate. Odyssey of the Mind is an extracurricular competition that fosters critical and higher-level thinking. Students try out to be on a seven-member team. Parents and teachers serve as coaches. Students demonstrate their ability to solve problems requiring spontaneous, divergent thinking at regional meetings using educational skits and spontaneous problem solving.

PORTFOLIOS AND AUTHENTIC ASSESSMENT

Dr. Joya Chatterjeee, principal at Westwood Elementary School in Santa Clara, California, explained that the school has moved from a traditional grade-based report card to a portfolio-based authentic evaluation system in order to realize a profound change in the instructional process. Many Blue Ribbon Schools have turned to portfolio assessment as a strategy for creating a classroom assessment system that includes multiple measures taken over time. Portfolios have the advantage of containing several samples of student work assembled in a purposeful manner. "Well-conceived portfolios include pieces representing both work in progress and "showpiece" samples, student reflections about their work, and evaluation criteria" (Herman, Aschbacher, and Winters, 1992).

The Summerville Elementary School in Summerville, South Carolina, uses portfolios to measure the effectiveness of their instructional strategies. They have students include works that show what they have learned. This may include teacher-made assessments, class projects or activities completed, writing samples, and completed exercises in any other subjects. The teachers' efforts to foster critical and creative thinking enable these students to become active learners rather than passive receivers, with the ability to do productive thinking, forecasting, decision making, and planning.

Portfolios allow students to evaluate their own work according to the high standards expressed in a rubric. Students are able to strive on their own to meet these high standards. Through authentic assessments, students are allowed to show that they have learned the given content to such a high level that they can actually perform the new skills in a real-life situation. Authentic assessments help students to develop their character because they help them to see that they are not just learning for the sake of test scores and grades; they are learning so that they can help make a difference in the world by using their knowledge to solve real-life problems.

SUMMARY

As this chapter demonstrates, the teacher, principal, counselor, school staff, and the parents are all key players in the promotion of character development in students. Blue Ribbon teachers use the latest pedagogical methodologies to enable their students to be successful academically. The students' success helps them develop their character through the effort they expend in doing their work as students well. Specifically, cooperative learning methodologies help students develop character qualities of responsibility, understanding of others, and team spirit. Learning styles instruction allows students to learn about themselves and take responsibility for their own learning. Whole language and thematic instruction help students develop thinking skills that are key to developing moral reasoning. Portfolios and alternative assessments enable students to show that they have worked hard at their job as students and have learned the required knowledge and skills. The Blue Ribbon Schools successfully engage their students in learning and thereby develop their intrinsic motivation. Students develop healthy self-esteem built on the realization of jobs well done.

The role of education is to help develop students into good people. Since students do not become good just because one tells them to be good, we have to look at how what they study and how they study it helps them develop good character traits (Vincent, 1994). The Blue Ribbon Schools help students develop their character by giving them the opportunity to do their work as students well by encouraging them through different instructional methodologies to work hard at their job of learning.

DARE We Count Drug Prevention Programs As Character Education?

What you think of yourself is much more important than what others think of you.

—Seneca

Many persons have a wrong idea of what constitutes true happiness. It is not attained through self-gratification but through fidelity to a worthy purpose.

—Helen Keller

Better keep yourself clean and bright: you are the window through which you must see the world.

—George Bernard Shaw

DRUG FREE SCHOOLS

The U.S. Government has already decided the answer to the values education controversy by funding anti-drug programs. In so doing they are telling us that no matter what our religious, cultural or social values are, there is something that *all* of us in this nation agree is a moral wrong—substance abuse.

The Anti-Drug Abuse Act of 1986 gave the Department of Education authority to carry out federal education and preventive activities in order to aggressively work to combat drug abuse by youth. The Drug Free School Recognition Program was established in 1987 in order to seek out and honor schools that had developed exemplary programs to combat student drug use and thereby focus national attention on these successful drug prevention efforts. This program was discontinued in 1995 in order to consolidate all school recognitions into one program—the U.S. Department of Education's School Recognition program. To win this national recognition, the school must give a satisfactory answer to the application's question "By what means does the school prevent the sale, possession, and use of drugs, including alcohol and tobacco, by its students on and off school premises?"

This chapter reports on the various substance abuse and health programs found in the Blue Ribbon Schools. It seeks to evaluate these programs in order to determine which, if any of them, can be considered a valid character education program. This chapter seeks to answer the following questions:

- Can a substance abuse program alone be considered a school's entire program for fostering the development of character in students?
- What has research shown about the effectiveness of substance abuse and drug education programs in schools?
- How have the Blue Ribbon Schools successfully become "drug-free schools?"
- What kinds of health education/sex education programs are effective for promoting character in students?

A REACTIVE APPROACH
TO CHARACTER DEVELOPMENT

Anti-drug programs guide students in making informed moral decisions; but the name itself implies a reactive more than a proactive approach to character development. Substance abuse programs could be considered as contributing to the students' "moral knowing" domain of character education because of their emphasis on decision making based on informed knowledge. The inclusion of drug, sex, and alcohol education in the schools represents a paradigm shift in the public's attitude towards the schools as agents of character education (London, 1987). Before the 1960s the consensus had been to consider these issues the realm of the home, not of the public schools. In fact, prior to the 1960s, cigarettes were probably the only destructive substances brought to schools. Now, because of hard data that shows substantial increases in substance abuse among young Americans, the public has changed its general opinion and is asking the schools to once again teach traditional values that include the sacredness of life, the value of sex within marriage, and how to say no to drugs and alcohol (Wynne, 1989). The U.S. Department of Education handbook, *What Works: Schools without Drugs* (1987) states that "In America today, the most serious threat to the well-being of our children is drug use." It seems the general public strongly agrees with this statement. In the 28th Annual Phi Delta Kappa/Gallup Poll of the Public's Attitudes toward the Public Schools, the majority of the respondents said that the number one problem facing schools was drug abuse (for years, the number one problem facing our schools had been "poor discipline" (Elam, Rose, Gallup, 1996)). In fact, in the 32nd, 31st and 29th Annual Phi Delta Kappa/Gallup Polls, the respondents were asked if they favored a "zero tolerance to drugs and alcohol" stand in the schools and 86 percent to 90 percent of the public were in favor of this policy in these surveys (Rose, Gallup, Elam, 1997; Rose and Gallup, 1999; Rose and Gallup, 2000). Finally in the 32nd Annual Phi Delta Kappa/Gallup Poll, 85 percent of the respondents said that drug and alcohol abuse education should be given more emphasis in the public school (Rose and Gallup 2000).

ARE DRUG EDUCATION PROGRAMS CHARACTER EDUCATION PROGRAMS?

Less than one fourth of the Blue Ribbon Schools answered the question, "How do school programs, practices, and policies foster the development of sound character, democratic values, ethical judgment, and the ability to work in a self-disciplined and purposeful manner?" by mentioning the school's drug education program as its "character development" program (See Table 5). This is a decided decrease from the one third of the schools found in the first edition research and documents a general move to a more comprehensive approach. According to Larry Nucci (1991), drug education programs are moral education programs if they induce students to consider how drug use has meaningful consequences for the welfare of self and others. Due to the fact that drugs block, retard, and distort the most crucial human capacities— perception, planning, physical coordination, and moral judgment (Hawley, 1987)—one can conclude that a person of character should not use drugs and some instruction in this area should be included in any moral or character education program.

Lickona (1991) has argued that for drug education to be effective, it must be part of a broader program of moral values education that helps students value themselves, aspire to worthwhile goals, and reject all forms of self-damaging behavior. He states that a good drug education curriculum helps students make a *moral* judgement about drugs: Doing drugs is wrong because it is self-destructive, it leads to wrongful behavior such as stealing and lying, it causes suffering, and it is against the law.

Character education is much broader and more encompassing than drug education alone, as it addresses *all* moral issues. However, learning about drug and substance abuse is important in order to address moral knowing and moral feeling in this area so that a person then chooses to do the right moral action, which in this case is to refrain completely. Drug education can be seen as a subset of character education (See Figure 4). In July, 1994, Senate Bill 513, known as the Dodd Amendment to the "1993 Improving America's School Act" was

DARE WE COUNT DRUG PREVENTION PROGRAMS?

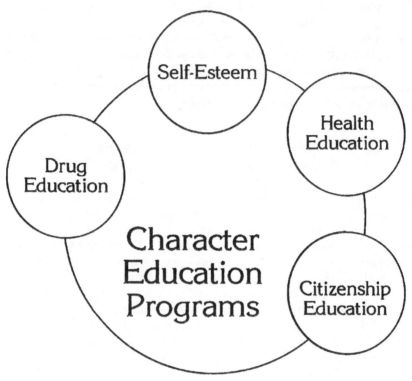

Figure 4.   Subsets of Character Education.

passed. This added the word "character" to the act: "Violence and drug abuse
have numerous personal and societal roots and *character* education is an important component of any comprehensive strategy to address the serious problems of violence and drug abuse." This addition allows schools, public and private, to use "federal drug education funds" to initiate or support their character
education programs.

WHAT DRUG EDUCATION PROGRAMS
ARE USED IN THE BLUE RIBBON SCHOOLS?

Table 7 lists all of the different drug education programs found in the Blue Ribbon Schools. In subsequent sections of this chapter, the drug curricula most
commonly found in the Blue Ribbon Schools are described and assessed with

Table 7.   Drug Education Programs used in the Blue Ribbon Schools to Develop Character

Category	Count	Percent of Responses
BABES	12	3
DARE	180	40
Good Choices	14	3
Here's Looking At You	60	13
Jump Rope for Heart	18	4
Just Say No	62	14
McGruff	93	20
Meology	7	2
Pride	13	3
Project Charlie	14	3
Quest	47	10
Red Ribbon	65	14
School Developed Program	78	17

456 Cases, 29 Missing Cases

regard to effectiveness and appropriateness as components of character education programs.

DARE

The most popular drug curriculum program, used in 40 percent of the Blue Ribbon schools, is the DARE Program (Drug Awareness Resistance Education), created in 1983 by the Los Angeles Police Department. Rosenbaum and Hanson (1998) state that DARE is used in 70 percent of the nation's school districts. Obee Elementary School is a small PreK–6 school with an ethnically and economically diverse student body located in Hutchinson, Kansas, a small city in a rural area that uses DARE. They describe the program as a series of classroom lessons, led by a police officer, that teaches students that popularity can be found in positive behavior; that belonging need not require them to abandon their values; and that self-confidence and self-worth come from asserting themselves and resisting destructive temptations. In short, DARE teaches students not just that they should refuse drugs and alcohol, but how to do so. Most importantly, students are taught eight ways to say "no" to drugs.

Steve Duke, the principal at the Quailwood Elementary School in Bakersfield, California, states that "the DARE program has been highly successful."

Sixth graders receive lessons related to the dangers of drugs, alcohol, and tobacco. The weekly 40-minute lessons emphasize positive approaches for avoiding these substances. The district has provided funding for having one police officer on campus one day a week for 15 weeks to be a model for students. The DARE officer plays sports, eats with the students, and informally talks to the students throughout the day in addition to conducting the classroom presentations and discussions. Three sessions are also taught by the officer in each K–5 classroom. The positive response to this program by students, parents, and staff has been outstanding.

The DARE curriculum focuses on teaching pupils the skills needed to recognize and resist social pressures to use drugs; it teaches decision-making skills, builds self-esteem and helps students to choose healthy alternatives to drugs (Ennett, et al., 1994). The program is now used in all states. This second edition finds DARE used in even a higher percentage of schools than five years ago. The County Line Elementary School in Georgia echoes what many schools reported:

> One of the most exciting additions to our school has been the DARE Program. DARE is a unique drug prevention education program designed to equip elementary school children with skills for resisting peer pressure to experiment with drugs and alcohol. This program is offered as a cooperative effort. Every class, K–5, is included in the DARE program. During one phase of the program, high school students, who have vowed never to take drugs, visit with the fifth graders and talk personally about peer pressure and ways to say "no." A DARE graduation ceremony is held at the end of the study. Parents, community members, local Board of Education members, and County officials are invited. Students are recognized for their work in the DARE Program with a DARE T-shirt and certificate. Many parents have commented that this program has opened the door to conversations with their children about the dangers of drug abuse.

Given its widespread use, the effectiveness of DARE has been evaluated by several researchers. Early DARE evaluations (1987–1989) were generally favorable; the participants showed decreased drug use, and increased self-esteem and sense of responsibility to self and to police relative to control groups (De-Jong, 1987). However, more recent metaanalysis of a group of evaluations (late 1989 to present) comparing the DARE curriculum to other drug education (if any) offered in control schools, show that the DARE program does not significantly reduce the actual use of drugs (Rosenbaum and Hanson, 1998). (A review of all existing DARE evaluations to date can be found on-line: hyperreal.com/drugs/politics/dare/dare.evaluations). These evaluation results contrast dramatically with the program's popularity and prevalence and lead to an important implication: perhaps DARE is taking the place of other, potentially more beneficial drug education curricula that students could be experiencing (Ennett, et al., 1994).

Who teaches DARE and how it is taught may provide possible explanations for the program's limited effectiveness. Lori Wiley (1998), has reviewed the DARE lesson plans and finds them to be more of a self-esteem program and a way for the police to interact in a friendly way with students than a real character education program. Perhaps greater emphasis in the DARE core curriculum on social competencies and less emphasis on affective factors might result in greater program effectiveness (Ullman, et al., 2000). The reader is encouraged to examine the DARE- Drug Awareness Resistance Education Curriculum themselves by contacting: Los Angeles Police Department, Juvenile Division, 150 N. Los Angeles Street, Los Angeles, CA 90028, Telephone (213)485-4856.

Here's Looking At You

One of the most widely used alcohol and drug education abuse prevention curriculum program in the nation is Here's Looking At You. This "state of the art" K–12 curriculum uses a variety of participatory activities to enhance self-esteem, promote good health, improve decision making, develop students' coping skills, and provide information on alcohol and other drugs. The curriculum is divided into grade level packages: K–3, 4–6, 7–9, 10–12. A revised version of the program is called Here's Looking At You 2000. These two programs were found in 13 percent of the Blue Ribbon Schools. The Dorothea Simmons School, a moderate sized K–5 school in suburban Ambler, Pennsylvania, piloted the revised program. Rita Klein, the principal, acted as the district trainer:

> Students in third, fourth, and fifth grades receive eight weeks of lessons taught by the health and classroom teachers and the guidance counselor. This program included drug and alcohol information, self-esteem, decision making, and development of refusal skills at each level. High school students visited the school and talked with fourth- and fifth-grade students about the natural highs available in a teen's life.
>
> The effectiveness of the "Here's Looking at You 2000" curriculum was evident in reviewing the pre- and post-tests given. . . . These tests showed a marked improvement in students' knowledge of drug and alcohol related information. The effectiveness of the refusal skills segment of the program was seen in the videotape the fourth grade students prepared. Parents were invited to see the tape . . . and they expressed positive feelings about the program and recommended its continuation. They mentioned the increased communication in the home about this subject.

A comprehensive short-term and long-term evaluation of the program found that, just as Rita Klein reported for Dorothea Simmons students, there was a significant short term knowledge gain about alcohol and alcoholism on the part of the recipients of the program based on the pre-and post-test scores. However, when this group was evaluated in a long-term, longitudinal study, their attitudes toward alcohol use and their actual alcohol drinking behavior was indistinguishable from those students who had not been exposed to the program (Kim, 1987).

Another comprehensive evaluation study found that the program had only "minimal impact on the psychosocial variables assumed to be involved in drinking behavior and had essentially no measurable carry-over effect on problem drinking behavior" (Hopkins, et al., 1988). Other critics of this program state that it is an affective education curriculum for grades 3–6 which uses values clarification techniques to teach about drug abuse and decision making and therefore it should not be used in the schools (Kilpatrick, 1992).

The curriculum is also rather expensive, so readers will have to decide if it is worth the cost, given these results. In order to obtain a curriculum review package contact: Here's Looking at You 2000; Comprehensive Health Education Foundation (CHEF); 20832 Pacific Highway South Seattle, WA 98198, Telephone (206) 824-2907.

Just Say No and Celebrate Red Ribbon Week

The federally sponsored programs Just Say No and Red Ribbon Week are each found in 14 percent of the Blue Ribbon Schools. The sixth of the National Education Goals 2000 states: "By the year 2000, every school in America will be free of drugs and violence and will offer a discipline environment conducive to learning" (U.S. Department of Education, 1991). Currently, all school districts receiving federal funds must establish standards of conduct for all students regarding drug use, possession, and sale, as well as provide a K–12 developmentally appropriate drug prevention education program. Research conducted by the Office of Substance Abuse Prevention (OSAP) has shown that ages 10–16 are the ages when alcohol and drug use attitudes and beliefs are being formed and when alcohol and other drug use is initiated. Therefore prevention efforts are strongly encouraged during the elementary and pre-teen years (U.S. Department of Education, 1993).

County Line Elementary School in Georgia celebrates Red Ribbon week by having students make t-shirts with original designs and the "Say No To Drugs" slogan. All students, faculty, and staff receive stickers and the school doors and signs are decorated with red ribbon bows and red balloons to signify that the school is drug free. Students conclude the observance of Red Ribbon Week by marching through the building and declaring war on drugs and by dressing in camouflage on the last day of the campaign.

At Pond Springs in Austin, Texas, Red Ribbon Week is five special days when teachers and students show their commitment to remaining drug free. Each day students wear a visible sign such as crazy socks, and mismatched or bright clothes to match a slogan of the day such as "Our Future's Too Bright to Use Drugs."

The Blue Ribbon Schools are following the national guidelines for implementing substance abuse programs. Nevertheless, the research shows that although these programs are able to show positive gains in knowledge, they are unsuccessful in changing attitudes and the drug-using behaviors of students (Bangert-Drowns, 1988). A large comprehensive study of 5,000 students, 240 schools, commissioned by the California Department of Education study of the DARE and Red Ribbon Week programs found that as students age, they become progressively more convinced that drug prevention programs are ineffective. As these programs rely on lectures and assemblies to promote the evils of drugs, they lack credibility with students and fail to reach them (Texeira, 1995). A growing body of research is finding that the most effective drug education programs help children deal with peer pressure to use drugs by engaging them in group discussions and role-playing, rather than by having an adult stand in front of the class lecturing (Bangert-Drowns, 1988). Peer- or student-led programs have achieved greater reduction in drug use than teacher-led programs partly due to greater fidelity in curriculum implementation by peer leaders and arguably because of higher credibility with high-risk students (Botvin et al., 1990).

The federal document *What Works: Schools without Drugs* (U.S. Department of Education, 1989) blames the widespread drug use in part on the influence of television and movies that make drugs and drinking seem attractive. A good classroom curriculum is a start, but it cannot do the job alone. In order for a positive reduction in drug abuse to occur, a comprehensive approach must be implemented: families, schools, and communities must work together. Parents need to be educated, society needs to promote and reward the right kind of behavior, and the media need to change their message and stop the glorification of the drug world.

McGruff the Crime Dog

McGruff the Elementary School Puppet Program is used in 20 percent of the Blue Ribbon Schools. This substance abuse program uses a puppet, called McGruff, with a weekly series of tapes and lessons. It is targeted for grades 1 and 2 and seeks to promote student confidence and self-esteem around the entire topic of drug awareness, safety issues, and abuse. At the Hill Elementary School in Austin, Texas, McGruff the "Take the Bite Out of Crime Dog" is used in primary classrooms to teach students in a non-threatening manner about the dangers of drug and alcohol abuse. Hill is a very large urban school with a diverse student population of over 700 students who speak seven languages besides English. Hill students come from a socioeconomic mix ranging from lower- to upper-middle class income families. McGruff, the Crime Dog, through his actions, is able to speak an international language to all of the students.

Project Charlie

Project Charlie is a drug abuse prevention program for elementary school children based on building self-esteem, teaching social competencies, and discouraging the use of drugs as a way to avoid problems. Project Charlie is found in 3 percent of the Blue Ribbon Schools. According to the curriculum authors, the program emphasizes feeling good about yourself without sacrificing anyone else's well being. The Dr. Joey Pirrung Elementary School in Mesquite, Texas, a suburban area of Dallas, is a K–6 school with a very diverse student body that has had a dramatic increase in enrollment over the past five years. They use Project Charlie in their classrooms and explain that the program approaches drug abuse from a different point-of-view, that is, students who feel good about themselves will want to take good care of themselves. When they have choices to make in life, they will know how to make wise decisions.

However, Project Charlie uses values clarification techniques instead of directive instruction and has come under criticism by some parents. According to the *Watchman Expositor*, the Arlington *Citizen-Journal* reported on July 29, 1990 that "Project Charlie approaches drug abuse prevention from a perspective other than telling kids what they shouldn't do." The curriculum explains to the teachers that they should not instruct the students by "advising, providing answers, or solutions." How, then, are the teachers of Project Charlie to help students make difficult decisions? In the lesson plan entitled "Decision Making," the curriculum instructs the teachers with this advice: "As children ask questions, tell them to use their own judgment as you do not know any more than they do" (*Watchman Expositor*, 1996). One should note that character educators often make use of indirect methods (such as questioning and discussion) as well as direct methods (such as explaining why something is right or wrong) but in all cases for the purpose of guiding children toward morally correct conclusions that adults have judged to be in the children's best interest.

Readers who would like to review this curriculum themselves should contact: Project Charlie, 5701 Normandale Road, Edina, MN 55424, Telephone (612) 925-9706.

Quest

The Quest program is a commercially prepared curriculum in self-esteem and decision making that emphasizes how to deal with drugs and respond to social pressures. Quest International, a nonprofit educational organization, was established in 1975 to "help create a world that cares more deeply about its young people." Quest develops and makes available comprehensive, broad-based programs, and services that enable young people to gain the self-confidence, good judgement, and social skills they need to cope with the challenges they face in today's world. The Quest curriculum was found in 10 percent of the total sample of Blue Ribbon Schools: the *Skills for Adolescence* curriculum for grades 6–8, first written in 1985, was found in 5 percent of the Blue Ribbon Schools and the *Skills for Growing* curriculum, written in 1990 for grades K–5, was found in 20 percent of the schools. Some of the Blue Ribbon Schools cite the use of the Quest program as their character education program, others as their drug education program, and/or as their guidance program. The Quest program curriculum guide states that it is meant to be a "life skills" program that helps to develop positive social skills, decision-making skills, character, and citizenship in children.

At the Westwood Elementary School, a school with a growing population of linguistically diverse students in suburban Santa Clara, California, all of the students participate in the *Quest: Skills for Growing Program*:

> The program is included as part of the curriculum at each grade level and teaches skills in self-discipline, responsibility, good judgment, and getting along with others. A unique quality of the program is that 100 percent of the Westwood staff has participated in the training. The staff integrates this program into daily classroom activities such as daily classroom meetings, conflict resolution activities, and leadership role-playing.
>
> An important aspect of *Skills for Growing* is the link between home and school. It helps parents resolve family conflicts with love and limits. This schoolwide program also allows us to use a common language for respect, tolerance, and acceptance. Some students' opinions were: "I liked cooperating on the friendship chain." "It helps me deal with situations in everyday life." "It helps me communicate in a way that does not make both of us angry."

Many of the students at Westwood are refugees from Ethiopia, South America, Vietnam, and Eastern Europe, with a considerable number of Korean, Spanish, and Chinese students. Quest letters to the family allow students to share with their parents what they are learning in school.

Critics of Quest, such as, Kilpatrick (1992), state that it is a humanistic education curriculum that uses values clarification techniques to enhance students' self-esteem. He states that it is an affective curriculum that is non-directive and allows students to choose for themselves whether or not to take drugs. Kilpatrick says that the real problem is that Quest is not clearly a drug education program because it has units on thinking, feelings, and emotions, decision making, communication, and action with only one unit on drug education.

Humanistic or affective education is concerned with the formation and development of emotions, feelings, values, attitudes, and morals (Beane, 1986). It is important for students to develop this moral feeling aspect if they are to avoid drugs, however, for Kilpatrick, the preferred curriculum would be more directive —"Don't take drugs"—and less values clarification. Kilpatrick cites an evaluation of Quest made by Professor Stephen Jurs at the University of Toledo in 1985 in which he found that program participation was followed by an increase in drug experimentation relative to a comparison group that did not experience Quest.

Quest has responded to Kilpatrick's allegations with a thirteen-page document correcting the misconceptions he raises. In particular, the document notes that "Quest's programs are based on the principle of skills acquisition, and teach traditional civic values, including self-discipline, good judgment, responsibility, honesty, and positive commitments to family, school, peers, and the community. By promoting these values, Quest's programs are clearly *not* non-directive. The program defended cites Dr. Jurs as saying that Kilpatrick has erroneously summarized his research findings. Dr. Jurs clarified that there was evidence of increased drug use by about 2 percent of the students who had taken the *Skills for Living* compared to an increase of about 5 percent among students not taking *Skills for Living*. This, he noted, was a positive finding— Quest students showed less drug use than non-Quest students.

Carol Apacki, Quest Program development writer, explained in a phone conversation that Quest has mirrored what has been the "best thinking" on educational methodology over the years that it has been in the schools. In the 1970s values clarification methods were used, in 1980 a child-centered/learning styles approach was used, and then in 1990 a more directive approach was used to revise the curriculum so that it would stress values such as citizenship, responsibility, honesty, good judgment, and self-discipline. She stated that Quest has responded to criticisms of its program with revisions that rely less on the previous "affective education techniques" and more on the current "directive approach." In its current programs it balances decision-making exercises with a "no use" stance toward drugs and it supplements self-esteem activities with a list of school service projects. The new edition of *Skills for Adolescence* even includes criteria for making decisions:

1. Will it lead to trouble?
2. Is it against the law, rules, or teaching of my religion?
3. Is it harmful to me or to others?
4. Would it disappoint my family or other important adults?
5. Is it wrong to do? (Would I be sorry afterwards?)
6. Would I be hurt or upset if someone did this to me?

Many Blue Ribbon Schools state that they foster character development through the use of the Quest curriculum. According to St. Albert the Great School, a very large K–8 school in suburban North Royalton, Ohio, The Quest *Skills for Growing* program frames moral and spiritual development in practical terms that include emphasizing conflict resolution skills, cooperative group work, dynamics, decision-making skills, drug awareness education, and promotion of confidence and self-esteem. Grayslake Middle School is located in a rapidly growing suburb north of Chicago with a growing Hispanic population. They use The Lions *Quest Skills for Adolescence* program to direct students in a decision-making model that promotes accountability and ethical judgement based upon family and social values, and encourages students to view themselves as part of a larger whole. According to the teachers, the Quest program has helped to build a welcoming and caring school climate as it emphasizes the need for a consensus regarding rules in the classroom community and respect of diversity.

The new Quest curriculum is more directive and does include some character education components, but it is mostly a "life skills" development program that emphasizes the development of social and emotional competencies. The old Quest curriculum, even though it was written by the "current educational experts" of that time, could actually be considered one of the causes for the sorry state of values education in many American schools today. Readers can review the Quest curriculum themselves to decide if it would be an appropriate component of their school's character education program by contacting *Quest International* at 537 Jones Road, P.O. Box 566, Granville, OH 43023-0566, Telephone (800)446-2700.

School Developed Programs

Seventeen percent of the Blue Ribbon Schools mention that they have developed their own drug education program. Many times these programs are a school motto that all adopt to show their commitment to saying "no" to drugs. Examples are:

> NOMAD—No More Alcohol Or Drugs
> RATS—Reject All Tobacco
> HOTS—Hazards Of Tobacco
> WHO—We Help Ourselves
> GROW—Gaining Responsibility, Opportunity, and Wisdom
> CHICKEN—Cool, Honest, Intelligent, Clearheaded, Keen, Energetic, and Not
> Interested in drugs

The China Grove Elementary School in North Carolina uses different programs at different grade levels:

> 3rd grade—Here's Looking at You, 2000
> 4th grade—I'm Special
> 5th grade—Be Smart, Don't Start
> 6th grade—DARE

China Grove is a K–6 school with a heterogeneous population of almost 800 students, 11 percent of whom are African American and over one-fourth of whom are from lower-income families.

Other Programs

The *Discovery* textbook series has been adopted by several of the Blue Ribbon Schools, including St. Damian's in Oak Forest, Illinois. The textbook series goes from grades K–8 and provides a comprehensive program of personal development, decision making, and drug and substance abuse prevention.

Another substance abuse program implemented in these exemplary schools is *Babes*, "Beginning Alcohol and Addictions Basic Education," which was found in 3 percent of the schools. *Babes* is an Alcohol Awareness Program for the primary grades. It has lessons that focus on self-esteem and drug awareness and emphasizes the development of a positive self-concept with the ability to say no.

The Extra Step Program (ESP) is a prevention program for children ages 5–12 who come from homes where chemical dependence, divorce or other stresses are present. These children stand a high chance, 40 to 60 percent greater than other children of becoming chemically dependent themselves. Royalview Elementary School in Willowick, Ohio, uses this program. The children meet in small groups of 8 to 10 for ten sessions of approximately one to one and a half hours in length. Some of the topics covered including: Feelings (anger-happiness, defenses, alcoholism/chemical dependency, It's OK to say no, decisions, families.) The content of each of these sessions is largely experiential, which has proven successful in working with this age group. Royalview is a K–5 school with a caring climate located in a suburb with a student body of 98 percent white, 20 percent of whom qualify for free lunch, 13 percent for special education services.

Teachers in the Como Park Elementary School in New York are trained in the Growing Healthy curriculum, a nationally recognized program for substance abuse prevention, which is described below under health programs. In addition, Como Park students are trained in the Prevention is Primary (PIP) program, which has been used in their district for many years and includes drug and alcohol prevention instruction.

Me-ology is yet another drug prevention education program found in the Blue Ribbon Schools. Me-ology, a program developed in the early eighties, has also been criticized for using values clarification techniques (Kilpatrick, 1991).

The Mary C. Howse Elementary School in West Chester, Pennsylvania, an ethnically diverse K–5 school uses the Good Choice/Bad Choice program that provides opportunities for students to develop decision-making strategies. This program is consistent across all grade levels with the expectation that students will make responsible decisions in accordance with their developmental level.

Project Smokefree is an interdisciplinary project developed by the American Cancer Society that teaches students about the dangers of tobacco use and stresses refusal skills useful in alcohol and drug prevention. All disciplines are actively involved in instruction, each with a hands-on project. Each year a schoolwide assembly initiates Project Smokefree. Students learn that tobacco is a gateway drug and that early refusal will result in a healthier and happier lifestyle. Clear messages are presented in this program in order to ensure that students will be provided with the necessary information to make intelligent choices with regard to tobacco, drug, and alcohol use. At Homewood Middle School, a racially and economically integrated middle school in a suburb of Birmingham, Alabama, students got involved through Project Smokefree in city council meetings in order to support the passage of a smoke-free ordinance in Homewood. Officials said that students' participation had actually affected the outcome of the vote. Students also wrote letters to the President of the United States regarding tobacco access for minors.

Students Teaching Students

There is a movement, especially in the area of substance abuse curricula, to have students who have quit using drugs talk to other young people. Some programs include Kids Teach Kids, which is a mentorship for drugs and alcohol prevention and Peer Outreach, which helps students develop a positive self-image, explains peer pressure, and provides factual information on drugs and alcohol. Let's Talk Turkey and Stars are two programs in which students talk about the risks of smoking. Research reviews of substance abuse programs have found significantly more attitude change and less drug use behavior on the part of peer-taught students as compared to adult-taught students (Bangert-Drowns, 1988).

RESEARCH RESULTS

In response to the 1985 Drug-Free Schools Act, more than 2,000 substance-prevention curricula flooded the market and by 1991, schools were spending almost $125 million on these curricula. Since most of the programs had not been properly evaluated, a five-year study was commissioned by the Department of Education. It found that the majority of these 2,000 curricula did not do much good (Adair, 2000). William Kilpatrick (1991) criticizes many of these drug prevention programs—Quest, Positive Action, Project Charlie, Here's Looking at You, Me-ology, and Values and Choices—because they were developed in the 1970s and early 1980s and are modeled on Carl Roger's therapeutic education scheme and values clarification techniques that put a heavy emphasis on feelings. Research studies have shown that drug education programs alone have minimal effect. Although there is an increase in knowledge by students who are in the program, it is very hard to change students' attitudes and behavior by a curricular program alone. On the long-term basis, the actual drug use of students is the same as students who have not been exposed to the program (Bangert-Drowns, 1988). In some cases, with a nondirective drug education program, there has been an actual increase in drug use; students choose to use the less serious drugs, but more students show greater drug use (Hopkins et al., 1988; Kim, 1987). Consensus is developing that a curricular program alone will not change students' attitudes and actions. What is needed is a comprehensive, multimodal approach.

WHAT DOES WORK?

The U.S. Department of Education (1999) has published a guide to selecting drug prevention curricula—*Making the Grade: A Guide to School Drug Prevention Programs*—in which fifty of the most popular prevention programs in the U.S. are evaluated. It states that consumers should watch out for outdated theories, avoid curricula that emphasize open-ended decision making, values clarification, and therapeutic educational strategies. The department's research has shown that the drug use prevention field has evolved from a reliance on simplistic approaches to one of combining multiple strategies to address multiple risk factors for substance use. Programs that target a single risk factor, such as low self-esteem or poor school achievement, are unlikely to have a significant impact (U.S. Department of Education, 1993). The *Third Triennial Report to Congress: Drug Abuse and Drug Abuse Research* from the Department of Health and Human Services (1990) also cites research that shows that although site-specific interventions have had limited impact on reducing drug use; there is evidence that a comprehensive approach is effective.

Perhaps the Murdock School, a very large school of over 1000 students in the suburb of La Mesa, California, is one of the best examples of this multi-pronged effort.

> In the educational community and the community at large, Murdock School is known for high standards of behavior and an educational environment that is conducive to learning. Through a comprehensive and cooperative approach at Murdock, students and parents are presented with the knowledge and skills to help prevent substance abuse now and in their future. All aspects of the school community coordinate their resources to promote healthy alternatives to illegal drug use.
>
> Ongoing skills in responsible decision making, refusal skills, and positive self-concept building are encouraged through a teacher presented curriculum. The school counselor collaborates on total school and community activities that include community speakers, letter writing to local government officials, poster contests, and classroom lessons. Murdock's staff and parents conduct an intensive parent education program. Through this joint effort between the district, school, and community, Murdock School is promoting a drug-free lifestyle.

As Murdock's broad-based program indicates, drug prevention is not simply a matter of developing good curricula, it needs to be a community-wide effort involving teachers, parents, students, and community members working together to fight drug and alcohol use and abuse by any member of the community. Clear messages need to be given about the moral implications of abusing alcohol and/or using drugs. Older students should be involved in encouraging younger students to resist drugs. These messages need to be clear in the school policies, in community social events, and in the media.

Kilpatrick (1992) found that the most successful schools do not limit themselves to providing drug education courses. A more important factor is the school's atmosphere of expectations. A strong school policy against substance abuse—clearly articulated, consistently enforced, and broadly communicated—is the foundation upon which any program should be built. Kilpatrick states:

Their first priority is to create a drug-free environment and a sense of pride in achieving and maintaining a drug-free school. Such schools take academics seriously and assign significant amounts of homework. In addition, they emphasize extracurricular activities. They attempt to create a school atmosphere rather than a group therapy atmosphere. They focus on science, history, art, and the marching band rather than on self-esteem. They enlist the help of families, business, police, and community groups (pp. 50–51).

Visits to the Blue Ribbons Schools revealed that the most successful drug prevention programs are those that are integrated as an essential part, although not the only part, of an all-school effort to promote good character in the students. Whether the school uses one of the character education curricula outlined in chapter 3 or integrates character education throughout the curriculum as done in the Princeton School District in Ohio, and the Plano School District in Texas, students are able to see that people of character, for many reasons, do not use drugs because they have no need for drugs. They get their "high on life" from doing good deeds, from helping others, and from being a positive leader among their peers. They have learned to use the character values to help them make good choices. Using their moral knowledge and moral feelings, they have chosen to perform good moral actions. As Daniel Goleman (1995) writes in *Emotional Intelligence*:

Information is not enough. The most effective programs supplement the basic information given with the development of essential emotional and social skills. These programs taught children to find ways to solve interpersonal conflicts more positively, to have more self-confidence, not to blame themselves if something happened and to feel they had a network of support in teachers and parents to whom they could turn (p. 257).

SEX EDUCATION

There is no specific question in the Blue Ribbon Schools application regarding sex education programs in the schools. Therefore, there was little information given regarding this area of the curriculum. Some schools did report on their health education program in the same category as that regarding the keeping of their school drug, alcohol, and tobacco free; others reported that it was part of the program they used to promote good character.

Only seventeen states and the District of Columbia include sex education as a mandated part of the school curriculum, specifying that the program should promote abstinence until marriage; however, they usually specify that such a curriculum should begin at grade six (McClellan, 1987). The Urban Institute and the National Association of State Boards of Education, in a 1982 survey of 180 school districts in cities with populations over 100,000, found that three-fourths of the city school districts provided some instruction in sex education in high school or junior high school and two-thirds provided it in elementary school (Kenney, 1987). "Should sex education be included in the curriculum?" was asked in the 30th Annual Phi Delta Kappa/Gallup Poll of the Public's Attitudes toward the Public Schools (Rose and Gallup, 1998). Eighty-seven percent of the national total said that it should be. This issue had also been explored eleven years previously in 1987 and at that time 76 percent said that it should be. Most of the schools in this Blue Ribbon sample were K–5 organizations, which would account for the general lack of program information in this area.

NEED FOR CHARACTER-BASED SEX EDUCATION

The Medical Institute for Sexual Health (1996) has developed *National Guidelines for Sexuality and Character Education* that state that character-based sex education should be directive, using thoughtful curricula, accurately interpreted medical data, and ethical reasoning to guide students toward right decisions about sex—that is, sexual abstinence until they are ready to establish a mutually faithful, monogamous relationship within marriage. Abstinence education presents young people with the moral dimensions of sexual conduct. It helps them apply core ethical values such as respect, responsibility, and self-control to the sexual domain.

Research has repeatedly shown little correlation between participation in a unit on sex education and level of sexual activity (this is similar to the findings on drug education). Simply incorporating a unit on sex education into other course work may increase students' knowledge, but it rarely changes their behavior (Buie, 1987). In fact, some will argue that it is the introduction of "too much explicit information at too early of an age" that has led to the dramatic increase in sexual activity among the young.

A five year project sponsored by the W. T. Grant Foundation studied and distilled the active ingredients of successful programs. The key list of emotional skills to be covered included self-awareness; identifying, expressing, and managing feelings; impulse control and delaying gratification; and handling stress and anxiety. A key ability in impulse control is knowing the difference between feelings and actions, and learning to make better emotional decisions by first controlling the impulse to act, then identifying alternative actions and their consequences before acting (Goleman, 1995).

Character-Based Sex Education in the Public Schools, a position paper adopted by the Character Education Partnership (1996a), states that character-based sex education must help young people develop the virtues that underlie the ability to make and live out good decisions about sex. Lickona says that the best hope for developing sexual self-control is directive sex education—teaching students why sexual abstinence is the only medically safe and morally responsible choice for unmarried teenagers (Lickona, 1994).

In 1981, the federal government approved the Adolescent Family Life Act, called title XX, that approved public funds for abstinence-only sex education programs. The goal of abstinence-only programs is to convince teens that the only morally acceptable sexual behavior takes place within marriage.

Character-based sex education should help young people understand that while condoms may reduce some of the physical risks of premature sexual activity, serious risks remain. These risks include pregnancy, disease, and the negative psychological consequence of temporary sexual relationships. Character-based sex education should help students develop the values and moral reasoning in supporting abstinence. In teaching abstinence, the school should stress that abstinence can be regained. If the school discusses condoms/contraception, it must do so in a way that does not undermine its advocacy of abstinence and related character goals.

The National Guidelines for Sexuality and Character Education (Medical Institute for Sexual Health, 1996) concur that abstinence sexuality education is directive sex education; it emphasizes making the right decisions. Through ethical reasoning, medical evidence, videos, role-plays, and real-life stories, abstinence education unambiguously promotes the reasons for waiting to have sex. It assumes that young persons respond positively when instruction is well reasoned and supported, and when it comes from an adult whom they respect and trust. According to an Alan Guttmacher Institute study, one in three schools now employs an abstinence-only/character-based approach to sexuality. Evaluations of a number of these programs show that they are having a positive impact (Lickona, 2000).

Sex Respect is a nationally known program used in several Blue Ribbon Schools. Developed by Colleen Kelley Mast, Sex Respect provides teens with information, identifies the emotional, psychological, and physical consequences of teenage sexual activity, and helps students to develop positive and healthy attitudes. The program's effectiveness has been documented in a series of evaluation reports for the federal office of Adolescent Pregnancy Programs (Lickona , 1994). For more information on this curriculum contact: Sex Respect, Inc., P.O. Box 349, Bradley, IL 60915, Telephone (815) 932-8389, www.sexrespect.com.

Values and Choices is another curriculum mentioned by the Blue Ribbon Schools. The curriculum focuses on seven values essential for maintaining positive human relationships: equality, self-control, promise keeping, responsibility, respect, honesty, and social justice. The curriculum includes abstinence messages throughout the fifteen lessons. It also includes a lesson on birth control as the second-best alternative to abstinence, and therefore cannot be considered a true character-based program.

Forever Friends is a program used at the Pine Tree Middle School, an ethnically diverse school in Longview, Texas, where one-third of the students qualify for a free lunch and 22 percent of the students move each year. Pine Tree girls in need of mentoring have lunch with women leaders in the community as part of

Forever Friends, a program to prevent teen pregnancy. This mentor program for at-risk girls encourages young women to set goals for themselves and avoid loss of education due to at-risk factors like drugs or teen pregnancy.

Learning About Myself and Others (LAMO) is another sexuality program found in some of the Blue Ribbon Schools. This program encourages parents to attend classes with their children at the school and to work together answering the teacher's questions. This helps build a climate of trust and open communication between parent and child. Take-home materials help to continue the discussion.

AIDS Curriculum

AIDS instruction began in most school districts about fifteen years ago. Responsibility for the curriculum was given to the nurse in some schools, to the guidance counselor in other schools, or to the science or health teachers, who were to teach it as one unit in their classes. Some of the Blue Ribbon Schools explained to me during visits that condoms were demonstrated as part of the original AIDS health classes curriculum, but parents protested and demanded "abstinence only" instruction. These Blue Ribbon Schools immediately modified the lesson plans in the curriculum to meet the desires of the parents, and they have had no problems in this area.

Our nation's leaders are urging educators to undertake an intensive educational effort that has a chance of influencing the sex-related and drug-related behaviors that place young people in risk of becoming infected with HIV. Effective AIDS education should encourage students to be abstinent and not offer "protected sex" as a "responsible" second option. The clear expectation of abstinence is the only message consistent with character education, since it alone truly respects the self and others. Any sex education worthy of the name must help students develop self-control and the ability to apply core ethical values such as respect and responsibility to the sexual domain (Lickona, 1993b).

"HIV, You Can Live Without It" is a curriculum for grades 5–12 which emphasizes that abstinence from premarital sexual activity is the best and only sure prevention of AIDS and other sexually transmitted diseases. It provides coverage of the topic of AIDS age-appropriately in the sensitive upper elementary grades within a directive, abstinence-based, family-centered conceptual framework. For more information contact: Teen Aid, E. 723 Jackson, Spokane, WA 99207, Telephone (509) 482-2868.

HEALTH CURRICULUM

Growing Healthy is a comprehensive, sequential K–7 health curriculum. It is designed to equip students with the knowledge and skills to make choices that are conducive to good health and to help children to establish good health habits. Miriam Remar, principal at Howard Reiche Community School in Portland,

Maine, explains that the school dedicates a minimum of one class period per week per grade level, ranging from twenty to sixty minutes, to the curriculum. It includes information on health, substance abuse, the anatomy and biology of the body, and sex education. The curriculum uses a hands-on approach to guide students through the decision-making process, so students can relate the information and concepts presented in their daily life. Teacher in-service training for implementation of Growing Healthy takes four days. Teachers usually integrate the curriculum into the science or physical education course. Evaluations of this curriculum have shown a positive correlation between the degree of in-servicing received by the teacher and the success of implementation (Smith et al., 1993).

Family Life Education was also mentioned by a few of the Blue Ribbon Schools. The Hillside School in Montclair, New Jersey, is a magnet middle school with a very diverse student body. The school uses this curriculum to help their middle-grade students learn to deal positively with the emotional, social, and physical changes experienced at puberty. The curriculum also deals with drugs, alcohol, and character development. Responsible decision making is the major focus of the curriculum; however it does not emphasize abstinence as the best choice and therefore cannot be considered a character-based curriculum. A goal of the curriculum is to foster increased communication between parents and children about sexuality. The Hillside School has guest speakers to address the students on issues such as dating, fighting, and drugs.

CHARACTER BUILDING HEALTH EDUCATION

According to Kathleen Sullivan of the Project Reality organization, health curricula are more effective than sex education curricula because they help students to understand not only the physical aspects of sex but also the emotional aspects, which are very much related to character education. No contraceptive will ever be able to prevent the emotional trauma involved in having intimate relations with someone who is not ready or able to make a true commitment.

A true "composite" approach to sex education includes character education as an integral part of the program. It helps build self-esteem by teaching students that there is a profound purpose for their lives, showing them how to develop caring relationships of all kinds, and encouraging them to think beyond the present and to set long-term goals. Students thus are given the skills they need in order to make moral decisions about the appropriate use and care for their body.

CHILD ABUSE AWARENESS

We Help Ourselves (WHO) is a program used in the Plano School District in Texas to encourage students to voice their concerns and opinions about child abuse. Arlene Carnes, the counselor at Saigling in this district, explained the program to me during a visit to the school. The Junior League in Plano started the program. It is a curriculum that includes videos for different grade levels. Carnes comments:

> It talks about strangers, stranger dangers, verbal abuse, physical abuse, and sexual abuse. Then it also talks about inappropriate touching. There are little puppets that go with the primary grades and then the older students do role plays as news commentators. One issue, which we just discussed, included a role play of a girl who comes home from school and gets a phone call. Saying it is a radio station, they ask her to answer who is the first president. She gives the answer, they say she has won, and ask her for her address. They ask, "Do your parents work outside the home?" "Well yes", she replies "but why do you need to know that?" They hang up. She realizes that she has given out too much information. Then the students brainstorm and discuss what she should have done, what she should do now, and then they make some decisions.

Come in from the Storm is another curriculum used in the Plano schools which deals with abuse—sexual, verbal, and physical. Parents are very involved in most of the Blue Ribbon Schools, approving these different curricula and giving their input on how they would like a program to be delivered. Parents have requested that boys and girls be separated for these classes, and the counselors and teachers have honored the parents' request.

RESEARCH RESULTS ON
HEALTH/SEX EDUCATION CURRICULA

Research studies have shown that students who have taken comprehensive sex education programs (those that also teach about contraceptives) were significantly more likely to have sexual intercourse than teens in sex education courses which did not discuss contraceptives (Dawson, 1986). In addition, health programs, which are simply knowledge dispensers, lead to high incidents of different types of abuse. Like the findings on substance abuse programs, knowledge alone is not enough to change behavior. Effective sex and health programs need to be multi-faceted and an essential element of a comprehensive character education program (Lickona, 1993b). These programs should teach moral values, develop healthy self-esteem, and foster attitudes that lead students to choose chastity as a virtue of a person of character. Schools must recruit parents, faith communities, and other community groups as partners in character-based sex education. All of the Blue Ribbon Schools that I visited had succeeded in their schools in this area.

SUMMARY

As this chapter shows, many of the Blue Ribbon Schools indicated that their drug education program is the main way in which they fostered the development of character in their students. However, research has shown that substance abuse and drug education programs alone have not been effective in changing students' behavior and have in fact increased students' use of these chemicals. Many of the programs that different Blue Ribbon Schools use are based on values clarification techniques and are the exact opposite of a character-building curricula. A drug prevention program alone cannot be a school's entire character education program, for research has shown that drug education will only succeed when it is part of a comprehensive character education program that involves the entire community.

Very few of the Blue Ribbon Schools reported on their health education and/or sex education programs, as there was no specific question in the application form regarding this area. However, some did mention these programs as part of the way in which they foster character or as part of their health and substance abuse prevention curricula. Research has shown that the effectiveness of sex education programs is similar to that reported for drug education programs: they are only effective when they are based on fostering the development of character through the living of core moral values.

6

Motivating Students

In praising or loving a child, we love and praise not that which is, but that which we hope for.

—Goethe

Teaching that impacts is not head to head, but heart to heart.

— Howard Hendricks

In teaching, and almost any other profession, they won't care how much you know until they know how much you care.

— Anonymous

WILL KNOWING THE GOOD LEAD TO DOING THE GOOD?

This book began with Meno's question to Socrates, "Can virtue be taught?" and it has tried to show how the Blue Ribbon Schools indeed help to develop students' virtue, values, and character. However, the less-than-encouraging research reported in the previous chapter regarding the effectiveness of drug education programs suggests that mere knowledge of something being the good or the better thing to do does not necessarily lead to our choosing to do this action. This bears on an ancient question asked by many philosophers, (e.g., Plato, Aristotle, Augustine): "Will knowing the good necessarily lead us to doing the good?"

In chapter 1, Lickona's model of good character was described as a combination of moral knowing, moral feeling and moral action (Lickona, 1991). It is a valid construct that can be used to categorize all of the different Blue Ribbon Schools' programs for character development. Programs that teach core virtues and decision-making skills emphasize moral knowing; those related to discipline and citizenship emphasize moral doing. In this chapter we look at how motivation, guidance, and self-esteem programs promote the moral feeling that serves as a bridge between moral knowing and moral action.

Developing the Affective Side of Character

This chapter looks at the programs in the Blue Ribbon Schools that attempt to develop the affective or feeling side of students, focusing on inspiring students to *want* to live the good character values. It reports on the various motivational programs found in the Blue Ribbon Schools, reviews their curricular components, and cites research that evaluates their effectiveness. The chapter tries to answer the following questions:

- Can and should schools try to develop the affective and emotional side of students?
- What are some effective ideas that schools can use to motivate students towards living a life of good character?
- Which guidance programs are more effective in promoting character development?
- Do self-esteem programs promote genuine character development in students?
- Why are so many Blue Ribbon Schools using ineffective programs based on techniques that range from values clarification to new age philosophy?

There are two sources for the information reported in this chapter. First of all, there are the programs mentioned in response to the main question, "How do school programs, practices, policies, and staff foster the development of sound character, democratic values, ethical judgement, good behavior, and the ability to work in a self-disciplined and purposeful manner?" In addition, there are answers given to another question in the section on student environment that was often referred to in answering the question above: "What specific programs, procedures, or instructional strategies do you employ to develop students' interest in learning and motivate them to study?" The answers given to these questions, as seen in table 5, fell into three categories: motivation programs, guidance programs, and self-esteem programs. These categories provide the organizing paradigm for this chapter.

EMOTIONAL INTELLIGENCE

It is important for students to develop the emotional side of themselves in order to not only know the good, but also love the good. Every teacher should read Daniel Goleman's book *Emotional Intelligence* (1995) in order to understand the important role emotions play in the successful education of students. Goleman shows in this text the importance of developing the emotional aspect of human potential, for there is growing evidence that fundamental ethical stances in life stem from underlying emotional capabilities. Emotional intelligence is a set of traits and qualities that make us more fully human, and that matter immensely for our personal destiny: "Emotional intelligence-abilities such as being able to motivate oneself and persist in the face of frustration; to control impulse and delay gratification, to regulate one's moods and keep distress from swamping the ability to think, to empathize, and to hope" (Goleman, 1995).

The teachers at Shreve Island Elementary School in Shreveport, Louisiana, studied Goleman's book and tried to integrate these ideas in various aspects of the school. They decided to implement "A Peace-Able Place," a violence prevention program that focuses on conflict resolution, anger management, respect for others, and effective communication (CARE), all skills necessary for developing students' emotional intelligence. A visit to the school is the best way to experience a school where emotional intelligence is fostered.

From the moment I entered the school, I found it to be a most inviting place. I observed a very warm and caring environment, child-centered, and supportive. During my visit I saw teachers visiting with students, the principal acknowledging children by name as well as sharing "hugs" and support staff recognizing children in such a way as to bring smiles to their faces. One parent said, "Shreve Island is an all inclusive school. There is something for every child and every child is able to build a strong self ego." Students said that their school was a "fun" place, "awesome," "cool," and "neat." They wanted to come to school. I sense that Shreve Island is not only preparing a generation of children to be good problem solvers, life-long learners, and good citizens; they are also working hard to help a generation of youngsters to be kinder and gentler.

MOTIVATION PROGRAMS

Student motivation is a very important factor in character education. Motivation is related to the students' inner desires and is thus closely associated with their values (Frymier, 1974). Values represent what people believe in, what they are committed to and what they cherish. Values give direction to behavior. A school tells students what it values by what it rewards and by what activities it deems are important enough to sponsor and include during school time. Typically, motivation is a durable phenomenon, although it is not fixed. Students who are not motivated to learn in schools can be helped by nurturing a positive self-concept. Giving students positive feedback helps them to take responsibility for their own learning. Students come to realize that their success can be attributed to their own personal effort and abilities.

At the time of nomination, all the Blue Ribbon Schools appeared to be effective in motivating students. However, some of the schools cite their move from unmotivated and undisciplined school bodies to highly motivated school bodies as one of the reasons they should be nationally recognized. These schools suggest that the implementation of some of the following ideas throughout the school resulted in more motivated student bodies. These student motivation ideas fall into four different categories: awards, ceremonies, high academic expectations, and school mottoes (see table 8). Ideas are included here if they satisfy either of two criteria: either they were mentioned so often by schools that they might be considered as an integral part of elementary school student motivation, or they seemed so interesting that other schools might want to consider them.

AWARDS

In *Reclaiming Our Schools, A Handbook on Teaching Character, Academics and Discipline*, Edward Wynne and Kevin Ryan (1993) state that awards and ceremonies are important ways of emphasizing and transmitting character values. A school—and, in fact, a culture—shows what type of character it values by the awards, recognitions and ceremonies (or celebrations) it sponsors. If all of the awards go to athletes (including the monetary "award"), the school or society says it values athletics. The Blue Ribbon Schools do give awards for athletics, but they also recognize and celebrate good character, hard work, effort, and good citizenship. There is no better way to build up children's "self-esteem" than for them to win an award that was well

Table 8.   Motivational Methods Used in the Blue Ribbon Schools

Category	Count	Precent of Responses
Activities	21	7
Assemblies	8	3
Awards	79	27
Catch Students Being Good	28	10
High Epectations	61	21
Mascot, Mottoes, Pledges	14	5
Positive Reinforcement	51	16
Other methods	33	11

Valid Cases, 290, Missing Cases 195

earned. Almost one-third of the Blue Ribbon Schools stated that granting awards was one of the ways they promoted character development in students.

Awards have been found to be effective motivators for students, especially when they help students to link their success in achieving the reward to their own efforts (Alderman, 1990).

It can be noted that some of these awards the Blue Ribbon Schools give directly express aspects of character development in the very name of the award:

- Athlete of the Month (must show good sportsmanship)
- American Legion Award for Leadership
- Good Citizen Award
- Knights of The Month
- Most Improved Student of the Month (sign on school van)
- Presidential Academic Fitness Award
- Student of the Month Award
- Super Kids Awards
- Terrific Kids Program

Other schools use acronyms to tell what their award stands for:

- DUDE—Doers of unusual deeds of excellence
- TOPGUNS—Totally organized pupils who are gentle understanding neat and sensible
- VIP—Very Important Person

The Rudy Award is given at the R. J. Neutra Elementary School in Lemoore, California. This award for fifth graders was developed around the movie, *Rudy*. Rudy Ruettiger overcame tremendous obstacles to achieve his goal of playing football for the University of Notre Dame. A student who displays the "Rudy" characteristics and spirit is presented a trophy that is four feet tall and a $100 savings bond to further his/her education. Fifth-grade teachers have developed a unit on character in which they use the book *Rudy's Lesson for Young Champions*. This story is about an eagle that overcomes peer pressures, gangs, and temptations. He learns to make worthwhile decisions that allow him to soar like an eagle. Neutra Elementary School is a K–5 building with 506 very diverse students: 15 percent Filipino, 11 percent African American, 8 percent Hispanic, and with 50 percent of the student body on free lunch. Neutra is located in the San Joaquine Valley on the Lemorre Naval Air Station halfway between San Francisco and Los Angeles.

David Derby, the principal at the Mountain View School in California, explains in the school application why awards are important:

Awards can be said to serve four functions. First, they are a vehicle to motivate students to become active participants in the activities of their school. Second, they are a *blueprint* for parents and teachers to use in planning, encouraging, and setting goals with children. Third, they are a means of affirming that the nurturing of responsible, well-rounded individuals is important. Fourth, they are a significant form of recognition for students who have met the criteria for the award.

Some schools have set up awards based on their school mascot. The Tarkington School located in Wheeling, a middle-class suburb northwest of Chicago, Illinois, has "The Tarkington Tiger." Tarkington is a K–6 school with 674 students in a diverse student body, both racially, economically and linguistically. A visit to the school revealed that Arvum Poster, the principal, was the key factor in creating and maintaining the school "ethos" or "climate"—the spirit of enthusiasm among members of the group for one another, their group, and its purposes (Kilpatrick, 1992). Mr. Poster came from another school in the same district, which had won the Blue Ribbon Award in 1990–1991. When he came to Tarkington, he purposefully sought to create a nurturing, happy, and excellent environment where children were encouraged to develop the many facets of their unique personalities and talents—with an eye to the school's model, the Tarkington Tiger. The "Tarkington Tiger Traits" are a list of academic and behavioral expectations of students that are posted throughout the building. Students are encouraged to participate in activities that require self-discipline, good behavior, and sound character—what their school award is all about. Students who are nominated by their peers or teachers for having done something nice are awarded "Paw Pats on the Back."

Kilpatrick (1992) would likely compliment Mr. Poster on what he has done at Tarkington:

> The primary way to bring ethics and character back into schools is to create a positive moral environment in the school. The ethos of the school, not its course offerings is the decisive factor in forming character. The first thing we have to do is to change the moral climate of the schools themselves (p. 226).

Tarkington School has a happy climate. Climate refers to the shared attitudes, beliefs, and values of a community of people or of a group (Wynne and Ryan, 1993). A Tarkington Tiger greets you on the carpet as you enter the school; another hangs in the lunchroom and smiles at you from the walls. Students love giving one another tiger paw waves using the three middle fingers of their hand.

The Terrific Kids Program sponsored by the Kiwanis Club is used by both the Mayo Elementary School, a K–5 school in Mayo, Maryland, a suburb south of Annapolis, with a white student body and the Carver Elementary G.T. Magnet School in Wendell, North Carolina, a K–2 school in a rural, lower income area with a very diverse student body of 62 percent white and 33 percent African American. This program reinforces exemplary citizenship characteristics and is an attractive program for all students of all kinds of backgrounds. Two students each month are selected from each class based on their good citizenship qualities such as good attendance, responsible behavior, and respectful and caring attitudes. The students receive an award certificate, a bumper sticker, and a pencil. A photograph of each Terrific Kid is taken and displayed in the main hall for students who demonstrate exemplary citizenship skills. While each school believes that all of their kids are terrific, they have a goal to help each child be recognized sometime during the year as a "terrific kid," and about 90 percent of the students are awarded each year.

There is also a consistent trend emerging in some of the Blue Ribbon Schools, in both inner-city as well as in white, middle-class districts, to discourage competition among students for awards and recognition. In these schools, awards and recognition are available for *all* students who meet the criteria; they are not competitively "won." Instead, students are encouraged to participate in all curricular and extracurricular events and to measure themselves against the standards and criteria that must be met to receive the award, not against peers.

Alfie Kohn (1993), in his book *Punished by Rewards,* criticizes our American system for what he considers the excessive use of awards. He, however, would prefer this non-competitive system, as he feels that the most destructive way to administer rewards is to limit the number that are available; if awards are to be given, they should be distributed equitably to all who manifest the desired behaviors at the appropriate level and quality of performance. For instance, the Schuster Elementary School in El Paso, Texas, reports that "students are encouraged to compete against norms, instead of each other. Non-competitive games were even found in physical education classes." Schuster is a PreK–6 grade urban school with a very diverse student population of 363. More than half of the students are Hispanic and 64 percent of the students are from lower-income families.

Assemblies and Ceremonies

The ceremony that goes along with receiving the award is perhaps just as exciting as actually receiving the award. Ceremonies are important because they teach the participants that there are certain values that we all collectively and publicly acknowledge are important (Wynne and Ryan, 1993). The main ceremonies utilized in the Blue Ribbon Schools are the assembly and the morning announcements. There are assemblies to announce and explain the weekly/monthly/yearly character traits and assemblies to award those who have developed and manifested the character trait. Assemblies provide students with the opportunity to practice "good audience behavior." During assemblies, students who have excelled in reading, math, and spelling, as well as attendance and citizenship, are given their awards. Sometimes these are simple certificates, and sometimes they are coupons to use at local merchants and fast food restaurants. This helps students to see that community businesses are also interested in promoting good character and good citizenship in young people.

Schools use the morning announcement time to explain the weekly character trait and to identify those who have been "caught doing something good." They also award students with visual displays such as banners, an Honor Roll, a Hall of Fame bulletin board, or a bulletin board highlighting excellent student work. Some schools use the school marquee and newsletter to announce the names of students who have excelled in some way. The Forest Park Elementary School in Albany, New York, a K–5 school located in a suburban area has a Morning Assembly Program (MAP). The MAP establishes a positive focus for the day as it promotes self-esteem and a sense of responsibility while providing a forum to celebrate student achievement, recognition, and appreciation within the school community. As students assemble in the cafeteria for the MAP, they are first greeted with a warm "hello" by the principal and then sing a familiar song. MAP is led daily by student anchors and provides a community-like start to the day. Here birthdays and special accomplishments are recognized, school-wide events and life skills of the week are introduced, and school pride is enhanced. A connection between what is being learned and lived in school and the expectations in the world of work is always made.

In addition, some schools have special clubs for students who agree to pursue the character goals of the club. Fairfield North Elementary School is a K–5 school of almost 900 white, mostly middle-class students from the suburb of Hamilton, Ohio.

Fairfield North has a "Principles Club" which is an all-inclusive, school-wide effort to reinforce self-concept and basic principles of cooperation, perseverance, and responsibility. Themes such as "Responsibility" are worked on for one month. Simple goals like "cleaning up your work area" or "handing in homework on time" are stressed. Children who are observed by any teachers as meeting one of these goals are given a badge to wear. At the end of the month, the principal hand-delivers small favors to all students who have demonstrated the principle of the month. Since our major emphasis is on reinforcing positive behaviors, each student who has received even one month's reward will receive special recognition in the spring.

Engaging Instruction

The Blue Ribbon Schools make schoolwide efforts to motivate students, but as every good teacher knows, motivated students are the result of excellent and engaging instruction in the classroom.

Christi Wiens is the current principal at Mountain View Elementary School in Fresno, California. She explained to me during my school visit that the cornerstone of the instructional process at their school is the belief of the faculty that "how they teach children is as important as what they teach them." Mountain View is a newly formed suburban K–6 school that continues to experience enrollment increases each year. The student body consists of a growing number of linguistically diverse students encompassing thirteen different languages.

We know that we cannot force students to be motivated, but we can create an environment that enhances motivation. In fact, our Faculty and Staff Handbook summarizes our philosophy well: Children learn best when they: (1) feel someone cares about them; (2) are curious about what they are learning; (3) are actively involved in the learning process; (4) receive appropriate feedback for tasks completed; (5) see a chance for success; (6) are interested and challenged in what they are learning; and (7) feel they are doing something worthwhile.

The Blue Ribbon teachers know how to teach to all students in a challenging, motivating, and rewarding way. A major principle of current motivation theory is that tasks associated with a moderate probability of success (50 percent) provide maximum satisfaction. Moderate probability of success is also an essential ingredient of intrinsic motivation (Clifford, 1990). Intrinsic motivation is motivation due to reinforcers that are inherent in the activity being performed (Gage and Berliner, 1991). Knowing that one can succeed in a learning task, if one applies himself/herself, is essential for a student.

The Argonaut Elementary School in Saratoga, California, serves a diverse, affluent population from the Silicon Valley. The ethnic makeup of the student body of 517 is about half Caucasian and half Asian. Parents have high expectations for their children and for the school. The principal, Sheri Hitchings, explained:

Research has proven that intrinsic motivation is a powerful long-term effective means to success; therefore, our staff strives to create a stimulating learning environment based on mutual respect and trust where students may experiment and take risks. Asking students what they want to learn is one of the highly motivating teaching techniques used by our teachers. Teachers strive to make learning relevant and to develop intrinsic motivation as well as extrinsic rewards.

At the St. Joseph's Montessori School in Columbus, Ohio, a teacher explained that:

The Montessori materials are developed to be challenging and exciting. The hands-on manipulative materials often attract the child to the work and to learning much more than before. These materials have proven to promote learning and make natural extensions in learning. Responsibility for work lies with the student. Much of the learning is on topics children are drawn to; sparking their imagination has caused great active participation in and enthusiasm for attaining knowledge. We are proud of the excitement and interest in our students.

St. Joseph's is a private, PreK–8 grade school with a diverse student population of 236.

Kohn (1993) would agree with the way these Blue Ribbon Schools engage students in learning, as he advocates the promotion of learning conditions that facilitate intrinsic, rather than reward-based, motivation.

> The job of educators is not to make students motivated, but to set up the conditions that make learning possible. The challenge is to offer a stimulating environment that can be perceived by students as presenting valid and valued options that can lead to successful learning and performance. It is necessary to establish the conditions that facilitate motivation, to create the right curriculum, and the right school climate (p. 194).

Many of the Blue Ribbon Schools would agree with Kohn as they emphasize the importance of the teacher's role in tapping the students' intrinsic motivation by engaging them with meaningful instructional tasks. Kohn (1993) summarizes intrinsic motivation as the desire to engage in an activity for its own sake—that is, just because of the satisfaction it provides.

The teachers at Bellerive School in Creve Coeur, Missouri, are firm believers that true learning comes from a desire within the student to learn. The subject matter need not necessarily always be fun, but it must be meaningful. Teachers know that they must convey expectations of students sensitively and realistically, because each student will learn differently; therefore their curriculum is structured to bring out the best in students. The school's application explains:

> [S]cience and social studies units culminate with celebrations in each grade level's yearly or monthly themes. One first-grade monthly theme is "Bernstein Bears At Bellerive" and they have a Bear Day. Second grade has "From Squiggly Sprouts to Towering Timbers". . . . Fifth grade uses a different piece of literature each year for their theme. This year it is "Follow the Yellow Brick Road" based on *The Wizard of Oz.*
>
> Bellerive teachers have a positive attitude toward students and they believe that all students can learn. They encourage students in their academic work and provide appropriate incentives and rewards. Sometimes rewards are in the form of assemblies, bound books of students' work, a bulletin board of photographs, or pizza parties. These and other strategies assist our students to become independent and prepare them for a lifetime of self-education.

This system of awards and ceremonies can only be considered character forming if the students continue to manifest these behaviors even when there are no more rewards to be earned. "Children who come to believe that their prosocial behavior reflects values or dispositions in themselves have internal structure that can generate behavior across settings and without external pressures" (Kohn, 1993).

OUTDOOR EDUCATION

Outdoor Education is a program that St. Clement's Episcopal Parish School, in El Paso, Texas, uses to allow students to step outside the classroom to explore the world around them. The Outdoor Education program is concentrated in a number of trips to the outdoors for grades 2–9. Each outdoor trip has as its goal to motivate the students to learn about themselves, others, the world, and their place in it. By teaching children how to live in the outdoors, children by necessity learn the important lessons of responsibility, cooperation, tolerance, and leadership. Second through ninth grade students are brought along progressively with each grade bringing new experiences and new challenges. Each trip involves extensive classroom preparation. Students study all aspects of the area they are to visit and discuss the outdoor skills necessary to complete the trip. While on the trip, students are responsible for journaling observations and for completing assignments pertinent to the goals of the trip. Through our program, a child not only gains an appreciation for the world around him/her but learns and practices essential life skills.

St. Clement's Episcopal Parish School is a very diverse PreK–9 school in a large, urban area with a student body of 60 percent white and 38 percent Hispanic students.

Mottoes, Pledges and School Songs

Schools have found, as have successful organizations, that mottoes, slogans, and symbols strengthen school spirit, and unite and motivate school members to strive toward a common goal. There is positive effort on the part of the teachers and administrators in these outstanding schools to create an image, a common goal around which the whole school unites. I found the most comprehensive school theme to be at the Terrell W. Ogg Elementary School in Clute, Texas. Ogg is a PreK–5 building with a very diverse student body of 600 students; over half are low-income families, with 58 percent Hispanic and 10 percent African American students. The Campus Theme is "The Land of Ogg." Each year the principal watches the movie classic with grades 1 through 5 and then explains the importance of brains, heart, and courage. Teachers believe in their students' "brains," and critical thinking skills are taught across the curriculum. "Heart" is necessary for our students to succeed despite the obstacles of poverty and speaking another language in an English environment. "Courage" is needed for students to resist the pressures of a society where substance abuse is an increasing danger. Instead of a cafeteria, Ogg provides a restaurant called the Munchkin Munch-In. Students are taught to exhibit good manners and positive behavior in both the cafeteria and in public places. Students make and maintain centerpieces and post the menu on a chalkboard near the cafeteria.

Other Blue Ribbon principals explain their school goals: "We create climate: we do not just maintain it." "Good climate is promoted, not taken for granted."

Several schools specifically mentioned in their application that the positive climate at their school is one of the reasons they should be nominated as an outstanding school.

The Jefferson Center for Character Education STAR (Success Through Accepting Responsibility) program, explained in chapter 3, is also a schoolwide systematic program for improving school climate and is used in the Parkway School in a suburb of New Jersey. Parkway has a diverse student body of 350, 12 percent of whom are Asian. STAR teaches these children personal and social responsibilities through the use of the monthly themes that become the school motto for the period.

From New York to California, schools use mottoes, just as they use awards— to express their values and unite the whole school around certain character traits that all strive to obtain:

- Be All You Can Be
- BE PLAN—Be Fun, Be Neat, Be Kind, Be Polite, Be Prompt, Be Careful, Be Honest, Be Alert
- Everyone Helps One
- OLYMPIC CREED—Always strive to do one's best
- Onward to Excellence
- PROJECT PRIDE—Personal responsibility in developing excellence
- RESPECT—Responsibility encourages student performance, enthusiasm and creative teaching
- Rising to the needs of others
- Say Yes to Friends
- Sharing is Caring
- What I'm going to be is up to me.
- You can if you think you can.
- You must give your best.

These nationally recognized schools recognize and reward student achievement through schoolwide systems of awards and school-wide activities that promote school spirit.

Pledges are one way that schools also promote character education by presenting a goal towards which students strive. At the Samuel Gompers Elementary School in Detroit, Michigan, a PreK–5 very diverse school of 357 students, 93 percent of whom are African American and from poverty level backgrounds, students begin each day with the following pledge:

Today I pledge to be the best possible me. I believe that I can accomplish anything I want to achieve. I come to school prepared to learn. I am responsible for my learning. I will listen to my teachers, follow directions and work hard. I will succeed. I am responsible for my behavior. I will have a positive attitude. I will respect myself and others, I will be cooperative, I will be a good friend. Today I pledge to believe in me.

An important part of the character education curriculum at the West View Elementary School in Spartanburg, South Carolina, is the Paws to be Polite program that focuses on table manners, answering the telephone, introductions, and other aspects of etiquette. Students listen to daily tips on the morning announcements and weekly television program. Each unit culminates with a special event such as a table manners unit ending with a special meal in the cafeteria. Students set the table properly with tablecloths and silverware, and practice serving their plates from bowls on the table. Character education begins anew everyday at West View with the following affirmation led by the principal emphasizing how we think, what we do, and who we are:

> Be PAWSitive with your thoughts
> For your thoughts become your words
> Be PAWSitive with your words
> For your words become your actions
> Be PAWSitive with your actions
> For your actions become your habits
> Be PAWSitive with your habits
> For your habits become character
> Be PAWSitive with your character
> For your character becomes your destiny

School Songs

Many of the Blue Ribbon Schools have written their own school song that includes the character traits for which their school stands. These songs are sung at every assembly and many schools start the day with the Pledge of Allegiance to the Flag followed by the school song. The McCoy School in Carrolton, Texas, is one of the five Blue Ribbon Schools to also receive the character education specialization award. They shared their school song with me during my visit. It was written by Kathy Struck, their fifth grade teacher to the tune of "Home, Home on the Range:"

Oh give me a school, where integrity is cool, where respect is the name of the game. Where seldom is heard, a discouraging word, and we're responsible every day.

School School at McCoy, where cowboys ride with pride.
We are fair and true, We make good choices too,
and our cowboy smiles are wild.
Hee haw

Mottoes, awards, ceremonies, pledges, and school songs help students to feel a sense of control over their own lives by giving them the guiding concepts that will help them to make judgments about what constitutes good moral behavior. The above-cited methods show how these Blue Ribbon Schools were able to motivate their students to achieve by: (1) emphasizing a schoolwide atmosphere of high ideals and values, (2) rewarding students who succeeded in developing the specified character qualities outlined by the school awards, ceremonies, and mottoes, and (3) recognizing the value of engaging instruction, which taps a student's intrinsic motivation.

Positive Reinforcement

Paul Chance (1992) disagrees with the assertion that intrinsic motivation is the only valid reward. Chance cites research showing that, although intrinsic rewards are important for maximally efficient learning, students need to have three forms of positive reinforcement: encouragement (praising, complementing, and applauding students), extrinsic rewards (special privileges, certificates, and prizes) and intrinsic rewards (pleasure in learning, satisfaction from a job well done). Many of the Blue Ribbon Schools would agree with this position as they indicate that "catching students doing something right" as well as awarding good behavior and citizenship are key elements of their schoolwide effort to promote character development in students.

Positive reinforcement is the key at the Dr. Joey Pirrung Elementary School in Mesquite, Texas. Kindergarten teachers give daily stickers or stamps as reinforcement of correct behavior. First grade teachers tie the incentives to their thematic instruction. Many of the second and third grade teachers have a class store with children earning money to be spent in the store. Some teachers offer individual and whole class rewards. Most of the teachers give weekly citizenship grades, and all teachers are generous with positive notes. The ultimate goal is for all students to practice self-discipline. Pirrung is a very diverse K–6 school in a suburb of Dallas with a student body that is 10 percent Hispanic and 12 percent African American; it has had a dramatic increase in enrollment over the past five years.

GUIDANCE PROGRAMS

Guidance Programs That Develop Character

The many different guidance programs mentioned by the Blue Ribbon Schools as ways in which they promote character are found in table 9. Guidance programs can be considered traditional "character development" when they follow a curriculum or program aimed at developing moral values or virtues. Judgment can best be made about the philosophy of a guidance program by looking at the curriculum to see if its components focus on content or process.

MegaSkills is perhaps a good example of a "character development" guidance program. It is a community-building program used by the Perley School in South Bend, Indiana. There are ten "MegaSkills" that the program seeks to develop: confidence, motivation, effort, responsibility, initiative, perseverance, caring, teamwork, common sense, and problem-solving. MegaSkills is a classroom curriculum and a school-wide program with parental involvement and training. It seeks to help students to develop strong study skills and good work habits; stimulate their creative thinking; involve families in educational activities at home; and build student self-discipline in coping with pressures, making individual choices, and developing a strong value system. Memphis State University researchers evaluating MegaSkills as implemented in the Tennessee schools found that those who participated in the program doubled the time they spent on homework and decreased the time spent watching television. In addition, parents spent two to two and a quarter hours more per week with their children. [These research results are reported in the MegaSkills information package and by Dorothy Rich (1991) in an *Educational Leadership* article entitled "Parents Can Teach MegaSkills to Their Children."] For more information on this curriculum, contact The Home and School Institute, MegaSkills Education Center, 1500 Massachusetts Ave., NW, Washington, DC 20005, Telephone (202) 466-3633.

Table 9. Guidance Programs and Self-Esteem Program Found in the Blue Ribbon Schools

Category	Count	Precent
Advisor System	6	2%
Character Education Guidance Lessons'	10	3%
Children Are People	6	2%
CLASS	14	4%
DUSO	11	3%
Kids on the Block	15	5%
Leadership Programs	5	2%
Magic Circles	9	3%
Positive Action	15	5%
PRIDE	25	8%
Project Self-esteem/Project Essential	11	4%
Rainbows for All	7	2%
Random Acts of Kindness	13	4%
School Program	43	13%
Self-Respect & Responsibility	29	9%
Super Me, Up With Kids	4	1%
Tribes	6	2%
Workshop Way	5	2%

Valid Cases 334, Missing Cases 151

Children Are People Program

The Children Are People (CAPs) program was found in several of the Blue Ribbon Schools. It is a basic part of the primary social studies and K–5 health curriculum at Independence Primary, Forest Elementary, and St. Thomas More School in Ohio. These three schools each represent a different socioeconomic mix of students, but the CAP program is successful at each. Independence is a K–4 school of 315 students from white- and blue-collar middle-class families located in Independence, Ohio, a suburb fifteen minutes from Cleveland. Forest is a K–6 school of 359 middle-class white students in North Olmstead, Ohio; and St. Thomas More is a Catholic, K–8 school in Cleveland with a diverse student population from lower-income families that include single-parent homes and racially mixed children.

The objectives of the CAP program are to foster self-awareness, positive self-concept, decision making, values, ethics and self-discipline, and prepare students for responsible independence in the future. Students learn how to develop friendships that are rewarding and encourage individual growth. Character, good behavior, and sound judgment are developed by teaching strategies that help children cope with rejection, frustration, disappointment, and failure. The CAP program deals with students' emotions and helps to incorporate the discussion of emotions into the classroom in a comfortable way.

Robert Sylwester (1994) reports that emotions are an area that even today we do not understand fully. Yet we realize they are very important for the overall health of our students and in order to have a stimulating and emotionally positive classroom. The CAP program seeks to teach these emotional competencies to children. These competencies include self-control, zeal, and persistence, and the ability to motivate oneself. As Goleman (1995) explains: "Whether there is a class explicitly devoted to emotional literacy may matter far less than how these lessons are taught. There is perhaps no subject where the quality of the teacher matters so much since how a teacher handles her class is in itself a model—a de facto lesson in emotional competency—or lack thereof" (p. 279).

Dilemma Discussions

Guidance program curricula are usually based on versions of Kohlberg's cognitive-developmental theory of character development (Power, Higgins, Kohlberg, 1989). Kohlberg maintained that moral reasoning is the most important factor in understanding and predicting moral behavior. His psychological theory and his educational interventions studied the relation between moral reasoning and moral behavior. Character development programs subscribing to Kohlberg's theory present students with moral dilemmas for discussion. The purpose is not to solve the dilemmas, because they usually can have two or three defensible solutions, but to aid students in developing more complex reasoning patterns. Critics maintain that Kohlberg's theory is more concerned with *how* we think about moral issues, that is, the structure of thinking—rather than *what* we think or what we do (Ryan, 1981).

One example of this type of program found in the Manoa Elementary School, a PreK–6 grade school in Honolulu, Hawaii, is the Foundation Program on Career Education and Guidance. It provides opportunities for students to examine their behavior, values, and judgments through class discussions, role playing, and other activities. The goal of the program is to develop a positive self-concept and an enthusiasm for learning along with a sense of responsibility to self and others. The program helps students practice cooperation skills and develop responsibility by problem-solving situations that they encounter as safety patrols, and as library, cafeteria, and office monitors.

Another dilemma discussion program is the Developmental Guidance Program, found in several Blue Ribbon Schools including the Los Encinos School in Corpus Christi, Texas. Los Escinos is a large, very diverse K–6 urban school with 86 percent Hispanic students, and 60 percent students from lower-income families. The goal of the Developmental Guidance Program is to help students become purposeful, responsible, and honest. The counselor provides organized thematic units in all of the classrooms in forty-minute sessions every other week. The units include such topics as self-awareness, respect, decision making, interpersonal relationships, responsibility, and drug education. These topics are all approached through moral dilemmas relevant to students' ages and interests. The counselor helps students recognize the importance of their own worth and take personal responsibility for their choices and their behavior. Emphasis is placed on making decisions, being an individual, and respecting the feelings of others. The school considers this developmental guidance to be an essential component of its character development program.

A Three-Pronged Approach

Joseph M. Roma, the principal at the Parkway School in New Jersey, explains that the school uses a three-pronged approach to teach values that involves character qualities, discussions of moral dilemmas found in good literature, and role models:

1. Standards of excellence, honesty, and cooperation are set for the social and moral behavior of students and communicated on a daily basis within the framework of the classroom environment.

2. Teachers, through the study of literature and moral dilemma discussions, heighten the students' awareness of moral issues and possible solutions to problems. As problems are discussed, children realize that people change their views when they gain a new perspective on a situation and may change the basis for their own moral judgments.

3. Students are exposed to the lives of outstanding personalities to foster emulation of strong character traits. Classroom situations are created for learning character traits through dramatic productions, role playing, and creative writing.

Positive Action

Another guidance program that promotes character is the Positive Action program. Positive Action is found in 5 percent of the Blue Ribbon Schools to "teach students a love of learning, how to feel good about themselves and how to become productive citizens" (Alred, 1994). The curriculum includes a scope or sequence chart that outlines for the teachers the character traits taught and reinforced in each successive year. Some of the traits listed on this chart include: cheerfulness, citizenship, cooperation, courage, diligence, generosity, honesty, kindness, patience, punctuality, respect, responsibility, temperance, and tolerance.

The parents of students at Cherokee Elementary School in Arizona initiated the Positive Action program so that each child would develop a positive self-image. The parents teach the curriculum as a total self-improvement plan that encompasses physical, mental, and emotional growth with a holistic program for self-improvement based on family values. Cherokee is a K–5 school of over 1,000 students, so it is important for each student to feel that he or she is personally important and not just a number in the school.

Linda Kamiyama, principal at the Waiahole Elementary School in Hawaii, explains that Positive Action encompasses guidance, character development, and drug education. "We combine this program with our self-esteem building and character development activities so that students have numerous opportunities to develop into responsible, resourceful, and self-assured individuals." Waiahole is a "bona fide community school" of 175 students, 88 percent of whom are Asian and 70 percent of whom are from lower-income families.

Positive Action develops pro-social skills using a "structured learning" approach similar to the teaching of academic competencies. Components include modeling, role-playing, performance feedback reinforcement, and transfer and maintenance strategies. At Oklahoma's Monte Cassino School, which uses Positive Action, individual achievement is recognized with ICU ("I see you") notes written by students and teachers. ICU notes give positive acknowledgement to students when they exhibit pro-social behaviors such as sharing and caring for others.

The Britt David Magnet Academy in Columbus, Georgia, a K–6 school with a very diverse student body, 43 percent African American and 7 percent Hispanic, explains how it uses the Positive Action program in its classes. Positive Action is a daily curriculum that teaches positive self-concepts using real-life situations. This curriculum is designed to enable students to choose positive actions over negative ones. Some of these positive actions include respect, responsibility, self-honesty, self-improvement, and a healthy drug-free lifestyle.

The lessons are another way of connecting the family and school since many require parental involvement. The Positive Action program provides classroom lessons that are integrated with all school activities to build a positive environment campus-wide. At Britt David, the Positive Action "Word of the Week" is announced each day right after the Pledge of Allegiance and the playing of a patriotic song. The morning announcements provide an opportunity to recognize students and to remind students of the positive word of the week. These are words that promote positive self-images and attitudes that are discussed in individual classrooms during the "Positive Action" lesson.

The Mary E. Roberts School, a K–4 school of 350 homogeneous students from the suburb of Moorestown, New Jersey, conducted a schoolwide evaluation following the implementation of Positive Action. The results showed the program was effective. Ralph Scazafabo, the principal was pleased with the program results: "This project has demonstrated how a program designed to change students' attitudes toward adults, peers, and self can have a dramatic effect on total school-wide climate." For more information contact: the Positive Action Company, 264 Fourth Avenue South, Twin Falls, ID 83301, Telephone (800) 345-2974, www.positiveaction.net/model.html

Project Essential

Project Essential is a character education curriculum that seeks to ensure healthy development by teaching children character traits such as self-control and respect for others. This unique education program is designed to enable children and youth to develop and maintain an inner sense of personal capability and self-worth as they grow to become the best they can be. Central Elementary School in Olathe, Kansas, uses this curriculum and describes its four basic principles: (1) improving self-control of emotions; (2) taking responsibility for yourself; (3) understanding the consequences of mistakes and correcting them; and (4) realizing that each person has rights. Central is a very diverse K–6 building of 235 students; 66 percent white and 47 percent from lower socio-economic backgrounds. They find the interactive, hands-on program that includes activities in all learning modalities, such as songs, stories, puppets, games, journal reflection, skill practice, teamwork, group discussion, and other age-appropriate activities excellent for their student body.

A longitudinal evaluation of 353 fifth graders in public and private elementary schools in the Kansas City area who had been in the program since first grade found that Project Essential children showed: (1) significant differences in knowledge regarding concepts such as responsibility, empathy, rights of others, emotions, and goal-setting; (2) were better able to admit errors, accept consequences, and learn from them; and (3) took responsibility for their own actions, and learned to fulfill their own responsibilities (Teel Institute, 1998). Chapel Lakes Elementary School in Lees Summit, Missouri, a homogeneous K–5 school of 466 students, 94 percent white, also finds Project Essential important for its students. "As we prepare our students for the future, we look to Project Essential to help us send citizens into the world who will understand the difference between reason and emotion in decision-making, accept and fulfill responsibility, and respect the rights of themselves and others."

Responsive Classroom

Positive interactions and respect among students and adults are fostered at Kilgour Elementary School in Cincinnati, Ohio, by an approach called The Responsive Classroom. Kilgour has implemented this program since its first nomination as a Blue Ribbon School in 1991–1992. The Responsive Classroom is a social curriculum based on the premise that social and academic skills are interrelated. The Responsive Classroom philosophy builds students' social skills and a sense of school community. The program provides students an opportunity to learn, practice, and reinforce positive social interaction based on core values such as accountability, responsibility, honesty, and fairness. Positive social interaction is discussed and modeled by the teachers and students on a daily basis. Students learn these values through the social skills of cooperation, assertiveness, responsibility, empathy and self-control, that will prepare them for adult life and the world of work.

The Northeast Foundation for Children provides training in the Responsive Classroom approach and also disseminates a newsletter. There are six components of responsive teaching (classroom organization, morning meeting, rules and logical consequences, academic choice, guided discovery, and assessment and reporting) set within the context of the commonly shared values of honesty, fairness, and respect that are implemented through the school day. Teachers are also taught to model and use respectful language that nurtures social skill development by reinforcing and validating children so that they are empowered to achieve their full capability. Kilgour is a very diverse K–6 school of 460 students, 53 percent white, 45 percent black and 38 percent from low socio-economic background. In order to create the Responsive Classroom, Kilgour teachers take a firm stand against excluding others, making it clear that it is not allowed. Teachers sometimes have to intervene with reminders or loss of privileges. The goal is to have more peaceful, inclusive classrooms where all students feel safe and important. For more information contact the Northeast Foundation for Children, 71 Montague City Road, Greenfield, MA 01301, Telephone (800)-360-6332.

TEAM BUILDING

Team building is one of Roguewood Elementary School's goals. Teachers use team building as a strategy to help students learn to work together, by teaching them how to include and accept others and by promoting a positive, caring environment wherein all students feel intellectually and emotionally safe. The main focus of team building is collaborating cooperatively, taking risks, solving problems, and accepting responsibility. The common goal is the achievement of skills and knowledge that have applications in the real world. Roguewood is a homogeneous PreK–5 school in the small town of Rockford, Michigan.

GUIDANCE PROGRAMS
SUPPORTING FAMILY ISSUES

Other guidance programs help children to deal with difficult family situations. I'm In Charge is a latch-key training program found in several Blue Ribbon Schools. The program is designed to give students the important skills they will need for times when they may be left on their own. Tribes is a program developed by Jeanne Gibbs for students who are at risk. It is used at the Fairfield North Elementary School in Hamilton, Ohio, in order to build positive character traits and behaviors through a "hearts and minds" approach. "Fairfield is a very large school of Caucasian students. Nevertheless, the student population is diverse as 14% come from lower-income families and 25 percent qualify for special education services. Classroom teachers have been trained to use a variety of inclusive activities to create a strong supportive, caring classroom community. Students are broken into "tribes" or groups that work together like the American Indian tribes functioned. The "tribe" is a group of five to seven students who meet together regularly during the school year to discuss personal concerns and feelings, plan, and solve one another's personal problems together, and at times work on appropriate classroom projects together. The teacher serves as the facilitator, as the students in these supportive peer groups work to improve their self-image and academic achievement. Tribes has evolved with the incorporation of current research and best practices that support character development throughout the school. The Tribes manual contains complete "lesson plans for meetings" in which social development classes and cooperative learning experiences provide a rich background for children who lack a cohesive family unit in their homes. The "tribe" at school becomes their own cohesive peer unit. The program can be reviewed on the Internet site: www.tribes.com.

Rainbows for All God's Children is found in several of the Blue Ribbon Schools. This program, used by its full name in most schools, but referred to just as "Rainbows" in some public schools, is a peer group for those who have experienced loss in their lives. The curriculum includes discussions about anxieties, fears, feelings, frustrations, and beliefs that children often experience as a result of death, divorce, and family separation. This program is explained well in the St. Damian School Handbook:

> We are aware that a child does not come to school and leave his/her feelings outside the school door. When children experience the loss of a parent through death or divorce, they experience many feelings that are new to them.

The Rainbows for all God's Children Program is designed to implant in these children a belief in their own goodness and the value of their own families. Rainbows is a support group program for children living in a single-parent family or a blended family. Small groups are arranged by age and meet with a trained faculty facilitator.

Currently at St. Damian, a large Catholic K–8 school located in suburban Oak Forest south of Chicago, there are six teacher-facilitators who work with groups of five or more children. Students meet with a facilitator once a week for twelve weeks when a parent dies or a divorce takes place in a family. The facilitator helps the students work through their grief, build a strong sense of self-esteem, and begin to accept what has taken place in their family. A culminating celebration is held at the end of the twelve weeks for these students and their parents. The celebration helps them to understand that a change in life can be an occasion for a new beginning. Students in the program feel comfortable in seeking out their facilitator whenever they have a problem or just need to talk.

Understanding Students with Special Needs

Kids On The Block is used in 5 percent of the Blue Ribbons Schools with their primary-grade students. Developed by Barbara Aiello in Washington, D.C., Kids On The Block is a national program that uses commercially produced, life-sized puppets who represent children who are non-handicapped, mentally handicapped, deaf, blind, and learning disabled. The program addresses a variety of interpersonal and intrapersonal issues using a one-hour-long puppet performance. The presentation helps develop awareness of the challenges faced by students with special needs.

The Locke Hill School uses the Kids on The Block program to foster acceptance of handicapped children and teach students to recognize and accept student differences and special needs. Locke Hill uses high school peer leaders, teachers, and Junior League volunteers who are trained to use the puppets with the children in grades K–2. The puppeteers are well informed about each handicapping condition as a result of the workshops given by professionals in each disability area, which they have attended in order to become puppeteers. They are able to respond to childrens' questions, usually using the puppets throughout the presentation. In addition, parents of disabled students are encouraged to speak to the class of their child's peers so that students receive accurate information about their fellow classmate's condition, having an opportunity to ask questions and add to their understanding of the student's personal victories and challenges. Locke Hill is a diverse and large K–5 school in San Antonio, Texas, with 817 students, one-fifth of whom are Hispanic, one tenth have special learning needs, and one tenth are at poverty level. Research into the program has shown that it is effective in increasing young children's knowledge and understanding of handicapped persons (Snart and Maguire, 1987).

To better prepare conscientious citizens, disability awareness is stressed at the Forest Park Elementary School in Albany, New York. Teachers work with students through the Circle of Friends program to increase their sensitivity for others who have handicapping conditions. Specifically, children who do not have a handicap use a wheelchair, wear a blindfold and wear cotton balls in their ears. The benefits are twofold: children who do not have disabilities become more accepting of those that do, and they become less fearful of the adaptive equipment used by children with handicapping conditions. Blue Ribbon Schools have found that inclusion of children with special needs into regular classrooms gives students the opportunity to practice the character qualities of kindness, compassion, and patience.

SELF-ESTEEM PROGRAMS

Almost 15 percent of the Blue Ribbon Schools equate character development with their self-esteem programs (see table 2). In such programs, it is important that the student be given the correct things to esteem: values such as responsibility, industriousness, honesty, and kindness—not values such as good looks, popularity, or possessions. Students will feel good about themselves because they know they have done well (worked hard) and have tried to do the right thing. Research has not shown the reverse to be true, that is, that students will do well in school because they feel good about themselves (Kohn, 1994).

Self-Esteem as Reverence/Respect for Oneself

High self-esteem by itself does not assure good character. However, unless students respect and appreciate their own worth and dignity, they have little to offer to others (Van Ness, 1995). Typically, self-esteem is defined as the personal judgment of worthiness expressed in the attitudes the individual holds towards himself or herself (Kohn, 1994). Self-esteem comes from a Greek word meaning "reverence for self." At a philosophical level, self-esteem is a central feature in human dignity and thus an inalienable human entitlement (Beane, 1991). Nationwide, teachers tell us that the number one problem in the schools today is a lack of respect: a lack of respect of children towards themselves, other students, their teachers, and their parents. Self-esteem allows them to value and respect themselves and thereby to value and respect others. Attributing intrinsic value to children because of their unique qualities and gifts is self-esteem education that is appropriate both in and outside the curriculum (Baniewicz, 1995).

Affective Education

Self-esteem programs are one kind of affective education, that is, concerned with the formation, content, and role of emotions, feelings, values, attitudes, predispositions, and morals (Beane, 1985). Most educators would agree with Bloom (1977) and others that education involves an artful blend of instruction in the cognitive, affective, and psychomotor domains. Many of the programs cited in this book dealing with the areas of character education, citizenship, substance abuse, and peace education include aspects of affective education—educating moral feeling or the "heart side" of character. Controversy arises when affective education is emphasized as more important than the cognitive, and when the content of the affective curriculum is based on a subjective, self-discovery philosophy (held by humanists) rather than on an objective, truth-discovery philosophy (held by "realists"). Controversy also arises when people have different understandings of what self-esteem is. Too many people see self-esteem as "permission to do what I want to do as long as it makes me feel good." By contrast, ethical self-esteem—the kind that is properly part of good character—is permission to do what I want as long as it results in good moral behavior.

Self-Esteem Based on Truth Discovery

The realists propose that self-esteem comes through focusing on truth-discovery. Their theory is that changes in achievement cause changes in self-concept, that is, self-esteem develops as a by-product of other reality-based factors. The pedagogical focus, then, centers on activities of problem-solving, seeking relevant meaning from facts, skills development, and discovering academic and moral truths. Truth, here, means conformity to fact, fidelity to the standard (Paul, 1990). Real self-esteem develops when a student works hard, learns something worthwhile, and learns how to accomplish challenging tasks. Edward Wynne states that students will then develop the virtue of "diligence" (Wynne and Ryan, 1993). If they are graded strictly but justly rewarded and praised when they have earned it, they will come to develop a sense of self-respect. Educators who want to help children "feel good about themselves" will do better by treating them with respect, not merely showering them with praise. Research has demonstrated the validity of the realist model for developing self-esteem, showing a correlation between students' academic success or failure and the resultant high or low self-esteem (Calsyn and Kenny, 1977). The Blue Ribbon Schools in this study promoted "achievement self-esteem" by implementing the latest pedagogical methodologies in order to ensure academic success for all students and thereby promote their feelings of self worth and accomplishment. (These teaching techniques are described in chapter 4.)

Humanist Affective Education

The humanists (Carl Rogers, Abraham Maslow, Arthur Combs) set up a system of affective education based on the human experience philosophy of John Dewey. Dewey proposed that values develop through the cyclical interaction of the individual with his or her environment. Values are open to question and change. This "developmental" approach to affective education proposes that the school's role is to help the child formulate values or beliefs through experiences (Beane, 1985). The content of the humanist's curriculum is based on the premise that self-esteem comes through focusing on self-discovery. The theory is that changes in self-esteem cause changes in achievement. The pedagogical focus in these programs centers on activities seeking self-discovery. The teacher becomes the facilitator of student self-discovery. Contemporary self-esteem programs are criticized because of their lack of consistency, absence of clear direction and purpose, and lack of thoroughness in program planning (Beane, 1985; Leo, 1990).

There are no data to show that these self-esteem programs can make a difference in raising students' self-esteem or basic view of themselves (Kohn, 1994). No researchers have been able to show that high self-esteem inclines people toward pro-social behavior or steers them away from anti-social behavior. Some studies have shown a positive correlation between self-esteem and school participation, school completion, self-direction, and various types of achievement and chances for success in life (Beane, 1991; Canfield, 1990), but such correlations could mean that self-esteem was the result of these outcomes rather than their causes.

One can even challenge the desirability of focusing on self-esteem in the classroom, because this kind of affective education program may lead to a preoccupation with self instead of with community. As stated by Kohn (1994), "Affective education should be embraced but in the context of building community rather than attending to each individual separately. . . . Whether our objective is to help children become good learners (that is creative, self-directed, lifelong learners) or good people (that is secure, responsible, caring)—or both, we can and need to do better than merely concentrating our efforts on self-esteem" (174).

There are several commercial self-esteem programs that are currently in use in many of the Blue Ribbon Schools. Most of them are used as one component of their school-wide program for fostering the character development of their students. Some of these programs, however, should not be used if a school is really serious about character development, because they give students mixed messages, that is, telling students that the most important criteria to use in judging actions is whether or not the actions make them feel good about themselves. Therefore, after each program mentioned in the next section, the author will give criteria for judging the program's effectiveness in fostering character in students.

DUSO

The DUSO (Developing Understanding of Self and Other) guidance materials were mentioned in 3 percent of the Blue Ribbon School applications. The DUSO curriculum is designed to help primary students build self-esteem, social awareness, respect for others, and decision-making skills. DUSO 1 is targeted for children in kindergarten and first grade; DUSO 2 for children in the third and fourth grades. The curricular materials feature an awareness kit that includes puppets (DUSO the Dolphin), a teacher's guidebook, story books, cassette, and lesson cards. Using the method of open-ended short stories, students discuss appropriate endings with the teacher. Topics of these short stories include a child who wants to be first in line, a child who has an opportunity to share, and making friends. The process, or story completion, focuses on helping children to understand behavior, listen reflectively, express their feelings, and deal with conflict. The guidance counselors interviewed in the Blue Ribbon Schools were very positive about the DUSO curriculum. One stated that she thought it was the "most well-known program being used by guidance counselors in elementary schools across the nation." Many of the activities in both DUSO 1 and DUSO 2 contain stories, songs, writing, and art projects that are valuable assets to the classroom (National Association of Christian Educators/Citizens for Excellence in Education, 1996a).

However, DUSO also has a unit which uses imagery lessons in which children are told by their teachers to relax, close their eyes, and then imagine that they are traveling to strange planets and meeting friendly creatures. For this reason, some parents have complained about the DUSO curriculum, stating that its guided fantasy activities asking students to "visualize" are mind-altering psychological techniques that are like hypnotism. For example, a parent in San Diego, California, objected to DUSO because it "encourages a child to explore his inner self, to relax by meditation, and to acquire fantasy companions to help guide him through life's stresses." The main criticism of the program is directed at its philosophic basis. DUSO was written by Don Dinkmeyer, Ph.D. in 1971 and uses values clarification techniques. There are no absolute values in DUSO, no definitive right and wrong.

Most of the research conducted on the DUSO program is over twenty years old and consists of doctoral dissertation studies. The findings are mixed; several studies found no significant difference in self-concept in DUSO students and those who were in a classroom without DUSO (Galina, 1973; Quain, 1977); other studies found a positive effect (Eldrige, et al., 1973). In 1982, the DUSO curriculum was revised (with less values clarification activities) and subsequent studies (Stacey and Rost, 1985) showed that the revised program can be more effective on raising self-concept, academic skills, and other variables than the original DUSO "if given a chance to work." For more information on DUSO and these research studies, contact the American Guidance Service (AGS) at 4201 Woodlawn Road, Box 99, Circle Pine, MN 55014, Telephone (800) 328-2560.

Magic Circles

The Stewart Elementary School in the Princeton School District in Cincinnati, Ohio, uses Magic Circle discussions to foster democratic values and ethical judgements in students. The Magic Circles program was found in 3 percent of the Blue Ribbon Schools. It is an affective education curriculum and methodology for improving self-concept, teaching self-discipline, and values. It seeks to promote self-esteem through the self-discovery model. It was developed by Bessell, Ball, and Palomares (1972) as a means for promoting social adjustment and mental health by providing students with the opportunity to practice humanistic social skills such as empathy, congruence, and positive regard (Braun, 1989). The curriculum and accompanying small-group discussion are designed to promote practice in displaying empathy for others (perspective taking), understanding of self, accepting responsibility, and dealing with conflict, and are to result in increased self-esteem.

Magic Circles has come under fire by Phyllis Schlaflly as sensitivity training that pressures students to express their feelings and seeks to solicit intimate familial information and undermined religious values (Schlaflly, 1984). The curriculum authors reply that, when properly led, the process is a safe and rewarding experience; but some teachers have tried the process without adequate training. It is not meant to be sensitivity training and the teacher is not meant to be a therapist. When sensitive issues are brought up, the teacher needs to bring this information to the appropriate professional on the school staff (counselor, nurse, social worker) and allow them to follow through with action.

The Ivymount School in Rockville, Maryland, uses the Magic Circles discussion methodology but focuses on more concrete content such as discussing responsibility, respect for others, appropriate behavior, and other issues that contribute to students' ability to function in a society where those qualities are valued. Ivymount, which serves the entire Washington, D.C., metropolitan area, is a private school for children who have disabilities that require special education services not found in the public schools. One class developed a "Civil Rights" document for students, staff, and parents. Ivymount seeks to maximize every child's potential and prepare students for a less restrictive setting and eventually toward living as independently as possible.

The "circle discussions" used at Ivymount are more similar to the "circle meetings" Glasser (1990) proposes in *Quality Schools* than to the Magic Circle meetings, because they focus on discussing issues from the perspective of the character qualities valued by the group. Glasser recommends that classrooms be permanently set up in a circle configuration, instead of the standard rectangular rows with the teacher's desk at the head. In this way, at a moment's notice, students and teacher can begin to discuss any problems that need to be solved. The main purpose of Glasser's class meetings is to teach control theory to students, that is, to teach them that they choose to do everything that they do in order to satisfy one of their five basic needs. Control theory helps students to develop their character as it teaches them that the better they are able to control their lives and make good, responsible choices, the happier they will be.

Power of Positive Students

According to the counselor at Huffman School, in Plano, Texas, the school has a "wonderful" program for teaching self-esteem—Power of Positive Students (POPS). This program was developed by Dr. Billy Mitchell to infuse positive attitudes into all aspects of the school. The program seeks to help all students and staff to develop positive self-images: "We have on the morning announcements every morning a POP statement, that is, a positive thing we must do right after we do the pledge. For example, one day the goal might be to try to complement someone in the class for something they do that is good." Every day the staff focuses on the positive, teaching children to think positively and to plan for positive results. Special reinforcement bulletin boards have been designed around the school, and newsletters are periodically sent home to parents, mentioning all of the positive things happening.

Project Self-Esteem

Other schools use Project Self-Esteem, a program that says in their curriculum flyer that it emphasizes sound character, decision-making skills, and developing positive self-concept. Project Self-Esteem is an elementary level program to enhance self-esteem, improve memory and communication skills, stress individuality, increase sensitivity to others, and improve self-responsibility.

The National Association of Christian Educators/Citizens for Excellence in Education (1996b), have found that the curriculum is based upon a form of moral relativism (situation ethics) that uses self-interest as the primary motivator for character development. They give an example from the unit in the curriculum on stealing. The objectives for the unit are stated as the child "will be able to state the reasons why people steal" and "understand that stealing hurts oneself and the victim;" however no explicit judgment is made in the lesson concerning the wrongness of stealing (and teachers are instructed to refrain from making judgments about the rightness or wrongness of the act). Self-interest, not society, is the norm of behavior.

The National Association of Christian Educators/Citizens for Excellence in Education (1996c) explains that there are some good lesson plans and activities in these curricula programs, that is, DUSO and Project Self-Esteem, but the lessons are not directive enough to be effective in promoting character. If teachers have a strong background in character education, they could use these creative curricular ideas to stress the development of decision-making skills in students based on reference to specific character qualities such as responsibility, honesty, and justice. Using the situations mentioned in the curriculum, they can be more directive and ask students, "What would a *responsible* person do in this situation?"

Workshop Way

Workshop Way, a kindergarten through high school program developed by Grace Pilon, is found in several schools including St. Thomas of Canterbury School in New York. St. Thomas is a Catholic K–8 school of 214 white, middle-class students. Sister Helen Boyd, the principal at St. Thomas, explains the Five Step Lesson Program of Workshop Way: (1) Communication with a smile; (2) Power Step—reinforce one skill for a few weeks; (3) technical vocabulary drill (flashcards); (4) new lesson presented each day; and (5) living their knowledge. She explained that the goal of Workshop Way is to help children believe more strongly in themselves as learners and in their ability to learn. Workshop Way is designed to inculcate a love for learning by creating an environment in which each child is accepted, wherever he or she is in the learning process at this particular moment in time. Children learn through Workshop Way that mistakes are a means by which we learn and that taking risks and making decisions are all part of a very intelligent process.

Workshop Way is "a way for a teacher to organize time, content, and materials so human growth is not left to chance. It's a way teachers can give all students the conditions that release their remarkable human potentials." The most important goal in the Workshop Way is to "respect the child's dignity at all costs" (Pilon, 1988).

Critics of Workshop Way cite the fact that it gives priority to nurturing dignity and intelligent living habits and not to academics. It emphasizes changing a child's attitude in order to develop feelings of self-worth but does not associate positive self-concept with knowledge, skills, or right answers. Pilon would direct these critics to look at an evaluation study conducted by Douglas Rose of Tulane University that found that students in Workshop Way classrooms outperformed their peers on SAT scores (Harmon, 1990).

SUMMARY

This chapter shows why it is important for schools to develop the emotional side of students' character. School mottoes, awards, and ceremonies can be effective ways for schools to motivate students to develop and display good character. There are some guidance programs that are effective in promoting character development because they teach character qualities as part of their curriculum. A self-esteem program can promote genuine character development if it teaches that authentic self-esteem is based on the knowledge that one has chosen to do the better thing. However, there are many programs in use in the Blue Ribbon Schools today that do not meet these criteria and therefore cannot be considered to be part of character education. Perhaps this review of these programs will lead schools to evaluate the effectiveness of the programs they are using.

7

How Do Discipline Programs Develop Good Character?

To be what we are, and to become what we are capable of becoming, is the only end of life.

—Robert Louis Stevenson

A good teacher is one who drives the students to think.

—Anonymous

It isn't what the student is today that counts. It's what the student will be tomorrow.

—Anonymous

DISCIPLINE AS MORAL EDUCATION

Discipline is a fundamental element of moral education according to Emile Durkheim (1973). This concurs with what the National Education Association's Committee of fifteen wrote over one hundred years ago "the substantial moral training of the school is performed by discipline rather than by the instruction in ethical theory. The essence of moral behavior is self-control" (cited in Bennett, 1988). The criteria set up by the U.S. Department of Education's National Recognition Program state that "for any school to be judged deserving of recognition . . . the school should have an atmosphere that is orderly, purposeful, and conducive to learning and good character. . . . There must be a strong commitment to educational excellence for all students and a record of progress in sustaining the school's best features and solving its problems" (U.S. Department of Education, 1994).

Seventeen percent of the Blue Ribbon Award-winning Schools (see table 3) defined character development as "having good discipline and good behavior" and 11 percent (see table 2) stated that they used their discipline program to promote character development in their school. This second edition research finds fewer schools using their discipline program as their primary vehicle for character development. However, one could assume that all of the Blue Ribbon Schools maintained effective classroom and schoolwide discipline, even if they did not mention it in their answer to this particular question. Schools with good discipline have students whose behavior shows that they are living the third aspect of good character, moral action. They are choosing to perform the appropriate actions in different school situations.

This chapter summarizes the main ways the Blue Ribbon Schools promote character development through their discipline programs. It tries to answer the following questions:

- What are some important qualities of proactive discipline programs that help to foster the development of good character?
- How can a character development program help a school to create a safe and orderly environment?
- Why is it important that school rules be stated positively if they are to be an important means for promoting character development in students?
- What are the most effective discipline programs found in the Blue Ribbon Schools today?
- What are the "character development" advantages of having class meetings?
- Why is it important to teach children how to resolve conflicts and mediate disagreements peacefully in order for them to develop a good character?

DISCIPLINE PROGRAMS THAT EMPHASIZE CHARACTER TRAITS

Several Blue Ribbon Schools have discipline programs that could be considered character developing because they emphasize specific good character traits. Richard Curwin (1995) believes that discipline programs should not be based on a system of rewards and punishments, but should be based on values. The best way to set up a values-based discipline program is to develop the value principles prior to rules. The principles are general attitudes, such as being respectful, and provide the reason for following the rules. The Brookridge Elementary School in Shawnee Mission, Kansas, a large K–6 suburban school with a homogeneous student body, has "Five Key Behaviors" that it expects students to demonstrate at all times: caring, concern, courtesy, responsibility, and respect. The handbook states that:

We believe that the best decisions for managing student behavior are based on a value system that maintains the dignity of each student in all situations. Behaving responsibly is more valued than behaving obediently. It is our goal to help students develop appropriate behaviors through understanding and acceptance in lieu of excessive extrinsic rewards and punishments. We know that good teaching is holistic and discipline is an integral part of the entire teaching experience. Good discipline is related to fair rules, consistency of application, and most importantly, to outstanding teaching.

Similarly, the Perley Elementary School in South Bend, Indiana, has its "Five Cs—Caring, Courteous, Cooperative, Considerate, Committed to Learning" that define its expectations for character and behavior in its students. Perley is a K–6 school located in the inner-city section of South Bend. The students are from diverse socioeconomic and racial backgrounds. A visit to the school reveals that the five Cs hang at the front hallway and in each classroom. The five C's are reinforced many times throughout the day and thus encourage students to act appropriately and to use them to resolve problems appropriately.

As mentioned in chapter 3, the character traits promoted in the Plano, Texas, school district included courtesy, courage, discipline, honesty, human worth and dignity, justice, patriotism, personal obligation for the public good, respect for self and others, respect for authority, discipline, tolerance, and responsibility. To reinforce these traits, the staff refers to them during any disciplinary actions. Saigling Elementary has the most diverse population of the Plano schools. It has over six hundred students in PreK–5 grades. The student body includes over 10 percent Asian-American students. Arlene Carnes, the counselor, mentioned during my visit to the school, that when a student is disciplined with an in-school suspension, she discusses the incident with the student, reviewing the school's character traits and deciding which ones were negatively demonstrated by the student's actions. Then, to reinforce the meaning of the citizenship traits, the student reads books that demonstrate traits being used positively and writes a one-page essay discussing the traits. Finally, the principal, student, and parents discuss the essay.

SCHOOL RULES THAT PROMOTE CHARACTER

Schools express their focus on character development by the rules they promote. Like other institutions, schools need rules to accomplish their goals. Rules are guides to behavior. They tell the student what is acceptable behavior and what is unacceptable. Rules help children learn the skills and attitudes needed to live in harmony with others (Wynne and Ryan, 1993). When rules are a positive expression of expectations, they are character building. They tell students what kind of behavior is expected of them. Rules written negatively list every possible type of misbehavior imaginable but do not successfully communicate to students the correct behavior.

Several of the Blue Ribbon Schools have integrated school rules into the form of a 'school motto.' For instance, at the Wilkins School in Amherst, the school strives to teach students their ABCs:

> The ABCs of Amherst Students
> Act Responsibly
> Behave Respectfully
> Cooperate and Care

While helping students to reach the school goal of "being a star:"

> Reach for the STARS—
> Speak politely,
> Try hard,
> Act carefully
> Respect each other
> So everyone wins.

The three basic rules at Los Alamitos Elementary School in Los Alamitos, California, speak to all of their large and diverse student body:

> Be Caring
> Take care of yourself
> Take care of others
> Take care of this place

Finally, the Rice Creek Elementary School in Columbia, South Carolina, uses another acrostic:

> TABS
> Take care of your school and environment
> Act in a safe and respectful manner
> Be Responsible for your learning
> Solve problems peacefully.

The rules found at these schools are formed to convey clear standards of character-building expectations.

SCHOOL-WIDE DISCIPLINE PROGRAMS

Red, Yellow, Green is a system used by some of the Blue Ribbon Schools in their cafeterias that communicates to students' appropriate levels of conversation.

There are three cardboard circles that can be displayed. If green is shown, children are allowed to talk normally. If yellow, they may talk in a whisper. If red is shown, there is to be no talking.

The Pride Program (Positive Reinforcement of Individual Discipline and Enthusiasm) was found in several schools. This system helps students develop a sense of responsibility and respect for others by achieving good conduct and work habits that are goals every student can attain. Some school programs emphasize "manners," others emphasize "being a lady" or a "gentleman," but the common element is a group of agreed-upon behavior expectations.

The Boca Raton Christian School in Boca Raton, Florida, has an "Exit Etiquette Course" for its eighth-grade students. The course teaches proper table and telephone manners, making introductions, and proper etiquette in formal settings. After several sessions the entire class goes to a fine restaurant for a culminating activity. The class has the opportunity to put into practice what they have learned and to interact with a head chef. The program received much publicity in the community and was covered on local television and on the front page of the local newspaper. Boca Raton is a PreK–8 grade school located in southeast Florida on the Atlantic coast with a diverse student body, 13 percent Hispanic. Mary E. Griswold School in Kensington, Connecticut, has a Magnificent Manners (M&M) program. Students are randomly rewarded with candy M&M's for demonstrating proper behavior in the cafeteria. Griswold is a K–5 school of 582 in a quaint, family-oriented neighborhood in a suburban community in the rolling hills of Connecticut.

SCHOOL HANDBOOKS AND DAILY PLANNERS THAT PROMOTE CHARACTER

There is a clear trend found in one-fifth of the schools, especially in the applications from recent years, to have a schoolwide discipline code in a handbook. In the handbook, the motto of the school, the expected behaviors of students, and the rules of the school are clearly spelled out. It is important that school handbooks express their expectations positively, telling students what kind of behavior is expected of them instead of listing every possible type of misbehavior with its consequence. Some of the schools issue bookmarkers or folders listing the school rules or have classroom posters that illustrate the rules.

Daily Planners are used at Bryant Ranch School in Yorba Linda, California. Bryant Ranch is a K–6 school with almost one thousand students from diverse ethnic backgrounds. The 16 percent Asian students speak Mandarin, Korean, Vietnamese, Chinese, and Tagalog. The daily planners are very effective because they post the school rules and class schedule on the inside and help to keep the large student body organized and moving quickly. Students record their homework in the planners and parents can sign them. The planners can be used to teach character qualities, as they focus on different character values each week with catchy little sayings and pictures. For example, in the third week of October the focus was on motivation. Some of the sayings include: "Motivating yourself to learn is the key to doing well in school—and in life." "The secret of joy in work is contained in one word, excellence." Daily Planners can be purchased from the Premier School Agenda Company, 6161 28th Street, SE, Suite 11, Grand Rapids, MI 49546, Telephone (800) 447–2034.

TEACHING RESPECT IN SCHOOLS

Lickona (1991) says that respect and responsibility are the "fourth and fifth Rs" that schools not only may but also must teach if they are to develop ethically literate persons who can take their place as responsible citizens of society. In these Blue Ribbon Schools, the rights of self and others and responsibilities to others are both emphasized.

The Primary 4 Rs of Respect found in the Livonia Primary School in New York state are:

1. Respect the school and its property.
2. Respect your teacher.
3. Respect fellow students.
4. Respect yourself.

Livonia is a K–4 rural school with some 800 students, over 10% of whom are from lower-income families.

Similarly, the Pine Grove School has Four Basic School Rules:

1. We respect other people and their property.
2. We try to make each other's day as pleasant as possible.
3. In school we talk, not fight.
4. In school we walk, not run.

Pine Grove is a K–6 school with a homogeneous student body of almost 500 students located in the small town of Rowley, Massachusetts.

Finally, the Blake School has three rules posted in all classrooms and published in the handbook:

1. The Safety Rule—Do not endanger oneself or other.
2. The Respect Rule—Respect ourselves, classmates, teacher, and property.
3. The Welcome Rule—All children must be welcomed into any activity as long as they play according to the rules.

Blake is a private school in Hopkins, Minnesota, which includes both a K–8 building of seven hundred students and a high school of almost four hundred students. School wide rules as formulated previously convey clear standards of respect and responsibility to all members of the school body.

The Shepard Accelerated School in St. Louis, Missouri, wants its students to succeed now and in the future. It teaches self-development through a ten-week Respect Seminar by having each child learn the code of discipline. The Respect Seminar is conducted for thirty minutes a day for one week, teaching the students to communicate and to learn tolerance, respect, and caring. Each school day is opened and closed with the pledge for doing one's best, respecting oneself, one's parents, teachers, and schoolmates.

Shepard Accelerated is a PreK–5 grade school with a very diverse student body; 80 percent African American, 20 percent white and almost the total student body qualifying for free lunch.

TEACHING RESPONSIBILITY IN SCHOOLS

A recurring theme in these schools is that effective discipline means teaching children how to become responsible. Far too many young people have little idea of what it means to be responsible. The Governor Bent School in Albuquerque, New Mexico, uses the responsibility mode of discipline. There is an attempt to involve students in decisions regarding behavior and responsibility at school so they internalize rules and develop as problem-solvers. Governor Bent has a heterogeneous student body of over seven hundred students. This very diverse population includes 40 percent Hispanic, 40 percent white with one-third of the students from lower-income families.

Allen Mendler (1988), the author of *Discipline with Dignity*, has developed the responsibility model of discipline that teaches children how to be responsible by teaching them to: (1) accumulate knowledge; (2) see the options available; (3) learn to anticipate consequences; and (4) then choose the path that they feel is in the best interest of themselves and others. Responsible students learn that they have choices and that they need to plan their behavior (Mendler, 1993). When students misbehave, they should be encouraged to ask themselves, what would happen if others acted this way? Why are these rules needed for the effective functioning of our society?

The students at the Volker Applied Learning Magnet School in Kansas City, Missouri, would be characterized by others as an "at risk" student body. More than half of the student body of this middle school of fourth- and fifth-graders are of African-American origin and are from lower-income families. One-quarter of the students qualify for special education services. According to Dr. Rayna Levine, the principal:

> Knowing right from wrong is taught and reinforced at the school. Honesty is appreciated and commended. We use students' sense of fairness, equality, and justice when

discussing incidents. In this way, personal responsibility is built. Our goal is for students to assume personal responsibility for their actions and not blame others when things do not go as envisioned.

DISCIPLINE THAT DEVELOPS CHARACTER

Some character educators define "character" as "practicing good discipline and being positively helpful to one's peers and to all adults" (Walberg and Wynne, 1989). A discipline program that teaches self-control can truly be a character development program because it spells out specific qualities or virtues to be developed. It seeks to help students internalize the locus of control of behavior. The New Canaan Country School in Connecticut states in its goals its belief that "mannerly behavior contributes significantly to the learning environment as well as to the character development of students." New Canaan School is an independent K–9 elementary school founded with the mission of "helping every child in its charge to develop a character built upon sound moral, spiritual, and intellectual values." New Canaan is located in a very affluent, homogeneous community. The staff believes that helping young people learn the skills of self-control and motivation to become productive, contributing, and knowledgeable adult participants in society is one of the most important tasks that good teachers undertake. They would agree with other educators who maintain that these are teachable and learnable skills (Schultz, 1995).

Skill Streaming is the character development discipline program found in the Clara Barton Open School in Minneapolis, Minnesota, based on the following behavior principles:

1. Be courteous to others.
2. Use time wisely.
3. Respect property.
4. Respect the rights of others.

Classroom techniques target the development of fair play and concern for others. Clara Barton is a K–8 school with six hundred students located in a large city. The student body is diverse: 17 percent African American, and 6 percent Asian American. As situations occur, the teacher helps the students to process through the incident, practicing conflict resolution skills, and including students in the discussion. The students use the behavior rules as their guide. The goal of Skill Streaming is to develop an atmosphere of trust that fosters self-discipline and responsibility.

TRUE DISCIPLINE IS SELF-DISCIPLINE

At St. Thomas More School in Ohio, students learn the value of self-discipline when they turn in homework assignments on time; of courtesy when they raise a hand before answering; of punctuality when they come to class on time; and of good judgment when teachers emphasize that there is a difference between good and bad and right and wrong. Ethical judgements are formed when students begin to see and understand the connection between education and "real life." St. Thomas More School is a Catholic K–8 school with students from both suburban and urban middle- and lower-class economic backgrounds most of whom are the third generation coming from a European ethnic background.

Locke Hill Elementary School in San Antonio, Texas, uses Right Choice—a schoolwide program of direct instruction in self-discipline. The Right Choice discipline topic of the week is highlighted during morning announcements and in a class newsletter. Student broadcasts illustrate how the topic is relevant to students' lives. Class discussions deepen understanding of the topics as students relate real-life applications. Ethical judgment and character development are the focus of classroom rules generated by students and by teachers providing time for students to analyze and solve interpersonal problems independently. According to the Locke Hill teachers, "Right Choice provides a structure enabling us to fulfill our responsibility to instruct students in the character attributes our society expects them to display. It helps us to seize situations that arise as teachable moments for helping students practice and apply good judgment by making good choices. It provides a curriculum resource to fill gaps or affirm previous efforts to teach character education elements." Locke Hill is a K–5 school with a diverse student population of 817. Some students come from middle- to high-socioeconomic suburban neighborhoods, others come from single-parent homes and federally subsidized housing. All students are valued individually and given a program that provides academic challenge in a student-centered environment. The school has an inviting courtyard with six classroom gardens and a picnic area with tables and benches.

DISCIPLINE AS PART OF THE EDUCATIONAL PROCESS

The teachers at the Monte Gardens Elementary School in suburban Bakersfield, California, believe that discipline is an educational process in which students are taught expectations for behavior and reinforced for achieving those expectations. Monte Gardens has a large diverse student population which includes 10 percent Hispanic students and 10 percent Asian students. Effective and consistent communication with parents is another key factor in its discipline program. All teachers have a discipline program in place in their classrooms. Some use a unique money system at the intermediate level whereby bank accounts are established for each student in which he or she can earn money for good behavior or have money taken out for poor behavior decisions. The policy is to reward the positive.

Neubert Elementary School in the small middle-class town of Algonquin, Illinois, has an interesting "society-based" program:

> Keystone Kids is based on the "Driver's License" concept; a license is issued to each student that is good for the entire year. Failure to accept the responsibility for one's behavior results in a written "citation." One copy of the citation is recorded in the office by the "meter maid" while the student copy must be signed by a parent and returned. Three citations result in a detention and a hole punch on the driver's license, which means the student is not entitled to the benefits of a popcorn movie each semester. An honor roll in the hall lists the names of responsible citizens. A videotape presentation acquaints the children with the program at the beginning of the year and a certificate is awarded at the end of the year to the "responsible citizens."

The East Elementary School in Pendleton, Indiana, compares being in school to holding a job and has developed a program called "Learnball" which unites the classroom into a company.

> Learnball is a classroom management program that helps build character. Students may earn points for their "companies" through appropriate behavior, good grades, neatness, etc. The accent is on the positive, not the negative. Winning teams are rewarded by having their company's picture in the winner's place or by receiving special privileges. *The real reward, however, seems to be merely the satisfaction of a job well done!* This system has provided dividends of good behavior, pride in work, and the development of student leadership.

Students at East experience intrinsic motivation from knowing that they have done their very best. East Elementary is a K–8 school of over eight hundred students from blue- and white-collar families in the small industrial town of Pendleton.

THE TEACHER'S ROLE IN
PROMOTING GOOD DISCIPLINE

An interesting trend found in the later years of reports is an emphasis on the role of the teacher in promoting good discipline. According to Walnut Hill in Dallas, Texas, "Discipline" is derived from the word "disciple," which means one who receives training from another. Therefore teachers see it as their responsibility to model principles of self-discipline." Other Blue Ribbon Schools agree: "Good classroom control is largely dependent upon a well-planned, interesting program and mutual respect between pupil and teacher. A pleasant orderly environment is conducive to good discipline." "Effective classroom management, appropriate planning, and interesting material are the primary means for preventing discipline problems." Schultz (1995) asserts that teachers bear moral and ethical responsibilities for promoting responsible social behavior in the classroom. They elicit the best work and behavior from children by modeling this themselves. Teachers are asked to teach to different learning styles and thereby involve all students in learning. "With a focus on multiple intelligences, children at Governor Bent Elementary School (in Albuquerque, New Mexico) learn to recognize and appreciate the strengths of others. Students are applauded by their peers for their differences and those differences serve to strengthen and unite the community of learners within each classroom."

HIGH EXPECTATIONS

Many of the Blue Ribbon Schools explicitly mentioned having high expectations of students' behavior, encouraging them to be self-disciplined, and to take personal responsibility for their actions, and fostering in students a respect for others, thereby helping them develop their character. Some of the schools stated their discipline philosophy in their applications: "True discipline is self-discipline;" "Discipline stresses personal pride in being responsible;" "High Expectations is the key to discipline."

Sister Lora Ann Slavinski, the principal of St. Stanislaus School, a Catholic K–8 school with a diverse Polish and Hispanic student population in Chicago, Illinois, explains: "A consistent discipline program sets a standard which encompasses all aspects of character development. The staff sets the example by appropriate role modeling, respect toward others, compassion, and a professional demeanor with students. Expectations are high. Students are held accountable for their actions. Mistakes are not character flaws but opportunities to grow." A visit to the school revealed that the strong ethnic background of the students is a great influence on their character. A strong work ethic and an appreciation for the value of education is a part of the Polish culture; and the Hispanic students are taught by their parents to obey and be respectful.

The Royalview Elementary School in Willowick, Ohio, is a school with a caring climate. Staff members all share the responsibility for informing students of the schoolwide behavior expectations and reinforcing these expectations through the year. The Schoolwide Behavior Expectations are:

1. Keep hands and feet to yourself.
2. Walk throughout the building.
3. Be polite and courteous.
4. Use proper language.
5. Respect teachers and other adults.
6. Follow behavior expectations established for each classroom.

As a teacher explains, "We set high expectations for student behavior and consistently communicate these expectations with each other, students, and parents. Communication is the key. All of us, teachers, support staff, and administrators have made a concerted effort to contact parents at the earliest instance of inappropriate behavior. We also "listen" as well as speak to our students. When we speak, the message is one of shared responsibility for a safe, caring, and orderly learning environment. We desire to be an affective school as well as an effective school in our mutual quest to meet the national goals. The caring climate and atmosphere of "caring" has permeated our school community and has led to the success of achieving our school priorities."

THE PRO-ACTIVE APPROACH TO DISCIPLINE

John Leucke, the principal at Frankfort Junior High School in Frankfort, Illinois, explains that their goal has always been a proactive approach instead of a reactive approach to discipline. Frankfort is a relatively new school located on a seventeen-acre site in a rural setting forty miles southwest of Chicago. The school has a homogeneous student body of four hundred from a rapidly developing, upper-middle class suburban community. The Tiger Gold Card Program focuses on responsibility and good citizenship. Students earn a card and its privileges by observing the school rules:

- Respect the rights and property of others.
- Be on time.
- Be prepared.
- No gum or candy.

The gold card can be used in the business community for discounts when purchasing items at cooperating establishments. Mr. Leuke commented that the middle school students at Frankfort strive very hard to get and to keep their Gold Card. It is as important to them as getting a driver's license is for their older brothers and sisters.

One can ask, what is the character-development rationale for such a system? Rewards like this are successful in increasing the probability that students will act respectfully in school. But these rewards must be judged on whether it leads to lasting change—change that persists even when the extrinsic motivation is no longer there. Will they help students develop the habit and good character of a responsible person? Will the Frankfort Middle School students bother to follow rules in other situations—the mall, the family, and so on—where there is no pay off? Mr. Leuke thinks that the students will, as the Gold Tiger Card is something important to them and their peers. It represents a personal commitment that they have made to be responsible in their behavior. As developing adolescents, it is important for them to make this emotional commitment to following rules.

Students in grades 2–5 at the Barringer Academic Center in Charlotte, North Carolina, are actively involved in the *I Can Manage Myself Club (I.C.M.M.C.)*. This program allows teachers to observe, assess, and foster the social and emotional growth among students. Each student is given a card that allows him/her the freedom of several privileges within the school (for instance, walking alone in the hall with only a pass, participation in clubs, etc.) If students show that they are not capable of managing themselves, they are given a reflective period that allows them an opportunity to practice their skills in a supervised environment and thus earn back their ICMMC privilege. The school saying, "Are you doing the right thing even if no one is looking?" influences the entire culture of the school and helps students grow in self-discipline. Barringer is a PreK–5 school of 501 with a very diverse student body of 53 percent white, 42 percent black and 4 percent Asian, with 28 percent qualifying for free lunch and 13 percent qualifying for special education services.

CREATING SAFE SCHOOLS

Several of the schools reported that one of their claims to meriting the Outstanding School Award is the fact that they have changed in a few years from having poor discipline to very good discipline. They answered in detail the application question: "Summarize your school's overall approach to discipline. Describe any special procedures or programs used to maintain order and discipline throughout your school. What factors contribute most to order in your school?" These award-winning schools created safe schools through very conscious school-wide efforts to integrate character development throughout the curriculum and throughout the school community.

In order to ensure that their school is safe, several Blue Ribbon Schools have implemented programs to ensure children are safe from the harassment of others. Counselors at the Harold H. Wilkins Memorial/Clark School in Amherst, New Hampshire, initiated a project of bully-proofing the school in order to ensure that the school was a safe place for all. Using common language and consistent guidelines, bullying was no longer tolerated. As the counselors explained, "Bully proofing our schools involves parents and teachers in empowering all children to know how to deal with intimidating behaviors." Students at the school told the site visitor, "There are no bullies here. Teachers tell you how to deal with situations. If anyone bothers you, you should just walk away." Wilkins is a primary building with 682 students in grades 1–4. Research supports the effort to be proactive in the early grades in order to encourage positive relationships and mutual respect among students (Froschl, 1999).

The Benfield Elementary School in Serverna Park, Maryland, has implemented a comprehensive school-based character education curriculum called No Putdowns. This program focuses on violence prevention, character development, substance abuse prevention skills, and life-skill building. The program teaches students powerful behaviors, such as helping others, apologizing when wrong, walking away from a fight, using constructive words instead of fists and put downs, and sharing and including rather than excluding others. According to the teachers, "We continue to use the teachable moment and counseling opportunities to help instill the character traits revered by our community such as self-control, responsibility, self-worth, empathy, cooperation, respect, and tolerance. Our school's accomplishments were highlighted in the *Washington Post* and on a Channel 2 broadcast." Benfield is a PreK–5 homogenous school of 376 students serving a professional middle- and high-socioeconomic community with a strong commitment to educational excellence.

Pleasant Hill Elementary School in Springfield, Illinois, has a Fight Free Program. Each day is opened with an announcement stating that 260 students are fight free and reminding them to think what they would do if someone tries to create a problem. The class also recites a Fight-Free pledge at the beginning of the day. Each class has a Fight-Free flag that is displayed unless there is a problem. In that case, the flag is turned around and the school flag taken down by the student that created the problem. The same students then put the flag up the next morning for a fresh start. Stars are given to the classrooms that are fight-free at the end of each week and an extra fifteen minute recess is given to Fight Free classrooms at various times throughout the year. Pleasant Hill Elementary School is a K–4 school with a diverse student body, including 29 percent African American. Eighty percent of the student body qualifies for free lunch, for Pleasant Hill is in a poor neighborhood, with much crime and gang activity. According to Johnson and Johnson (1995b), preventing violence and resolving conflicts are interrelated. Violence prevention programs alone are not enough, for students also need to learn how to manage conflicts constructively. Students trained in conflict resolution will help schools become orderly and a peaceful place in which high-quality education can take place.

Second Step

Many of the Blue Ribbon Schools, including the Castle Hills Elementary School in San Antonio, Texas, have implemented a schoolwide (preschool through fifth grade) violence prevention and conflict resolution program called "Second Step." This program has improved the overall school climate, created an environment more conducive to learning, and helped to end acts of violence. The Second Step curriculum is a nationally known character education program that focuses on conflict resolution, empathy, anger management, and problem-solving. This violence prevention program is used throughout Castle Hills School to help children learn what to do when someone is trying to cause a problem. Alternative solutions to problems are taught in a manner appropriate for the age of the child. The Second Step Violence Prevention curriculum teaches children to recognize their own feelings and the feelings of others. Children learn ways to control anger and ap-

Table 10.   Discipline Programs Used in the Blue Ribbon Schools

Category	Count	Percent
Assertive Discipline/Modified Assertive Discipline	11	24%
Behavior Modification	6	1%
Bully Proofing/No Put Downs	6	1%
Catch Them Being Good	25	5%
Class Meetings and Problem-Solving	61	13%
Code of Conduct	40	9%
Conflict Management and Peer Mediation	95	20%
Cooperative Discipline	22	5%
Discipline with Dignity/with Love & Logic	15	3%
Etiquette and Courtesy	7	1%
Good Citizenship	9	2%
Handbook/Class Rules	93	20%
Moral Discipline	19	4%
Peacemaking	13	3%
Positive Discipline	73	16%
Quality Schools	17	4%
Respect, Responsibility	16	5%
School Wide	11	3%

Cases 470 Missing Cases 15

propriate ways to show anger. Each lesson is scripted for ease of use and frequently employs role-play and discussions as teaching techniques. Evaluations of Second Step have demonstrated that teaching the curriculum leads to decreases in aggression and increases in neutral and pro-social behavior in schools. The 1998 "Safe Schools Report" called the curriculum a "model program." For more information contact: Committee for Children, 2203 Airport Way South, Suite 500, Seattle, WA 98134-2027, Telephone (800) 634-4449.

Table 10 lists the various discipline programs or approaches mentioned by the Blue Ribbon Schools.

ASSERTIVE DISCIPLINE AND "MODIFIED" ASSERTIVE DISCIPLINE

The most common commercial program found in 24 percent of the schools is "Assertive Discipline" by Lee Canter (1976). The key to this program is that the students are told clearly what behavior is expected of them, how that behavior will be rewarded, and what the consequences will be when behavioral expectations are violated. Behavior modification is the predominant philosophy of education underlying Assertive Discipline. Although Assertive Discipline was found in a total of 24 percent of the Blue Ribbon School applications samples examined; it was most common in the 1987–1988 year. Assertive Discipline—with its emphasis on rewards and punishments—reinforces immature character development (Stages 1 and 2 in Kohlberg's theory: Punishment-obedience and Instrumental-relativistic) and therefore *cannot* be considered a good character education strategy. It is a model that fosters obedience to an authority figure rather than personal responsibility (Render, et al., 1989; Curwin and Mendler, 1988; Lickona, 1991).

In more recent years, there has been a definite trend toward using what schools call a "modified" Assertive Discipline program, in response to research showing that Assertive Discipline worked only when the teacher was present. The Susan Lindgren Intermediate Center in St. Louis Park, Minnesota, explains that its student discipline policy has been modified from a more Assertive Discipline "ticketing" approach to one that inserts reason between impulse and action. Students explained the change in these words: "Last year we had yellow and white slips. This year we have lessons." The focus is on helping the students understand about being good. The school's discipline program now utilizes a participatory process that involves all students. Guidelines for responsible behavior are developed cooperatively by the teacher and the students. The diverse student body in this large 3–6 middle school located in a suburb of Minneapolis includes Russian and Asian immigrants as well as white and African American students. Family income level is also diverse, from upper-middle-class income to over 15 percent from lower-income families. The staff at the Lindgren School strongly believes that when students have input into classroom and school policy, they become better executors of the policies. This practice is supported by substantial research indicating that people are more inclined to obey rules when they have had a significant part in determining them (Ban, 1994).

BEHAVIOR MODIFICATION TECHNIQUES THAT PROMOTE CHARACTER DEVELOPMENT

Behavior modification per se was mentioned in only a very few of the school reports but behavior modification techniques were listed in many applications: for example, rewarding appropriate behavior by giving first place in line, a star on the classroom or behavior charts, and the issuance of good behavior slips that can be refunded. Time-out often takes the form of a "Time to Think Room" or a special place in the room, and is mentioned as an effective method for modifying inappropriate behavior. At St. Mark the Evangelist Catholic School, staff explained, "In the formative years of a child's development, external rewards and punishment may be necessary but the ultimate goal is that the child internalize modes of acceptable behavior." St. Mark's is a relatively new K–8 Catholic school in Plano, Texas, with a diverse student body of almost 450 that includes Hispanic, Asian and Caucasian students.

Whenever behavior management is used in the Blue Ribbon Schools, staff try to preserve the dignity of the individual student. For example, Shirley E. Anderson, the principal at the Washington School, in Mundelein, Illinois, explains:

Our discipline program is based on the belief that all children can behave appropriately, all children have human dignity and worth, and that behavior is maintained by consequences. Positive consequences are most powerful.

Washington is a K–5 school of over four hundred students with almost 10 percent Hispanic students.

CATCH STUDENTS DOING SOMETHING RIGHT

In five percent of the Blue Ribbon Schools, The One-Minute Manager's philosophy of Spenser Johnson and Ken Blanchard (1982) has been applied and teachers, staff, and administrators seek to "catch students doing something right." With this proactive system, students are encouraged to act correctly because these positive actions are acknowledged. There is clearly a trend in the last few Blue Ribbon Award years, to emphasize a proactive approach to promoting pro-social behaviors. Another example of this is found at the Eric Norfeldt School in West Hartford, Connecticut, which stresses kindness, consideration, and respect for others. Students have rights and responsibilities. Norfeldt is a school of four hundred students. The school has a diverse student population due to its participation in a voluntary desegregation program that buses students from the inner city of Hartford to the school.

THE CLASS MEETING

The class meeting has become very popular in both private and public schools as both a means for solving classroom management problems and as a component of their character development and good discipline program. The St. Rosalie School, located in Harvey, Louisiana, a suburb of New Orleans, uses the classroom meeting in order to solve class or school behavior problems cooperatively. St. Rosalie School is a Catholic K–8 school with over one thousand students, representing diverse racial and ethnic backgrounds that include Italians, Cajuns, African Americans, Asians and various European groups. According to the teachers, the classroom meeting "helps develop students' self-confidence, self-respect, and ultimately self-discipline." It also helps to create a good moral environment, provides an experience in democracy, and involves students in making decisions about the life of the classroom (Lickona, 1991).

One procedure for conducting a problem-solving class meeting, using a circle discussion, is as follows (Pereira, 1988):

1. At the teacher's signal, all chairs are arranged in a circle so each participant has eye contact.
2. The agenda is announced and students are welcomed to add other items to the agenda.

3. A method is determined for allowing each person who wishes to speak.
4. No interruptions are permitted while students are sharing their ideas and comments.
5. All comments are recorded and discussed; consensus is arrived at regarding the planned course of action.
6. A timeline is agreed upon in order to implement the solution decided: tasks are assigned to volunteers.
7. The date of the next meeting is announced. At that time the outcomes of this new decision will be evaluated.

According to the teachers at Black Bob Elementary School in Olathe, Kansas, following the honorable tradition of Chief Black Bob of the Shawnee Indians, students explore new frontiers, discover their inner strengths, and cultivate life skills through the use of class meetings. These meetings facilitate a healthy peer climate. They provide a framework for students to speak positively about classmates, compliment peers and voice concern about classroom or school climate. Students demonstrate life skills of respect and courtesy when speaking to the class about their concerns. A variety of issues are discussed and possible solutions are brainstormed. Students look forward to the "compliment" component of class meetings. "I like class meetings because you get to give compliments and everyone gets one. You also talk about stuff and work out problems together as a class," explains Rebecca Antes, a fifth-grade student. Black Bob School also has Mediation Managers (M&Ms). M&Ms help other students solve conflicts peacefully during recess. All students learn to practice conflict resolution and problem-solving skills during the weekly class meetings. Kohn (1996) agrees that the class meeting is the best forum for resolving issues and making decisions that affect most of the class. It can help the classroom become a real "community," that is, a place in which students feel cared about and are encouraged to care about each other.

CONFLICT MANAGEMENT

The most popular movement today in all schools, including the Blue Ribbon Schools, is teaching students and teachers how to resolve conflicts or disagreements in a peaceful manner. This proactive mode teaches social skills, for example, negotiation skills, mediation skills, anger control, refusal skills, and problem solving. It teaches students how to listen instead of punishing them for not listening. Teaching all students negotiation and mediation procedures and skills results in a school-wide program that empowers students to solve their own problems and regulate their own and their classmates' behavior (Johnson et al., 1992). Johnson and Johnson (1995b) have found that a comprehensive conflict resolution program has three major components: (1) creating a cooperative context; (2) implementing a conflict resolution/peer mediation program; and (3) using academic controversies for instructional purposes.

West View in Spartanburg, South Carolina, uses a conflict management program suggested by Gwen M. Sitsch, *Coping with Conflict: An Elementary Approach*. Students are taught that we all have conflicts and therefore must have life skills to manage them. Conflict is seen as a problem that needs to be managed, since not all conflicts can be resolved. Classroom guidance lessons introduce students to four main skills to manage conflicts: (1) Get the facts about a conflict; you may find that they do not actually have a conflict. (2) Manage anger; it is okay to feel angry, but not okay to hurt ourselves, hurt others, or damage property when we feel angry. (3) Communicate with the person with whom we are having a conflict; listen and use "I" statements. (4) Sharing, apologizing, compromising, and negotiating. Teachers are trained in the four conflict management skills and are able to reinforce the skills as situations arise. Parents also attend workshops on conflict management skills and receive information on using these skills at home. The program has been implemented so successfully, that when I visited the school in October, Sam Bingham, the principal, stated that there had been no conflicts that school year.

At the Pioneer Elementary School, with its homogeneous population of 688 students located in the mid-sized city of Colorado Springs, "discipline is a growth from dependence to independence. Students resolve their own conflicts using "I" messages. Conflict management training promotes participatory citizenship and personal responsibility." Research on the effectiveness of conflict resolution programs has been very positive (Johnson and Johnson, 1995b). When conflicts are managed successfully, they can increase achievement, develop higher-level reasoning, and build problem-solving skills; they also energize individuals to take action, promote caring and committed relations, and help students to understand others.

Richard O'Brien, the principal at the Snug Harbor Community School in Quincy, Massachusetts, explains that his school has adopted a philosophy of nonviolence. The school also has a successful conflict manager program. All fifth-graders are trained in conflict management by the end of the year. These managers are cited by the students as someone they could go to if they had an academic or personal problem. Snug Harbor is an ethnically and linguistically diverse school with limited-English students who represent six different language backgrounds.

According to the teachers at the R. J. Neutra Elementary School in Lemoore Naval Air Station, California, the goal of conflict resolution is to provide students with the knowledge, skills, and practices that will motivate them to respond to conflict constructively, have a positive self-esteem, and encourage them to work actively for a more peaceful school. Teachers were trained to guide students to communicate better, solve their own disputes, and lessen tensions and animosity. They teach the students:

Six Strategies for Conflict Management:

1. Talk It Over
2. Take Turns/Share

3. Ignore it
4. Walk Away
5. Say you are Sorry
6. Go for help

Neutra School is K–5, with 506 very diverse students, 15 percent Filipino, 11 percent African American, and 8 percent Hispanic. Half of the student body qualifies for free lunch. Neutra is located in the San Joaquine Valley on the Lemorre Naval Air Station halfway between San Francisco and Los Angeles. It is a Demonstration and Innovation School in fine arts, technology, special education, and physical education.

The Barclay Brook School teaches its students the DINO acrostic:

Decide if it's important.
Investigate the conflict.
Negotiate a plan.
Only ask for help if you can't work it out.

Students giving a tour of the building to the site visitors pointed out the peace table, located on the playground. They said that "most students go there on their own or if a friend suggests it. Most kids don't need teachers to solve their problems." Barclay Brook School, located in the town of Jamesburg, New York, is a K–2 primary building with 313 students.

PEER MEDIATION

Conflict resolution is a method that enables people to interact with each other in positive ways in order to resolve their differences. Peer mediation programs take the next step: they empower students to intervene in the conflicts of others and thereby share responsibility for creating a safe and secure school environment. A peer mediation program's first objective is to ensure that *all* students have learned the basic skills required to resolve conflicts. Then a staff member, usually a guidance counselor or teacher, supervises 15 to 20 hours of training the student mediators. Peer mediators may be nominated by teachers or chosen by peers. Stomfay-Stitz (1994) suggests that all students serve as peer mediators on a rotating basis after mastering the basic skills. This gives all students the opportunity to benefit from having this special kind of social responsibility.

Cambridge School in Kendall Park, New Jersey, has a Peer Mediation program as part of a full-school peacemaking program. Fourth-, fifth-, and sixth-graders are provided with intensive training that enables them to help prevent, solve, and alleviate conflicts building-wide. The Peer Mediators are instrumental in upholding school policy by: (1) modeling good behavior; (2) using conflict resolution strategies; and (3) influencing other students to resolve conflicts in a peaceful manner.

To achieve this end, mediators meet weekly to plan schoolwide activities, engage in peer mediation activities, and review mediations that have taken place. Often teachers call on the expertise of mediators when students are engaged in conflict. The principal also engages the services of mediators when children are sent to his office. Mediators are assigned a post on the playground and in the lunchroom. Aides send children to them as conflicts arise. Mediators also function in a preventative manner, averting conflicts before they begin through early intervention.

Many of our safety patrol members double as Peer Mediators, applying their skills as needed. Peer Mediators visit classrooms during recess time on "in" days, and assist with conflict resolution and general role modeling. They are currently being trained to teach conflict resolution lessons in the younger grades. They create bulletin boards, skits, and songs to engage the rest of the student body in the conflict resolution process. Cambridge is a K–6 school with a very diverse student body: 13 percent African American, 14 percent Asian, 5 percent Hispanic, and 11 percent lower socioeconomic status.

PEACEMAKING

One example of a conflict resolution program that promotes peace is found in the Aikahi Elementary School in Hawaii, is "Peace on the Playground." Students are trained as mediators or Recess Refs to arbitrate disputes and help other students work out misunderstandings. Aikahi is a K–6 school with a culturally diverse population of almost six hundred students: 25 percent Asian and 12 percent from lower-income families. Another program used in this same Hawaiian school is "Peace Begins with Me," which promotes non-violent attitudes and behavior. The program teaches that each person is unique and has strengths and limitations, rights, and responsibilities. The concept of peace education is multifaceted and cross-disciplinary; it includes peace and social justice, economic well-being, political participation, non-violence, conflict resolution, and concern for the environment (Stomfay-Stitz, 1993). For more information on the curriculum "Teaching Students to Be Peacemakers" contact: David and Roger Johnson, 7208 Cornelia Drive, Edina, MN 55435. "PEACE," according to one Blue Ribbon School, means "Peers Excelling Against Conflict Through Education."

Cambridge School in Kendall Park, New Jersey, also has a peacemaking program that they consider to be of central importance to their school's curriculum. One of the Cambridge teachers is coauthor of a book *Learning the Skills of Peacemaking,* now being used nationwide and recognized by the United Nations. The goals of the peacemaking program are: to build community; to enable students to take responsibility for actions upon others; to create acceptance among all members of the school regardless of ethnic background, religion, gender, or handicaps; to provide all students and staff with a precise strategy for resolving conflicts peacefully; and finally, to provide uniform consistent standards and strategies that enable all members to coexist in a safe and respectful environment. The halls are lined with "Peace Pledges" children have taken to promote peace in their lives and in the school—for example, "I will make our school a more peaceful place by not fighting." Children are nominated by their peers for the "Peacemaker of the Week Award" based on how well they have shown respect toward others throughout the week.

The Holly Oak Elementary School in San Jose, California, has a "Peace Patrol." Thirty-five upper-grade students are trained in conflict resolution skills in an extensive one-month training period. They learn to recognize conflict and develop strategies that can be used to resolve them peacefully. Through accepting responsibility and helping others, students in the Peace Patrol are learning to help themselves. Larger school problems are brought to the attention of all students at the weekly schoolwide morning assembly. This serves as a catalyst for discussions in the class and on the playground. Peace patrol students discuss ethical values, develop interpersonal and peaceful conflict resolution skills, and become valuable contributing members of the Holly Oak Community. Holly Oak is a K–6 school with a very diverse student body; 13 percent white, 33 percent Hispanic, 41 percent Asian, 12 percent African, one-third with limited English, and more than half living at the poverty level.

From Moorestown Friends School in New Jersey to Argonaut Elementary School in Saratoga, California, and from Centennial Elementary School in Tucson, Arizona, to the Volker Learning Magnet in Kansas City, Missouri, peer mediation and conflict resolution are being taught to students as this decade's solution to discipline problems. While traditional discipline procedures teach students to depend on authority figures to resolve conflicts, peacemaking programs teach students how to mediate disputes and negotiate solutions themselves (Johnson, Johnson, Dudley, and Burnet, 1992). In the process, such programs are also developing strengths of character such as good judgment, perspective taking, self-control, and personal responsibility.

COOPERATIVE DISCIPLINE

A number of schools reported using Cooperative Discipline (Albert, 1990), a classroom management system that promotes self-esteem by reinforcing cooperative behavior on the part of students. Using a comprehensive approach, Cooperative Discipline deals with all three discipline types: corrective, preventive, and supportive. It addresses the topics of student motivation, avoiding and defusing confrontations, ways to reinforce desirable behavior, building student self-esteem, involving parents, and how to discipline cooperatively. A multimedia package for implementing this system can be obtained from the American Guidance Service, P.O. Box 99, Publisher's Building, Circle Pines, MN 55014-1796.

Carver Elementary G. T. Magnet School in Wendell, North Carolina, believes that when students are respectfully treated as important decision makers who have the right to make choices and participate in the design of their education, they behave more cooperatively and achieve more academically. After each class has developed their belief statements about respect, they discuss what they want their classroom to look like. The teacher uses questions such as: "If we are all learning in our class, what would that look like?" "What would we be doing?" "How would we feel?" Based on the shared vision, the teacher and students develop a list of my job (teacher) and your job (student). As a result of these discussions each class adopts a classroom climate contract. From the classroom contracts, schoolwide rules are developed. Students actively participate in the decision making and the resolution of conflict as it occurs. Restitution plays an important role in the plan. Students who choose not to follow a rule are asked: "Have you done your job?" "What do we believe about respect for others?" or a question that will help them understand what the rule or belief is, and how they chose their behavior. They are given opportunities to make things right for the person they have hurt or offended. They are also given the opportunity to have an adult or classmate help if they need assistance.

DEVELOPING GOOD DECISION-MAKING SKILLS

There is a clear emphasis in the Blue Ribbon Schools on developing good decision-making skills in students as a way to promote good behavior. At Spring Glen Elementary School in Renton, Washington, the principal explains that the values emphasized at the school are respect, responsibility, and safety. In order to promote these values, the teachers teach the students to use problem-solving strategies to make responsible choices. This results in a safe and respectful physical and emotional environment. Staff believe that appropriate behavior is self-motivated and is celebrated and recognized through clear, consistent consequences. Spring Glen is a K–6 school of about four hundred students, almost 10 percent of whom are of an Asian background.

Kelso's Choice is a program that teaches students the difference between big problems, those that need adult intervention, and small problems, those they need to learn to handle independently. At the Henry T. Brauchle Elementary School in San Antonio, Texas, school students are taught nine techniques, such as talking it out or moving away to prevent small problems from escalating. As a teacher explained, "Kelso's Choices serve as a foundation from which our discipline folders are built. Each student has a Kelso's wheel imprinted on his/her discipline folder. When a good choice or a poor choice is made their folder is marked as such. This allows communication from teacher to teacher, and teacher to parent. Classroom, cafeteria, and hallway rules are also built on Kelso's Choices." Kelso's Choices posters are strategically positioned in nearly every hallway and classroom wall. This program provides a blueprint for peer mediation and sets a solid foundation in which schoolwide and classroom positive reinforcements are built. Henry T. Brauchle Elementary School is only nine years old, but already has 1250 students. It is a PreK–5 school with a very diverse student body; 50 percent white, 40 percent Hispanic, 33 percent of whom qualify for free lunch, and 23 percent of whom qualify for special education services. For more information on Kelso's Choices contact Sunburst Technology, 1990 S. Batavia Ave., Geneva, IL 60134, Telephone (800) 321-7511, www.sunburst.com.

DISCIPLINE WITH LOVE AND LOGIC

Jim Fay's "Discipline with Love and Logic" (Fay and Funk, 1995) is mentioned in the 1991–1992 and 1993–1994 award-winning school applications. It is used at the Pioneer Elementary School in Colorado Springs. Pioneer has 688 students, 10 percent of whom are from lower-income families. The students come from diverse racial and ethnic backgrounds: 85 percent white and the rest equal percentages of Asians, African Americans, and Hispanics. The Discipline with Love and Logic_program is a system for developing natural and logical consequences instead of rewards and punishments. It involves the teacher giving the student encouragement that communicates love, support, and valuing each child as a person. The Three Rules of Love and Logic for the Teacher are:

1. Use enforceable limits.
2. Provide choices within limits.
3. Apply natural and logical consequences with empathy.

The philosophy of Discipline with Love and Logic is that it fosters personal responsibility and respect for self and others. It states that discipline involves building students *up* so they feel more capable and better about themselves, even after a discipline situation. It asks the teacher not to rely on *external* controls to maintain students' behavior, but to get students to develop *internalized* controls. Jim Fay's philosophy states that instead of *making* kids behave, the goal is to make them *want* to behave (Fay and Funk, 1995). This emphasis on developing intrinsic motivation clearly reflects character education's emphasis on helping students develop the desire to be good (moral feeling). The Four Basic Principles of Love and Logic are:

1. Share the control.
2. Share the thinking.
3. Balance consequences with empathy.
4. Maintain self-concept.

For more information on Teaching with Love and Logic you can call the Love and Logic Institute, Telephone (800) 338–4065, listen to Love and Logic

Audio-tapes, or consult the book *Teaching with Love and Logic* by Jim Fay and David Funk (1995).

JUDICIOUS DISCIPLINE

Judicious Discipline (Gathercoal, 1990) explains discipline in terms of constitutional rights and citizenship. In line with this approach, some classes write their own Constitution or Student Bill of Rights, which is based on the premise that each child has a right to learn and each teacher has a right to teach. At the Caroline Bentley School in New Lenox, Illinois, these rights are summarized as: "Every student has the right to learn, teachers have the right to teach, and no one has the right to interfere with the rights of others." Respect must be the basis of discipline. Caroline Bentley is a fourth- and fifth-grade intermediate school located in a middle-class suburban community that places a high value on education and has a strong sense of family values.

The Highlands Elementary School in Saugus, California, outlines the Basic Rights of Students in this way:

1. To learn without interference.
2. To work together with respect and understanding.
3. To have their property safe.
4. To be safe from bodily harm.

Highlands is a large K–6 school located in a middle-sized urban city setting with a diverse student population that is 10 percent Hispanic and 5 percent Asian students.

MORAL DISCIPLINE

There is a definite change in discipline philosophy in the 1990s. Seeking to help students internalize the reasons why someone should behave, schools have sought to practice Moral Discipline, that is, to use discipline as a tool for teaching respect and responsibility. This approach holds that the ultimate goal of discipline is self-discipline—the kind of self-control that underlies voluntary compliance with just rules and laws is a mark of mature character and is what every society expects of its citizens (Lickona, 1991). In 20 percent of the applications, the school is equated with societal institutions and students are taught behaviors that are required in the larger society. For example, in the Quincy Public Schools, located in a suburb of Boston, Massachusetts, the discipline program is based on the philosophy explained in the handbook, that all members of the community have rights and responsibilities as defined in the U.S. Constitution. Students are expected to respect the rights, feelings, and property of others.

POSITIVE DISCIPLINE

Sixteen percent of the schools reported using Positive Discipline instead of Assertive Discipline. Positive Discipline is based on the philosophy of Alfred Adler and Rudolph Dreikurs. It seeks to teach children self-discipline, responsibility, cooperation, and problem-solving skills by allowing the teacher and students to cooperatively set logical and natural consequences and limits. This method considers the students' needs for self-respect and positive reinforcement (Nelson, 1987). The Britt David Magnet Academy in Columbus, Georgia, is a very diverse K–6 school with a student body that is 50 percent white, 43 percent black and 7 percent Hispanic that finds Positive Discipline the perfect approach for their students. As they explain: "Positive Discipline allows students to make positive choices and consistently outlines steps taken by the student to rectify negative choices. If students choose a negative action, they are required to recognize their choice in writing and choose a positive action that would be more appropriate if put in the same situation again."

Cedar Island Elementary School in Maple Grove, Minnesota, also emphasizes positive actions:

> Our philosophy of discipline is based on the premise that students need to be recognized for doing the right thing and that they need to have clear rules about behavioral expectations and consequences so that they can choose their course of action. We work toward creating an environment that is respectful, orderly, safe, and predictable. We believe that effective discipline has to be self-motivated. Have few rules and emphasize positive action. Good behavior is infectious.

Cedar Island School is a K–6 school with a homogenous population of eight hundred students.

The County Line Elementary School in Georgia has found the same to be true. Its discipline program is based on the theory that the reward for good behavior is as important as the consequence for inappropriate behavior. Each teacher writes a classroom discipline plan with positive and negative consequences. The school's philosophy of discipline works toward prevention instead of intervention. Its policies are designed to teach positive behavior. The principal stated, "We pride ourselves on being proactive instead of reactive." Over one-fourth of the County Line students are from families of low income.

Class meetings modeled from *Positive Discipline* by Jane Nelson, Ed.D, are held in most classrooms at the Harold Wilkins Memorial School/Clark School, a primary school of K–4th grade students. Class discussions are held in all rooms. Classroom management is handled skillfully with a climate of mutual respect present. Use of *Positive Discipline* principles is setting a tone where students are encouraged to express their feelings and empathize with their peers when they are feeling very sad or very happy. It was gratifying to watch the actions in a classroom where students were sitting in a circle with their teacher practicing positive interaction. Ground rules were clearly established and understood by all members of the class. The basis of expressing feelings was saying a number (1 through 5). Going around the circle, children expressed how they felt by reciting a number. If the response was a one or a five, they could tell a little more. Most memorable was one student who said: "Both five and one. Five (very happy) because my guinea pig had babies and one (very sad) because I can't keep any of them." The exercise in expressing feelings freed students to share happiness and sadness and support each other. The Harold Wilkins Memorial School/Clark School in Amherst, New Hampshire, has two buildings which host one school of students, Clark school has 221 primary and first-graders, Wilkins has 461 second-, third-, and fourth-graders.

QUALITY SCHOOLS

Glasser's ideas, that is, control theory in the classroom, affective discipline, and reality therapy are used in several of the schools (Glasser, 1990, 1986). Historically, one could see the development of the different Glasser ideas as they came out in his different books. In *Control Theory in Classrooms* (1986), Glasser suggests that effective teachers are those who use cooperative learning instead of lecturing and who manage their classroom in such a way that all of their students do quality work in school. Nancy Martin, principal of the Conder Elementary School in Columbia, South Carolina, explains: "This program emphasizes agreements for individual behavior. It results in a consistent method of dealing with discipline problems throughout the school." Glasser's ideas as found in his books, *The Quality School (1990)* and *Choice Theory, A New Psychology of Personal Freedom (1999)* also found a home in Blue Ribbon Schools.

Many of the Quality School ideas are being implemented in the Blue Ribbon Schools as a way of fostering good discipline and character development. As the principal at St. Isidore School in Danville, California, explains, "Using the Quality Schools idea means that students are encouraged to take responsibility for their behavior. They design the classroom poster which outlines their expectations of what they can do without infringing on the rights of others." St. Isidore is a K–8 Catholic school of three hundred and fifty homogeneous students of suburban, middle-class, and white families.

Carver Elementary G. T. Magnet School also uses this model.

Our belief system is derived from the Quality School Model by Dr. William Glasser. We strive each day to move away from control and coercion toward creating quality conditions for students and staff. Reality Therapy is interwoven throughout the school environment: and the school day. By using the theories from *Teach Them to Be Happy, Helping Kids Help Themselves* children have learned to be responsible for their own behavior and choices, solve conflict more appropriately, and strive for quality work. The Quality School model provides a vehicle for a purposeful climate conducive to learning. We all know what our job is and what it is not. This knowledge helps facilitate a cooperative mentoring approach to teaching and learning. Our emphasis on learning is based on character education. Through Quality Schools, literature experiences, and everyday life situations students are given opportunities to develop thinking skills, problem-solving skills, conflict resolution, and to apply those skills in a secure and nurturing environment. Students are taught respect for diversity. Teachers use a number of strategies to promote skills by structuring activities where students work together in cooperative groups, individual projects, and whole school programs.

Durkheim would agree that most of the discipline programs used in these Blue Ribbon Schools are truly promoting character development and morality in the classroom. "Discipline is not a simple device for securing superficial peace in the classroom; it is the morality of the classroom as a small society" (Durkheim, 1973).

SUMMARY

As this chapter shows, in order for a school to foster the development of "sound character . . . good behavior and the ability to work in a self-disciplined and purposeful manner," it must have an effective discipline program that promotes self-discipline. Some of the programs that successfully do this emphasize character qualities, class meetings, and conflict resolution and peer mediation training programs. The latter promote character development by teaching students prosocial skills, thus ensuring that the school has an orderly and safe environment.

8

How Does Good Citizenship
Contribute to Good Character?

You will remember that all the End of study is to make you a good Man and a useful Citizen.

—John Adams in a letter to his son, John Quincy Adams

Great schools are the result of great cooperation. Let's remember that it takes both the white and the black keys of the piano to play "The Star-Spangled Banner."

—Anonymous

The only ones among you who will be really happy are those who have sought and found how to serve.

—Albert Schweitzer

EDUCATION FOR CITIZENSHIP AS
THE GOAL OF UNIVERSAL EDUCATION

"Citizenship" is a quality that most Americans would agree should be promoted in the schools. "Values education," as we have seen, provokes controversy and the question "Whose values are you going to teach?" An acceptable response would be "Values of citizenship, American democratic values, and the values upon which our country was founded."

Jefferson, Madison, and Adams each said that a well-constructed constitution was not enough to maintain our democracy; a free society ultimately depended on its citizens and on their knowledge, skills, moral, and civic virtues. The "habits of the mind" and "habits of the heart" that Alexis de

Tocqueville saw in the American democratic ethos need to be taught by word, study, and example (Quigley, 1996). Noted historian, R. Freeman Butts (1991) says that education for citizenship was the primary reason for establishing universal education in the American Republic. The purpose of universal school, Butts explains, is to develop among all students, whether in private or public schools, the virtues, sentiments, knowledge, and skills of citizenship. In short, the health and survival of our democracy rests on the character of its citizenry.

This chapter shows us how the Blue Ribbon Schools use their citizenship programs to assist in the development of the character of their students. Citizenship programs are usually found within the social studies curriculum but are also found integrated throughout the school in various other programs. This chapter presents answers to the following questions:

- What are the essential characteristics that make a citizenship program character education and not just civic education?
- What are the democratic values that we want to foster in our nation's schools?
- Why is it important to involve students in decision making in order to develop character and citizenship?
- What are some ways that students can develop good character by caring within the classroom?
- How does community service help students develop character?
- How do the Blue Ribbon Schools prepare students to live effectively in our culturally, ethnically, and economically diverse society and world?

CIVIC EDUCATION
VERSUS CHARACTER EDUCATION

One needs to note what a school means by citizenship, in order to judge whether its citizenship program can be considered character education. If the school considers citizenship only to be learning about voting and laws, observing national holidays, and knowing leaders and historical figures, it is limiting citizenship to civic education, not character education (Letwin, 1991). Character education is much broader than this.

Character education means coming to understand, care about, and practice virtue. It includes learning the moral principles of a democratic society, namely, the perpetual struggle to live rationally within the boundaries of democratic tradition. This moral code is based on cultural history and is accepted as the ethic of our society. It should give students the ability to separate good from evil, fairness from unfairness, justice from injustice, and truth from falsehood (Reische, 1987).

DEMOCRATIC TRAITS OF CHARACTER

The Communitarian Network's 1996 task force paper, *The Role of Civic Education*, explains that civic education is not synonymous with character education; however, the two are related, and their aims overlap in important respects. An effective civic education program should provide students with opportunities for the development of desirable traits of public and private character. According to the task force paper, the public traits of character needed for the healthy functioning of our constitutional democracy are "civility, respect for law, civic-mindedness, critical-mindedness, persistence, and a willingness to negotiate and compromise"(p. 5). The private traits of character needed include "self-discipline, moral responsibility, honesty, respect for individual worth, and empathy for others"(p. 5).

Citizenship education is character education if it focuses on helping students develop the moral knowing aspect of their character while learning about their civic responsibilities. It uses citizenship awards to promote moral feeling in students. Finally, it gives students opportunities to show good actions to others in the classroom, school, family, and neighborhood, so they manifest the third component of good character, moral action. When citizenship education involves cooperative learning, it provides still another way for students to practice good moral actions and develop morally by having the opportunity to work with others, make fair decisions, and develop prosocial skills such as perspective-taking (Lickona, 1991). Citizenship education can be one of the best forums for developing character in students because it allows the development of all three aspects of character.

> Citizenship practice in the earliest grades is most appropriate in the setting of the classroom and the school itself. Students begin to understand through participation such as role-playing, games, and active discussion how and why rules are made, why people have laws, how people negotiate agreements. Through games, simulations, plays, and other activities students can experience directly how disputes arise, how they can be resolved without conflict, why people need to agree upon rules or laws (Reische, 1987).

School Mission Statements Promote Citizenship

It is not surprising, then, that developing citizenship was mentioned as the mission and goal of one-third of the Blue Ribbon Schools (see table 4). For example, the mission of the Lewis Powell Gifted and Talented Magnet Elementary School in Raleigh, North Carolina, is "to enable students to develop the skills necessary to become capable productive citizens." Lowell is a large PreK–5 grade school with a very integrated student body of five hundred students; 43 percent African American. Similarly, the mission of the Saigling School in Plano, Texas, is "to develop students who are responsible citizens, who make good decisions, and who try to do their best." To accomplish this mission, they have defined three goals; one of which is that 100 percent of their students will exhibit good citizenship and character.

The objective of the Normandy Elementary School in Centerville, Ohio, is similar to Saigling's goal: "Normandy staff want to produce self-disciplined, morally sound, and socially aware citizens for the next century." Normandy is located in a suburb outside of Dayton and has a small homogeneous student body.

Mill Lake School is a primary K–3 school of 380 homogeneous students located in the small town of Spotswood, New Jersey. One of the school's goals is to develop good character, good citizenship, and positive relationships with others. Nancy Richmond, the principal explains the school goal:

> A commitment has been made to establish a foundation upon which future building blocks of good citizenship, community service, and personal responsibility can be laid. These basic concepts are addressed through age-appropriate activities and learning experiences which included social studies lessons, assemblies, awards, bulletin boards, community service, and guidance lessons.

PROMOTING CITIZENSHIP
IN THE SOCIAL STUDIES CLASS

The normal academic setting for instruction in both civic education and character-building citizenship is the social studies class according to the teachers at the Russell Elementary School in Missouri:

> Good citizenship is the major focus of the social studies curriculum at Russell Elementary School. The cooperative learning that takes place in these classes allows the students to assume various roles in a group to prepare them for roles in the community. Class meetings and student council speeches and elections allow students to experience democratic processes. Discussion of current events and multicultural units within the social studies curriculum contribute to developing the students' sense of citizenship in a global society.

At the Southwest Elementary School in Howell, Michigan, the social studies program provides opportunities for students and staff to be involved in promoting good citizenship and community service. Southwest is a PreK–4 small-town school with a homogeneous student population of over five hundred mostly middle-class, white students but also including over 10 percent lower-income families. Student activities include visiting nursing homes, participating in Scouts, recycling, and being part of a good citizen recognition program.

CIVITAS

The more recent Blue Ribbon award groups (since 1994) mention using the CIVITAS curriculum in their social studies classes. CIVITAS is the result of a collaborative project of the Center for Civic Education and the Council for the Advancement of Citizenship, with support from the Pew Charitable Trusts. The aim of CIVITAS is to provide an intellectual and scholarly curriculum for K–12 civic education in the schools. This consists of a common core of knowledge, skills, and values desirable for all students in the nation to achieve (Quigley and Bahmueller, 1991).

It is interesting to see how much the Blue Ribbon Schools value their citizenship program as an important component of their character education program. Joyce Westgate, the principal at Benjamin Franklin Elementary School in Binghamton, New York, describes their diverse student body as including students from middle- to lower-middle-class families. Students learn the habits of good citizenship in three ways:

> First is through example. Students witness the cooperation, hard work, and friendliness of the staff, administration, and faculty. Secondly, the Character Education Committee regularly plans events around positive character traits. One month highlights "Responsibility" with a new rap song taught in music classes and sung during assembly; another "Honesty" with public acknowledgment of honest actions; and yet another "Helpfulness" with classroom displays of photographs that show children gaining understanding by helping others. The third focus on citizenship is direct instruction through a series of activities emphasizing peaceful conflict resolution, problem solving, cooperation, self-esteem, and responsibility. (National Association of Elementary School Principals, 1995)

Judith Schulz, principal of the Independence Primary School in the Cuyahoga Valley of Ohio, explained that its schoolwide citizenship programs are very effective in fostering good character and leadership in students. It strives to develop values, such as responsibility for self, trust, and caring for others, and thereby helps to ensure that students are prepared to be responsible members of American society.

The Bellerive School in Missouri teaches the civic values of equality, freedom, justice, respect for authority, and respect for property in many of its programs and especially through its Bellerive Cadet Helper Program. As explained in chapter 3 on character education programs, the Bellerive Cadet Helper program is one in which students volunteer to participate as a service to the school, but one to which they also have to be chosen, based on their possession of good character and leadership qualities. Students are able to choose the teacher, job, and time they are available, but it is basically an opportunity for them to show they are good citizens of the school by helping out in another grade.

East Elementary School in rural Pendleton, Indiana, considers "love of country" as one of the several cornerstones that support purposeful citizenship. Students raise and lower the American flag each day. The flag is placed in every classroom and the Pledge of Allegiance is respectfully recited each morning. The annual all-school singing assembly emphasizes America's heritage. Individual classrooms study the important responsibilities of American leaders.

Current Events

At St. Rosalie School in Harvey, Louisiana, current events are addressed daily at all levels. From these topics come the opportunities for discussion of behavior and consequences: Why do we have certain opinions? Are they based on facts? How are we, school, and country, working in support of democratic ideals? From these discussions and role modeling, students gain insights into problem solving.

At the Elvin School in Alabama, current events are used to help students live values. For instance, students wrote protest letters concerning ethical issues in South Africa and wrote their Congressmen regarding political issues. The large, very diverse student body of 647 consists of 18 percent African American students and 40 percent students from lower-income families.

Ernest Boyer (1990) believes that civic education means helping students confront social and ethical concerns, even if it involves controversial issues. Students can apply what they have learned to make judgments, form convictions, and act boldly on values held. Schools that advocate citizenship programs for their role in character development provide students with opportunities in which they can find solutions to problems and can then act on these solutions. These programs help them to become active, questioning young adults who are prepared to take on the vital role of citizens in a democracy (Sadowsky, 1991). Moreover, they build personal character by challenging students to translate moral judgment and feeling into moral action as citizens of their classrooms, schools, and communities.

Law-Related Education

Ralph E. Noddin Elementary School in San Jose, California has Law-Related Education, a program for fifth grades that builds character and civic responsibility. It is an integrated social studies program that covers the concepts of American history and civics. It includes field trips to court, mock trials, visits from judges, probation officers, police officers, and attorneys. Through this program, students will examine what it means to be a good citizen, what it means to be fair, responsible, and just. Ralph E. Noddin Elementary School is a K–5 school of 507 diverse students: 10 percent Hispanic, 12 percent Asian, almost one-fifth qualify for free lunch. Noddin is a neighborhood school in a scenic setting surrounded by parks, homes, and small businesses located in the heart of Silicon Valley.

DEVELOPING DECISION-MAKING SKILLS

Recommendation No. 8 of the National Task Force on Citizenship Education states: "Because values and ethical issues are central to civic education, school should be encouraged to use moral education concepts, as well as . . . community-based experiences reflecting the values of the community" (Reische, 1987). Some schools have based their citizenship program on an application of Kohlberg's theories of moral development (outlined in chapter 2). Kohlbergian methods initially focused on encouraging interactive moral dilemma discussions among students at different levels of moral reasoning. Later, the focus changed to establishing within existing schools, models of participatory democracy called "just community schools" (Reische, 1987). The Blue Ribbon Schools use the moral discussion method extensively; however, instead of discussing hypothetical moral dilemmas, they tend to discuss real school issues. Thus, students truly participate democratically in making suggestions for the effective running of their school.

A good citizen must be a thinking citizen (Rowe, 1990). Social studies is one of the school subjects that provides a natural context for teaching thinking skills. The "town meeting" is a method mentioned in several of the Blue Ribbon Schools. It is a problem-solving framework that allows students to use thinking skills, techniques, and processes learned in the social studies content area to solve real school problems. Some schools use the "town meeting" to invite the community to discuss ethical issues. (Many of the character education organizations are now ending their annual meetings with a "town meeting" that allows participants of the conference to make suggestions to the organizational leaders and to problem-solve with the other members of the professional group.)

CARING AS A MORAL VALUE

Lickona (1991) says that respect and responsibility are the "fourth and fifth Rs" that schools not only *may* but also *must* teach if they are to develop ethically literate persons who can take their place as responsible citizens of society. He states that the effectiveness of a character development program is shown in students' actions. Lickona's comprehensive approach to character education emphasizes the importance of caring within the classroom and caring beyond the classroom. The Blue Ribbon Schools also strive to develop these two aspects of caring within their citizenship programs. This focus on caring is especially important in order to begin bridging the differences in the multiracial and multicultural community; it is a virtue that has truly global repercussions.

According to George Noblit and his research colleagues (1995), "Morally and culturally, caring is a belief about how we should view and interact with others" (p.680). Alasdair MacIntyre (1981), in *After Virtue* states that caring is a moral concept when it is something that is reaffirmed continually in everyday life. Alfie Kohn (1991) concurs, stating that caring is a natural quality in humans and that the school provides a logical setting in which to guide children toward caring about and helping other people. The outcome of good citizenship education is students who know how to care for all of the other people in their world—family, school, community, city, and nation.

Students are taught the attributes of caring and responsible behavior in grades K–5 at the Hill Elementary School in Austin, Texas. "Respect for difference is emphasized throughout our curriculum. Students at Hill interact with students from schools with a different ethnic and economic population mix. This helps both groups of children appreciate diversity." In addition, the integrated social studies curriculum helps students to value and cherish diversity in ethnicity, culture, and economics as an important "good citizenship" skill.

CARING WITHIN THE CLASSROOM

George Wood (1990) has spent three years in classrooms observing teachers who see their task first and foremost as nurturing the skills, attitudes, and values necessary for democratic life—that is, teaching caring. He believes that with proper attention to all the individuals within the school, educators can create an experience for students that demonstrates what it means to be compassionate, involved citizens. For it is only within a community that young people learn how important are such principles as working for the common good, empathy, equality, and self-respect.

One of the most common ways for students to show their good citizenship within the classroom is to participate in a buddy program, patrols, or a tutoring program.

CITIZENSHIP PROGRAMS FOUND IN THE BLUE RIBBON SCHOOLS

More than 10 percent of the Blue Ribbon Schools mentioned their citizenship program in response to the question, "How do school programs, practices, policies, and staff foster the development of sound character, democratic values, ethical judgment, good behavior, and the ability to work in a self-disciplined and purposeful manner?" Table 11 summarizes the programs that they mentioned they used.

Table 11. Citizenship Programs Mentioned by Blue Ribbon Schools

Category	Count	Percent of Responses
Buddy Program	59	14
Citizen of Week Award	64	15
Community Service	120	29
Develop Cooperative Skills	10	2
Global Concerns	19	5
Leadership Programs	10	2
Patrol/Scouts	65	16
Student Council	101	24
Tutoriing Program	51	12

Total N 419   Missing Cases 68

"BUDDY" PROGRAMS

Students show that they care for others by sharing their time with them. Educators can begin to promote the value of caring explicitly by exploring ways in which they can create a more caring culture in classrooms and in schools. Culture is based, in part, on such gestures of caring and other everyday ways of doing things (Noblit, 1995). Westwood School in Santa Clara, California, describes how its students care for one another through the buddy program:

> Our fourth- and fifth-grade classes are role models for the school. Their leadership program includes working with younger students in developing math and reading skills. Each student selects a buddy, and together they select books to read, stories to write, science, or social studies projects to do, and games to play. Consequently, it is a two-way street where both students benefit. A fifth-grade ESL student tutoring a first-grader reinforces his own English skill while the first-grader learns math problem-solving skills.

At Lowell Elementary School in Boise, Idaho, the fifth-and-sixth grade classes use "study buddies" in which children are paired with a partner in class to provide instructional and work habits support. In other grades, peer helpers work with students who are having difficulties academically or motivationally. Lowell is a K–6 urban school of four hundred students of growing diversity. The formerly all-white school body now has 8 percent of its students from other ethnic heritages. Lowell families have the greatest socioeconomic span of the Boise schools; 72 percent are low-income families, but the others represent middle-income, professional and even executive-level occupations.

In addition to the "study buddies," Lowell has a cross-grade buddy system in which all fifth- and sixth-grade classes are paired up with a primary class. Besides listening to children read, the upper-grade students teach "mini-lessons" to their buddies. The older students have special projects that combine social studies and science with research skills. They learn the material, then modify it to included hands-on, concrete examples to teach the concepts to the younger children. These "mini-lessons" have included subjects on manners, snakes, and plant growth. Buddies also have shared field trips and art projects and celebrate holidays together. This year the second-graders read to the kindergarten students. One of the students told about the program: "We have a buddy program, and it helps us to know someone little is looking up to us. My buddy cried this morning because she didn't know why I couldn't come." (She was touring this visitor around the building!)

GOOD CITIZENSHIP AWARD

Increasingly, schools are teaching citizenship and character in the same way that they are teaching reading and math. They are working with their communities to define those core values such as honesty, hard work, and respect for others and for oneself, that make it possible for our democracy to continue (National Association of Elementary School Principals, 1995). Although some schools do give grades to their students on their report card for citizenship, 15 percent of the Blue Ribbon Schools have found that a more effective way to promote good citizenship is to recognize those who demonstrate good citizenship in their actions.

Fort Washington Elementary School in Fresno, California, is a large heterogeneous K–8 school of six hundred students; 6 percent Hispanic, 4 percent Asian and 2 percent African American. It became a "Blue Ribbon School" because of its Exemplary Patriot Award Program.

> The award is based on (1) Academics, (2) Co-curricular Activities, (3) Athletics, (4) School Service and Leadership, and (5) Effort and Citizenship. The Patriot Program reflects a holistic view of the person and presents the students with the motivating challenge of striving to achieve the goals set out by the school in order to become responsible and well-rounded individuals. The school has prepared "A Guide for Earning the Exemplary Patriot Award" which defines in clear terms the character expectations and qualities needed in order to win the award. Specifically students are asked to be honest, responsible, respectful, dedicated, persevering, self-respecting, and concerned for others.

The effectiveness of the Exemplary Patriot Award Program was evaluated after five years of implementation. The program was found to be effective in developing a positive, purposeful school climate. Evaluators observed several key outcome variables. Specifically, scores on achievement tests improved and the number of students on the honor roll grew; daily attendance to school improved and incidence of school vandalism became none existent; and the number of students who participated in school extracurricular activities increased greatly (Sparks, 1991).

A visit to the school by the author also verified the effectiveness of this program. In fact, the Patriot's Award Program was seen as so effective that when the principal, Dr. Richard Sparks, moved into the district offices, other schools in the district were also encouraged to implement their own version of the award program. Mountain View School, also in Fresno, implemented the *Exemplary Bear Award;* and other schools are also beginning award programs.

Oakbrook School in suburban Laden, South Carolina, is a very large diverse pre-K–5 grade school that has also developed a good citizenship award program:

> Through a grant, the guidance program at Oakbrook has been coordinated with the citizenship program. A good citizen selected weekly from each homeroom is recognized in the newsletter and in the in-house TV broadcast, and receives a ribbon and a pizza coupon. Each month there is a special focus on topics such as: responsibility, respect for authority, decision making, good manners, and conflict resolution skills. The "Red Carpet" is given by the principal to the class with exceptional citizenship.

Most of Oakbrook's students come from middle-income families; however, 25 percent are from a lower socioeconomic background. Sixteen percent of the student body is comprised of minority students.

Kohn (1993) questions the use of good citizenship awards although he admits that they are common across the country. "Sometimes rewards are used in the hope of promoting undeniably worthy qualities such as generosity and concern for others. The evidence, however, shows that anyone who is rewarded for acts of generosity will be less likely to think of himself as a caring or altruistic person; he will attribute his behavior to the reward instead," (p. 173). The Blue Ribbon Schools would not agree with Kohn in this area. Although they would concur with him that "good values have to be grown from the inside out and that no behavioral manipulation ever helped a child develop a commitment to becoming a caring and responsible person," (p. 161) they would tell him that good citizenship awards are important because they teach specific character values to students, and the awards are open to all students who so manifest these values. By encouraging self-discipline these awards help students to develop control over their own life and help them to make judgments about what constitutes good behavior.

CIVIC ACHIEVEMENT AWARD PROGRAM

The Civic Achievement Award Program (CAAP), found in several of the Blue Ribbon middle schools, is a citizenship education initiative established by the U.S. Congress that provides students with the knowledge and skills necessary to become responsible citizens (Dolenga, 1990). The program, which is now fully funded by Burger King Corporation, targets fifth- through ninth-graders, because these are crucial years for inculcating the basic concepts and values that support

American pluralistic democracy. For information, contact the Civic Achievement Award Program, 1235 Jefferson Davis Highway, Arlington, VA 22202, Telephone (800) 356–5136.

The Moriches Elementary School in Moriches, New York is committed to "developing individuals who can adapt to our changing world." Moriches is a very large first- to fifth-grade school with almost one thousand culturally, racially, and economically diverse students. Thirty-six percent of the students are from low-income families; and the linguistically diverse students represent seven different languages. Moriches has a very large student transience rate of 25 percent so it is important that students quickly learn about the citizenship qualities the school seeks to promote in them:

> All students in the school understand the responsibilities of being a good citizen. Through citizenship awards and special awards given at monthly assemblies, students are recognized for their outstanding efforts. A bulletin board in the lobby lists the citizens of the month and special award winners. Democratic values are communicated to our students through mock elections, Student Council elections, and a lottery system for selection in school clubs. Elected student council representatives are given a forum for input on policies and procedures.

Almost all of the Blue Ribbon Schools report that their students are recognized for good citizenship and behavior through schoolwide recognition programs and assemblies. These different awards are described in chapter 6 on Motivation.

Giraffes

The fifth grade class at the Henry W. Allen Fundamental Elementary School in New Orleans, Louisiana uses the Giraffe Project, *Standing Tall* to promote good citizenship and character. This curriculum introduces students to "Giraffes"—real-life heroes, men, women, and children worthy of admiration. *Standing Tall* helps students distinguish media celebrity from lasting contributions, one time acts of heroism from the perseverance necessary to achieve long term results, selfishness from selflessness and the generosity to work for the common good. It helps students see service to others and to their communities as an integral part of their plans for a meaningful life. The purpose of the curriculum is to get students to stick their necks out for others by teaching about courage, compassion, and personal involvement in the community-at-large. The basis of the program is a story bank of hundreds of real life heroes whose lives show kids what they too can do. By the end of the curriculum, the class is in action, doing a service project they design to address a public problem that concerns them. Henry W. Allen Fundamental Elementary School is a large urban PreK–6 grade school; 98 percent African American and 85 percent low income. For more information on the Giraffe Curriculum contact The Giraffe Project, P.O. Box 759, Langley, WA 98260, Telephone (360) 221-7989, www.giraffe.org/giraffe.

Leadership Training

Programs to promote leadership are found in the Blue Ribbon Schools; and even more so in this second edition research of the latest winning schools. The CLASS Program, "Community Leadership Activities for Students" is one popular leadership program; another is the STOP Program (Students Thinking of Others and Peers) found in the Plano School District and other schools. The STOP program allows students to develop leadership qualities by encouraging them to think of others and to think about the consequences of their own actions. This extracurricular program permits all interested children to receive training in developing skills for responsible decision making and resisting peer pressure. One strategy teaches students the importance of being a responsible leader by developing their sensitivity to the new and lonely student. The counselor appoints STOP students to be "pals" or buddy partners with new students or students needing special friends. These students take them to class and lunch, call them to offer help with any assignments, buddy with them at recess, and just let them know that they have a "pal" to help them with problems and events. This program is also aimed at helping children build self-esteem and keep themselves drug free. Students in this peer support program learn and model ethical decision making in skits at student assemblies. STOP members also fill Christmas baskets, package groceries and give toys and the like to less fortunate families.

At the Westwood Elementary School in Santa Clara, California, students are expected to be leaders, acting as tutors, peer coaches, and problem solvers. The student body is ethnically, economically, linguistically, and religiously diverse, and students are taught to accept others and help others. Character education is a thread that runs throughout their curriculum, integrated within each subject matter, and taught at appropriate "teachable moments." Class meetings are held regularly by teachers to discuss school, class, and personal issues. Students are thereby given the opportunity to apply their character lessons by solving school problems and by getting involved in service to others as tutors, coaches, or conflict mediators.

The PLUS program (Peers Leading to Ultimate Success) is found at the Mount View Elementary School in Virginia. Mount View is a large K–6 school with a homogeneous population of white, largely middle-class students. The goal of the school is to "develop ethical standards of behavior in order for students to participate in society as responsible family members and citizens." Students are taught by trained high school students who introduce them to the wider world that the students will enter after elementary school. The lesson plans include an introduction to making course choices in high school, extracurricular options open to students, tips on how to make good decisions, and an explanation of the different ways in which older students communicate, cooperate, resolve feelings, and form friendships. All of these goals are approached in interesting and creative ways. This program helps develop peer leadership and provide young students with appropriate older role models.

Seven Habits

Pond Springs Elementary School in Austin, Texas, uses another innovative program with their fourth- and fifth-graders—Student Leadership Training (SLT). SLT builds around *The Seven Habits of Highly Effective People* written by Stephen Covey, but the "habits" have been modified to fit young learners' needs. The program has two week-long segments, one in the fall and one in the spring. Students name persons they perceive as leaders and leadership qualities to begin the "adventure." After a large group activity introduces the day's objective, students divide into four small groups to do the hands-on, cooperative group activities. Then the students return to the large group for a closure activity. By the end of the first week, students know an effective leader: "walks his talk, begins with the end in mind, is proactive and does the right thing." Students learn "beginning with the end in mind" means they must set personal goals. The fifth day is devoted to making yearly goals that are included in the parent/teacher/student goal setting conferences.

The spring session has students tell how they have used the SLT learning and how it impacted their lives. The spring week's objectives finish teaching the seven habits: "think win/win, applaud others, seek first to understand and then be understood and work productively in a group." The week concludes with a graduation ceremony. Parents are invited and community leaders make short speeches focusing on the leadership qualities sought for business and community leaders. Response to this program from parents and students as been overwhelming finding it "exciting and innovative." Pond Spring is a very diverse K–5 school: 10 percent Asian, 6 percent African American, and 8 percent Hispanic. The common language helps unite the students in the pursuit of a common goal. Other Blue Ribbon Schools promote leadership using Sean Covey's *The Seven Habits of Highly Effective Teens* and 2001 Blue Ribbon Schools cite using *The Seven Habits for Highly Effective Teachers.*

Patrols

Participation in patrols helps develop good citizenship in students by providing them with the experience of fulfilling a role within a group and serving as role models to others. The Safety Patrol at Anna Reynolds School in Newington, Connecticut, is made up of students in grade five and gives them an opportunity to learn self-discipline and control while helping them to discipline and work with primary students. Safety Patrols help reinforce school safety rules and good behavior before and after school.

Scouts

Scouting per se was mentioned in a very small percentage of the schools' applications as one of the programs that contributes to the promotion of character at the school because these organizations are not sponsored by the schools. However, visits to the Blue Ribbon Schools confirmed the fact that almost all of the schools do have Scouting activities available for the students and allow the organization to use their facilities. The Scouting program is one that does, at least in its stated aims, foster good character, and good citizenship in students because of the character-related criteria that it sets for each member:

The Boy Scout Law

A scout is:
trustworthy
helpful
friendly
courteous
kind
obedient
cheerful
thrifty
brave
clean
reverent.

St. John Bosco is a Catholic, K–8 school of almost eight hundred homogeneous middle-class students in suburban Parma Heights, Ohio. Sister Gretchen, the principal, feels that the Scouting troop provides an outlet for students to interact with adult leaders on camping trips, at meetings, and at outdoor events and provides these students with many opportunities for service to the community.

Sister Schools

Anna Reynolds School in Connecticut has a unique "Sister School Program" that pairs classes from its school with classes from an urban school. Teachers plan joint educational opportunities that allow students from the two communities to work and learn together. Classes from each school send letters, cards, and artwork to each other and visit each others' schools for picnics and other activities. This creates a climate that affirms diversity through personal contact and prepares students to live productively and harmoniously in a society that is culturally diverse.

Programs like these have been shown by research to enhance caring values, attitudes, and behaviors. They do so by providing students with opportunities to discuss caring, to demonstrate caring to others, and to participate thoughtfully in caring relations (Bosworth, 1995).

Student Council

One of the most common ways for Blue Ribbon Schools to involve students actively in practicing decision-making skills is to promote their participation in Student Council. At the Argonaut Elementary School in Saratoga, California, students are given an opportunity to influence classroom and school policy:

> We instill character and ethics traits through student council meetings that include school officers and two representatives from each class. Student opinions and concerns on timely issues are solicited by the class representatives who then present them during their student council meetings. The council then discusses these issues and makes recommendations to the school faculty, School Site Council, or other appropriate groups.

Sheri Hitching, principal of Argonaut School, explains that their citizenship and character-building programs immerse students in decision making. Students have many opportunities to be involved with democratic values and ethics, particularly in learning respect for one another and reflecting on individual responsibility.

Cadwallader Elementary School in San Jose, California, ensures that their students feel a commitment to the school by providing many opportunities for them to influence school policies and activities; one avenue is the Student Council. The Student Council voted to adopt two city blocks around the school. They were then responsible for picking up litter and keeping the surrounding community clean. Students also bring concerns and suggestions to the Student Council. For example, the Student Council received a complaint about misbehavior in the restrooms. The Student Council recommended that the restrooms be locked should this occur in the future. Based on this recommendation, offered by the students themselves, the problems in the restroom ended. Cadwallader is a PreK–6 urban school with a unique student body; one third of them are at poverty level and one-third of them qualify for special education services.

Student Suggestion Box

Students at Crest Hill School in Casper, Wyoming, know that the principal seriously studies the suggestions they put into the "Student Suggestion Box." They look forward to the biweekly assemblies with the principal when the suggestions are read to the whole school. Students know that their suggestions are taken seriously, studied, reported on, and are a vital part of the school, for they have seen how their suggestions have been implemented, even changing school policies. They have new lunch menu selections now, a Chess Club has been added, safety has been addressed on the parking lot, and there are grade-level dances.

The teachers at Baker's Chapel Elementary School in Greenville, South Carolina, believe that students should have some decision-making power in their own lives in order to teach them the democratic way of life and prepare them for later life. Half of Baker's Chapel students are African American and half of the students are from low-income families. Most of these parents have never completed high school. In the past few years, Baker's Chapel has transformed its poor image from that of a dull, mediocre, low-achieving school, to that of an award winning school where its large population of at-risk students achieve and excell:

> The classroom itself is the best place for students and teachers to get involved in activities that promote good citizenship, community service, and personal responsibility. Here there are thought-provoking discussions of current events which involve valuing, training in animal care, making Christmas cards for crippled children, gathering petitions to send to the principal, and practicing democratic practices in cooperative learning groups.

Tutoring Programs

One of the key goals of the Child Development program used in the San Ramon, California, schools is to "create a caring community within the classroom" (Kohn, 1990). Several of the San Ramon schools have won the Blue Ribbon Award. One of them is the Country Club Elementary School. It reports on the success of their tutoring program: "Our kindergarten read-aloud program utilizes upper grade level students who read to the young students. This promotes an interest in the kindergarten students to read, while the older students vie for the privilege of reading. Our older and younger students tell use they like this program."

CARING BEYOND THE CLASSROOM

The Value of Caring for Others

Research has found that an intensive experience in caring for others may have a profound effect on young people:

> There are many possible ways for young people to become involved in the community in a meaningful and contributory role: working with senior citizens, caring for and tutoring younger children, working in service-learning placements in health and community programs, and taking part in other types of volunteer activity. Those young people who have opportunities to care for others in such programs have been found to show an increased sense of social responsibility, a higher level of self-esteem, and better school attendance (Chaskin, 1995).

CARE Programs

Some Blue Ribbon School programs that promote character by giving opportunities to students to care for others are called CARE Programs with differing words for the anachronism: Citizenship, Achievement, Responsibility, and Education or Cooperation, Appreciation, Responsibility, (Respect), Effort, and Sharing. These programs promote social and emotional well-being, kindness, and helpfulness. The "KIDS" Program at Pioneer Elementary School in Colorado Springs, stands for "Kids involved in Doing Service." Students take their gifts and talent beyond the school walls into the community. Some of the KIDS projects include performing for convalescent homes, cleaning up the community, sharing with students at the deaf and blind school, food and clothing drives, recycling paper, and Thanksgiving food baskets. Pioneer is a very large school with a diverse student body of 688: 7 percent Hispanic, 5 percent African American, and 3 percent Asian students.

Community Service Projects

Community service projects undertaken by schools help students realize that character education includes service to others. These projects build self-worth and allow students to experience themselves as part of the larger network of people who are helping to create a better world (Berman, 1990). Some Blue Ribbon Schools stated that a measure of the success of their character development programs is the service activities in which their students engage and the percentage of the total school body who participate.

Fund-Raisers and Drives for Others

Among the student community service projects are the typical drives, bike-a-thons and jog-a-thons to raise money for medical research on cancer, diabetes, cystic fibrosis, or bone marrow; and to support an overseas child through UNICEF. At the Dennis Elementary School in Oklahoma City, students help to meet community needs, for example, by buying a new animal for the zoo. Its "Adopt a Family Program" enabled a class to provide food and clothing for a family in need either at a holiday or after a disaster such as a hurricane, earthquake, or drought. Dennis is a very large K–6 school with a homogeneous, middle-class student body.

At two schools in Louisiana, the Weaver and Rilliewux Schools, the students participate in community service such as caroling, making centerpieces for the nursing home, or sponsoring an Easter egg hunt for younger children. Both of these schools are very large urban schools with very diverse student bodies of 50 percent African American and 50 percent Caucasian and/or Hispanic students. These schools are in tune with the events of the times; they sponsored Earth Day, Environmental Awareness events, litter-control patrols, recycling drives, Heart Smart, the Smokey the Bear program, Statue of Liberty Renovation drives, and nutrition/safety awareness events.

Helping Hands

"Helping Hands" is a community service project found at several schools that fosters the habit of giving of oneself for the benefit of others. Indian Trail School is a primary K–3 school with a diverse student body of 341 from suburban Highland Park, Illinois. It believes that an essential aspect in the development of character is the idea of service. Its slogan is "Just Say Yes"—to friendship, senior citizens, food drives. This school believes that service in the classroom leads to service in the community. The students love to participate in service opportunities at the school.

At the Weedsport School in New York the philosophy is: "We will place more stress in the area of character development by involving students in community projects than by writing a character development curriculum. Teachers feel that children who are already very positive and caring may benefit more from the school community if they are encouraged to become active with senior citizens and handicapped in the community." Weedsport is a K–6 school located in rural Weedsport, New York. The school lacks ethnic diversity, but has students from diverse socioeconomic backgrounds; 17 percent are from low-income families and the majority of the others are from lower-middle class families.

Sister Mary Carol Gentile, the principal at St. Rocco School, in Johnston, Rhode Island, explains how "Community service gives students a chance to demonstrate social and civic responsibility, increase service skills, and act ethically in service settings. Our community service is making a difference through actions of caring, and by extending compassion to many in need."

Kathleen Gannon-Briggs, the principal at St. Isidore School in Danville, California, has made a schoolwide commitment to the development of character, values, and ethics.

> Students are encouraged to become responsible, caring citizens by getting personally involved with charitable efforts. Activities include monthly visits to a local convalescent home, coordinating "care packages" to sister schools in need (both in our country and one in Central America), outreach efforts in face of natural disasters, clothing drives for the poor, removal of litter from local neighborhoods near our school, and fund-raising for the homeless. We also have "service hour" requirements whereby students in the fifth through eighth grade must volunteer at least twenty hours of human service work each year.

St. Isidore is a Catholic, K–8 suburban school with a homogeneous student population.

Service Learning

Research for this second edition finds more and more Blue Ribbon Schools involved in service learning. This reflects the national trend that shows a great increase in service learning in the last decade. According to a report issued by the National Center for Educational Statistics, by 1999, 64 percent of all public schools had an organized form of community service for their students, half of them providing this through service learning (Billig, 2000). Service learning is a way of teaching and learning that engages students in active service to the community tied to the curriculum. Service learning fosters civic responsibility; it actively engages students as citizens; they are expected to solve authentic community problems; they use the subjects they are studying to help research solutions (Kielsmeier, 2000). Research on the effectiveness of service learning has mostly been evaluation studies of programs implemented. Nevertheless, the results show a positive effect on student personal, social, and interpersonal development, and help to develop students' civic and social responsibility, citizenship skills, and academic skills and knowledge (Billig, 2000).

El Marino Language School in Culver City, California, has a Service Learning Program which they call KidsCare. This service learning program connects students to the realities of local problems and needs, and is an integral part of their academic curriculum. EM students, parents, and teachers work in partnership with community members representing government, private, and non-profit agencies. The Service Learning Program is cross-curricular and involves hands-on, participatory experiences. Children participate in activities that contribute to the well-being of the community; they understand the importance of caring for the environment and helping those less fortunate through service learning. Because their emotional growth and self-esteem development are such important goals of the program, their individual responses are a critical part of each unit's pre- and post- evaluations.

The principal, Theresa Delgado, explains the program:

> The Service Learning Program involves all students, but is concentrated at three levels. As an extension of the social studies curriculum study of home and the community, second graders research the impact of homelessness and collect food and clothing for People Assisting the Homeless (PATH), a local community program. They learn compassion, appreciation of differences, and their responsibility to others.
>
> In the upper grades Service Learning is an integral part of the science curriculum. As a culmination of their study of underwater habitats and fauna, fourth graders participate in a major ecology unit, involving literature, art, and math skills, in addition to scientific methodology. They explore the fragility of the ecosystem by raising trout from embryos, and ultimately discharging them into Piru Creek and the San Gabriel River to help replenish and restore the natural balance.

El Marino Language School in Culver City, California, is a PreK–5 grade school of 647 very diverse students: 22 percent Asian, 9 percent African American, 26 percent Hispanic: almost one-fifth of whom are at poverty level.

Service Projects by Year

Sunset Elementary School in Miami, Florida, a PreK–5th grade school in Dade County, is a mini United Nations with a student body, 46 percent Caucasian, 32 percent Hispanic, and 21 percent African American, one-fifth of whom qualify for free lunch. Sunset is a Magnet School with international studies emphasizing foreign language instruction and a program called Global Tech 2007. This program studies pressing global issues and stresses community involvement as well as community service. Learning about these areas requires extensive research and the use of cooperative learning in a variety of settings. It also requires the use of materials and resources beyond the textbook and traditional classroom instructions. The ultimate goal of this endeavor is working and forming alliances with global counterparts. Another unique feature for Global Tech 2007 is its organization. The themes stay the same, allowing all students to participate in each thematic area of study as they progress through grade levels. Each year the child advances to a more in depth area of study addressing global and local concerns. Each grade level, across all four programs, also works as a team to develop one community service project. The following are each grade-level's themes, slogans, and service projects:

Table 12.   Service Projects by Years

Grade	Slogan	Theme	Service Project
Pk–K	"Helping Hands"	World Hunger	1) Clothing drive for refugee children 2) Making peanut butter and jelly sandwiches and soup for homeless
1st Grade	"World Travelers"	Families Around the World	1) Providing food and clothing to needy families 2) Preparing a video and brochure of family, family traditions, sharing in schools
2nd Grade	"Earth Patrol"	Environmental Issues	1) Fund raising for Miami to purchase rainforest acres 2) Creating learning/study area gardens on school grounds
3rd Grade	"Inventors'"	Inventions	1) Fund raising for lollipop sales for Miami Museum of Science 2) Sending third graders from an inner city school to the Museum of Science
4th Grade	"Health Crusaders"	Health Issues	1) Creating care packages for children in a pediatric wing at Miami Children's Hospital 2) Holding a "Health Summit" at a local hospital; Sending health and personal hygiene packages to children in Haiti
5th Grade	"Space Explorers"	Space	1) Fund raising to assist in the maintenance of a sister school's own planetarium

GLOBAL CONCERNS

From the very beginning of the award program, Blue Ribbon Schools showed that they were aware of global concerns. Reading the award applications from several years provides a review of recent global history. In 1984–1985, students gave to the Red Cross Drives for the starving children in Ethiopia, in 1989–1990 it was for the earthquake victims in Mexico, in 1993–1994 the concern was for those in India, and in 1996–1997 it was the children in Bosnia. Starting in 1991–1992 a specific question was added to the award application: *"How is your school preparing students to live effectively in a society that is culturally and ethnically diverse and an economy that is globally competitive?* In the answer to this question, many Blue Ribbon Schools also mentioned how learning to live with those who were culturally and ethnically diverse also helped to promote character.

Celebrating Cultural and Ethnic Diversity

Country Club School in San Ramon, California, hosts many events and celebrations that emphasize cultural and ethnic diversity. They include United Nations Day, Heritage Days, Mardi Gras, Bastille Day, Chanukah, Christmas, and Cinco de Mayo. Some private schools add to their celebration list their cultural religious holidays, such as St. Joseph's Day, St. Patrick's Day, and La Posada. For example:

> While the activities of the school are strictly secular, Laurel Mountain Elementary School in Austin, Texas, recognizes the contribution of the United States' diverse religious heritages to formulating a sound character, ethical behavior, and self-discipline. Parents assist teachers in helping children learn cultural songs for the music programs. Rabbis and ministers are invited in to discuss specific customs and traditions with students.

Laurel is a large suburban school with a heterogeneous school population with 5 percent Asian, 6 percent Hispanic, and 3 percent African American students.

Schools are making efforts to allow students to experience diversity in their day-to-day living by seeking to employ staff and faculty that represent diverse groups. Westwood School in Santa Clara has a principal from a minority background, a music teacher from Russia, an art teacher from France, a science aide from Africa and custodians from Portugal. In addition, the school tries to host guest speakers from various backgrounds and cultures. The Lowell School in Idaho has had assemblies with Native American dancers, a Japanese folktale performer, an Australian storyteller, Japanese students, and a parent from Norway — all of whom share their culture with the students.

Multicultural Studies

Respect for differences is emphasized throughout the curriculum at the Blue Ribbon Schools, both in the cultural studies in the classroom and through art, music, sports, and school celebrations. More and more schools are offering instruction in foreign languages at the elementary and middle school level. There is an emphasis on using multicultural literature, such as that found in the Heartwood Curriculum to teach character values such as respect and understanding of others. The literature-based Heartwood Curriculum allows teachers to integrate social studies, language arts, reading, music, and art. Flags of each country are displayed as part of the curriculum, and students learn to sing songs in different languages. For more information on the Heartwood Curriculum see chapter 3.

Moorestown Friends School in New Jersey, with its very diverse student population, tries to teach an appreciation of cultures and share this appreciation on a very personal level. The students are involved in service projects that tie into and support other cultures.

> Many Moorestown students come to school from families that instill sound values regarding the importance of cultures. Moorestown teachers also understand the necessity of teaching students to be responsible, global citizens and give them many opportunities to enhance their behavior and attitude toward becoming thoughtful citizens. Students are specifically taught about cultures and ethics in social studies, music, and library classes. Foreign language classes are also offered.

In the past few award winning years, schools documented their progress in developing technological skills in students. Schools use internet and e-mail capabilities to connect students in American schools with students from other countries. Computer programs that help to develop students' appreciation for other cultures and societies include The Voyage of the Mimi, Mayan Quest and Where in the World is Carmen Sandiego? Other computer programs encourage students to analyze situations, determine goals, consider options, make decisions, and examine consequences. Some programs mentioned include the Oregon Trail and the Decisions, Decisions series from Tom Synder Publications; for example, Decisions, Decisions: The Environment and Decisions: Lying Cheating and Stealing. These interactive programs allow students to work together on the computer to deal with real life situations and to solve problems.

Social Justice

St. Elizabeth School in Kansas City, Missouri, uses a social justice curriculum to help students problem solve the moral dilemmas in our world. The curriculum is designed on a three-year cycle and covers topics such as democratic justice, economic justice, world peace, equality, prejudice, and environmental issues. The students are very active in the learning process; they are expected to conduct extensive research outside of class. Students work individually as well as in groups. They exhibit what they have learned through presentations, writing assignments, discussion, and action. A teacher tells about a particularly poignant and powerful lesson in the study of the disparity of economic justice in our country.

The students were first given occupations and salaries and asked to create a budget based on their individual salaries. Then focusing on living a life of poverty, they were given a poverty level income and asked to redo their original budgets. It did not take long for students to see just how impossible it is to survive on such a low income. Student were then given a two week period during which they were to go to the grocery store and "purchase" enough items for a month spending no more than $160.00. Discussion ensued in the classroom about the reality of a life lived in poverty.

St. Elizabeth School is a PreK–8 grade Catholic school of 478 students; mostly an Irish American population with 6 percent Hispanic, and 4 percent African American.

EVALUATION OF THE
EFFECTIVENESS OF CITIZENSHIP PROGRAMS

The focus on citizenship and character seems to be paying off. Many of the schools featured in this chapter report that they are spending less time on discipline and behavior problems and more time on helping children learn (National Association of Elementary School Principals, 1995).

Joyce Westgate, the principal at Ben Franklin School in Binghamton, New York, reports that: "We have experienced fewer behavior problems, a kinder atmosphere, and observable positive actions that support exemplary citizenship as a result of our attention to building better habits of character. The best lessons of citizenship, however, are received through living in a caring, nurturing community where all concerned demonstrate good character every day."

Schools have a special and historic responsibility for the development of competent and responsible citizens and the Blue Ribbon Schools show that they are seeking to meet that responsibility by forming good character in America's future citizens. They do this by developing good citizenship in them.

SUMMARY

This chapter reports on the different ways in which the Blue Ribbon Schools promote the character of their students through their citizenship programs. A character-building citizenship program emphasizes the development of specific "democratic" qualities such as justice, respect, fairness, cooperation, persistence, moral responsibility, empathy, and caring. In order to develop these virtues, schools have given students opportunities in the classroom to practice actions of caring, concern for others, generosity, and kindness. Evaluations of these activities in the Blue Ribbon Schools and in other schools that have also implemented these programs have shown them to be effective in helping students develop their character and thereby act as good citizens.

9

Evaluating the Effectiveness of Character Education in the Blue Ribbon Schools

What people say you cannot do, you try and find that you can.
— Henry David Thoreau

The possibility that we may fail in the struggle ought not to deter us from the support of a cause we believe to be just.
— Abraham Lincoln

A ship is safe at shore, but that is not where a ship is meant to be.
We cannot discover new oceans unless we have the courage to lose sight of the shore.
— Anonymous

EVALUATING THESE RESEARCH FINDINGS

Aristotle begins the *Nicomachean Ethics* by explaining that "every inquiry, every action and pursuit, is thought to aim at some good; this is the end to which all things tend. Although it is good to attain the end for one person, it is finer still to attain it for a nation. Happiness is the end and goal of all human beings; and one who lives a life of virtue, the good life, is happy." (*Nicomachean Ethics*, 1094a1–5.)

This book can be seen as a compendium of moral and character education programs found within schools selected as among the best in the United States. It shows how these programs help students attain their ends, to develop their characters, to learn to live lives of virtue. However, as pointed out earlier, the presence of a particular character education program in a Blue Ribbon School does not necessarily mean that the specific program is also one of the best in the country. In each chapter, available research has been cited to help the reader evaluate the character education program for its effectiveness and desirability as a component of a comprehensive, schoolwide approach to character education.

This chapter addresses the importance of evaluating character education programs in order to assess whether or not they are achieving their end. It reports on the few programs that have been evaluated and gives readers guidelines on how they might go about evaluating the effectiveness of character education programs implemented in their own schools. It seeks to answer the following questions:

- How are schools' applications evaluated in selecting Blue Ribbon winners?
- Must schools have an effective character education program in order to be named Blue Ribbon Schools?
- How should a researcher or school set up an evaluation study of a character education program?
- What programs have been found to be effective in promoting character development? How do we know that they work?
- What key components can be extracted from the many programs cited in this book that have been found to be effective in promoting character in students?

THE BLUE RIBBON SCHOOL EVALUATION PROCESS

All of the Blue Ribbon Schools, through the selection and review process, were judged to be educating their students effectively, striving to strengthen subject matter content in English, mathematics, science, history, geography, art, and foreign languages, while using instructional techniques that motivate students to learn and study. These schools have environments that support and recognize excellent teaching, involve the parents and the community in the education of children and prepare the students to live effectively in a global world. These schools are safe and free from drugs, have a climate conducive to learning, and foster the development of sound character in their students. They had to show that they were meeting these goals in order to be named as worthy of National Recognition as Exemplary Schools. They were evaluated at several different stages of the application process before they received the Blue Ribbon Award.

A school's completion of all of the required parts of the application to the Department of Education's School Recognition Program is the first step in the selection process. These applications are then sent to the Chief State School Officers who review them and choose the schools from their state to nominate for consideration at the national level. These nominations are then reviewed by a National Review Panel that selects schools to recommend for site visits. Two-day visits are conducted to each school so chosen. (I participated as a U.S. Department of Education site visitor to two of the schools that had applied for Blue Ribbon Recognition). The responsibility of the site visitor is to verify that what the application reports is indeed happening in the school. The site visit is the qualitative evaluation of the school's application. The site visit reports are then forwarded to the Review Panel, which meets a second time to review all of the schools who have received site visits. The Panel then selects the final group of schools for recognition by the Secretary of Education. (As an illustration, in 1998–1999, 407 were nominated to the program, 273 schools were chosen for site visits, and 266 of these schools were chosen as Exemplary Schools.)

The National School Recognition Program uses an "expertise- oriented evaluation approach," that depends primarily upon professional expertise to judge an educational institution, program, product, or activity (Worthen and Sanders, 1987). Using a very specific checklist, in conjunction with observations, document analysis, and interviews, the site visitors gather information on school leadership, teaching environment, curriculum and instruction, student environment, parental and community support, success indicators, and organizational vitality. They then judge the school's application as accurate, understated, or overstated in each of these categories as meeting the criteria for recognition delineated in the program guidelines. To be given special honors in a particular area, the applications and site visits of the Blue Ribbon awardees are reviewed once again by a different panel of experts in the area. For example, in order to be given the "special honors in character education" recognition in 1998–1999, the fifty Blue Ribbon Schools that had applied for the special honor were reviewed by staff members from the Character Education Partnership. Five schools were chosen as having exemplary programs of character education.

In order to be nominated for Blue Ribbon recognition, all schools must show evidence that its policies, programs, and practices foster the development of sound character, a sense of self-worth, democratic values, ethical judgment, and self-discipline. The Blue Ribbon Schools do *not* have to have an explicit character education or moral education program in place in order to be chosen. However, they do have to show that the school programs and policies in general, whether or not they are called "character education," foster the development of sound character and good discipline and promote a safe, drug-free environment in which students are motivated to learn and prepare themselves to become participating citizens in our diverse global society. The many character-building ideas found in these schools contributed to the formulation of the Blue Ribbon Schools' Comprehensive Model of Character Development discussed in chapter 1.

AN EVALUATION MODEL FOR
CHARACTER EDUCATION PROGRAMS

How effective are the character education program(s) that the Blue Ribbon Schools have identified? If the current revival of character education is to succeed, it will have to successfully address the question of assessment of program effectiveness (Leming, 1993a). Ralph Tyler (1949), considered by many as the founder of curriculum evaluation, defined evaluation as "essentially the process of determining the extent to which the educational objectives of a school program or curriculum are actually being realized (p. 105)." *Evaluation,* according to Webster's dictionary, means "to determine the worth of or to ascertain the value of, to appraise." By evaluating character education, we are attempting to ascertain the value of these programs or efforts. In order to assess their effectiveness in the Blue Ribbon Schools, we have to know what objectives schools hope to meet by implementing these educational programs. Tyler's evaluation model consists of the following steps:

1. Establish broad goals or objectives
2. Classify the goals or objectives
3. Define objectives in behavioral terms
4. Find situations in which achievement of objectives can be shown
5. Develop or select measurement techniques
6. Collect performance data
7. Compare performance data with behaviorally stated objectives

It can be used as a basic model of evaluation upon which an evaluation of a character education program can be built.

In order to "establish," "classify," and "define" our objectives—Tyler's first three steps—a review of the character education paradigm presented in chapter 1 may be helpful. If we understand "good character" as the intersection of moral knowing, moral feeling, and moral action, we will want to see (1) how well students have met the objective of "knowing" particular good actions that they should do; (2) how well have they grown in their attitude formation so that they "want and will" to do the good; and (3) to what extent they actually "do" acts of good character. It is important to reach agreement about the primary objectives of the school's character education initiative in each of the three domains. Then the evaluation can be planned, choosing measures that match the aims of the program initiative. Marvin Berkowitz (1998) has developed a "Taxonomy of Character Education Types" which was adapted from the Character Education Partnership's survey of teacher preparation institutions. It serves both as a summary of the many types of character education programs found in the Blue Ribbon Schools and as a nice tool for choosing the primary objectives of a particular character education program.

Table 13.   Taxonomy of Character Education Types

Moral Reasoning/Cognitive Development

Discussion of moral dilemmas facilitates student development of moral reasoning capacities

Moral Education/Virtue

Academic content (literature, history) used to teach about moral traditions in order to facilitate moral habits and internal moral qualities (virtues)

Life Skills Education

Practical skills (communication and positive social attitudes [self-esteem] stressed)

Service Learning

"Hands-on" experiences of community service integrated into curriculum

Citizenship Training/Civics Education

American civic values taught as a preparation for future citizenship

Caring Community

Caring relationships fostered in the classroom and school

Health Education/Drug, Pregnancy and Violence Prevention

Program-oriented approach used to prevent unhealthy/anti-social behaviors

Conflict Resolution/Peer Mediation

Students trained to mediate peer conflicts as a means of developing constructive conflict resolution skills

Ethics/Moral Philosophy

Ethics or moral philosophy explicitly taught

Religious Education

Character education taught in the context of a faith tradition justifying morality from a transcendent source.

Adapted from CEP survey of teacher preparation institutions.
This list is not intended to be exhaustive. It is intended to provide examples of the various activities sometimes considered under the general term "character education."
Taken from *A Primer for Evaluating A Character Education Initiative* by Marvin Berkowitz, Ph.D., Character Education Partnership, 1998.
Used with permission.

Moral knowledge is perhaps the easiest to evaluate. Moral knowledge includes knowing *that* certain things are right and others wrong and understanding *why* certain behaviors are right and others wrong (moral reasoning). The measurement of moral reasoning by Kohlberg and his followers has yielded innumerable studies showing that it is possible to raise a student's moral reasoning one-fourth to one-half of a stage when students are involved in the process of discussing moral dilemmas (Leming, 1993b). However, because none of the moral dilemma studies included any form of behavior as a dependent variable, such studies can only be said to assess one aspect of character—namely, moral knowing—rather than full character development. Moral knowledge also includes knowing specific virtues or character traits, what they mean and what actions would show that you are living them. Virtues need to be operationalized so that behavioral indicators can be counted or rated (Vessells, 1998). Various test formats (i.e., true-false, short-answer, multiple choice) can be used to assess students' knowledge of the definitions of virtues and their recognition of situations that call into play the living of these virtues. These tests also can be used as both pre-test and post-test measures to assess growth in knowledge in these areas after completion of a character education unit or program. However, in practice, even elaborate programs of inculcating virtue do not ensure later virtuous conduct by all participants. That is why virtues should be applied as well as studied in schools giving students opportunities for displaying the desired character traits in good actions (Wynne, 1993).

Evaluation of moral feeling is more difficult for several reasons: the field is much newer; the psychometrics are less sophisticated, accurate, and reliable; and it is more difficult to measure beliefs, attitudes, and feelings. Evaluation of the emotional or attitudinal side of character often makes use of introspective questionnaires, self-report and projective measures such as sentence completion, picture interpretation, and rating scales. The validity and reliability of these measures is often not as great as for measures of moral knowing. In fact, one cannot reliably infer that internally good moral feelings and attitudes are necessarily behind observably "good" behavior, that is, one could be doing the action out of fear or punishment, for instance (Cline and Feldmesser, 1983).

Behavior is easier to measure than feelings, but in order to measure moral behavior programs, evaluators must agree concerning what behaviors show that students are living the specific character qualities that have been identified as important to the school implementing the character education program. Measurement of behaviors can be gathered through analysis of classroom conduct, (e.g., attendance and discipline referrals) and anecdotal evidence (e.g., observations of students during small or large group activities, teacher journals, or diaries). In addition, various survey instruments can be used to document behavior.

Tyler's fourth step requires "finding situations in which achievement of objectives can be shown." As this book demonstrates, there are different ways to understand what character is and there are different types of character education programs and/or initiatives that are considered as helping to develop character. It is critical to clearly identify which character component you are trying to address in your initiative so that you will know in what situation you can see the objective achieved. The more specifically and accurately you identify the intended results of your program, the more likely you will be to accurately assess its outcomes (Berkowitz, 1998). It is important to evaluate both the implementation of the program (process evaluation) as well as the final results or effects that are found after the program has been successfully implemented (outcome or product evaluation). (The reader may remember that some of the programs critiqued in this book, such as Magic Circles, and DUSO, have cited lack of successful implementation of the program as the reason for less than desirable results.)

INSTRUMENTS FOR EVALUATING CHARACTER

Continuing to the fifth step of the Tyler evaluation model outlined previously—when goals and objectives have been established, classified, and defined, and situations demonstrating achievement of character education objectives have been identified—measurement techniques must be developed or selected, and student performance data need to be collected. The data you choose to collect have to relate back to and match up with the goals and aims of the program.

Two approaches can be used to collect data for an evaluation of contemporary character education programs: informal and formal. Informal evaluation methods rely on qualitative data, that is, data gathered by the evaluator in the natural setting of the school by using unobtrusive, multiple data-gathering methods, such as participant observations and interviews (Worthen and Sanders, 1987). These generate data from anecdotal evidence, surveys of teachers, parents, and students, and highly subjective perceptions. Formal evaluation of character education programs uses quantitative data, that is, data gathered using standardized, objective, and reliable measurements, instruments, or tests, (i.e., both a pre-test and a post-test). It must also utilize proper experimental design, that is, compare character education program students to non-program students, and attempt to control for potential sources of bias (Leming, 1993a). A number of evaluators have argued that quantitative and qualitative approaches should be utilized jointly as the two strategies have complementary strengths. The Blue Ribbon Schools use the following survey instruments:

1. School Climate Survey is used at Black Bob Elementary School in Olathe, Kansas. This survey gives feedback on topics such as: academic programs, home-school communications, school facilities, student enthusiasm for learning, and parent involvement. Research for this second edition revealed that climate surveys are the most common instruments used for evaluation in the Blue Ribbon Schools.
2. Safe School Questionnaire (for adults) and Our Schools' Safety (Questionnaire for students) are used at both the Stockdale Elementary School in Bakersfield, California, and the Patterson Road School in Santa Maria, California. These instruments can be found in *Safe Schools: A Planning Guide for Action*, California Department of Education's Safe Schools and Violence Prevention Office, 1995, p 121–24.

3. School as a Caring Community Profile and the Eleven Principles Survey of Character Education Effectiveness have been developed by the Center for the 4th & 5th Rs at the State University of New York at Cortland, P.O. Box 2000, Cortland, NY 13045.

4. School Character Survey gives feedback that highlights the impact of the leadership and multi-faceted dimensions of the school that contribute to the development of a character-based school. It is available from Human Systems Development, 500 Evans Lane, Dayton, Ohio 45459, Telephone (513) 439-9315.

5. Character Education Components Survey from the School for Ethical Education is used at the Daisy Ingraham School in Westbook, CT. The school is working with Dr. David Wangaard to measure its students' ethical growth. The survey can be used to assess the design and implementation of a character education program. It can be obtained from the school for Ethical Education at 1000 Lafayette Blvd., Bridgeport, CT 06604.

6. "Hypothetical Scenarios" test measures students' responses to ethically based scenarios. It was developed by Stanley Weed of the Institute for Research & Evaluation, 6068 South Jordan Canal Road, Salt Lake City, UT 84118, Telephone (801) 966-5644.

7. Social Skills Rating System is a multi-source, multidimensional instrument of student social and academic functioning used by parents, teachers, and students to rate student behavior. It is available from the Northwest Foundation for Children. It quantifies students' social skills (cooperation, assertion, responsibility, empathy, and self-control), problem behaviors (externalizing problems, internalizing problems, and hyperactivity) and academic competence.

8. Student Survey—Motivation to Learn, Study Habits, Citizenship at School and Interactions with others have been developed by WickPartners, Inc. and are used at the Belmont Elementary School in Belmont, Michigan, to assess its Life Skills Character Education Program.

Formal evaluations are based on systematic efforts to define criteria and obtain accurate information about alternatives (Worthen and Sanders, 1989). It is very difficult to have a formal evaluation of a character education program with a true experimental design because of the subject matter: students in schools with many different teachers. Even when students are randomly assigned to experimental and control classes, the "control breaks down" as the year progresses, that is, students come in, leave, or are absent; teachers differ in their teaching techniques even when using the same curriculum, and so forth. Additionally, there is a consensus that because character develops incrementally over time, it is unrealistic to expect an evaluation of a program after one year to prove anything definitively. Evaluation of a character education program needs to have a longitudinal component.

Most evaluators would therefore agree with Cline and Feldmesser (1983) that the quasi-experimental design of Campbell and Stanley (1966) is the most effective for the evaluation of character education programs. A quasi-experimental design uses two basic strategies: the use of comparison groups and time-series analyses. Comparison groups are not strict "control groups" because it may not have been possible to assign the members randomly, or to control for newcomers or leavers. There may be other extraneous variables, such as, sex, race, age, and socioeconomic status, for which one cannot control. A school with limited funding cannot afford the cost of an experimental research evaluation with a control group. However, using the quasi-experimental design a school can gather data on its students before they begin the character education program and after they have experienced the program. This will be a valid evaluation. Time-series design means that measurements are taken before the program begins, during the program, and after the program ends. If both comparison groups and time-series can be combined in the same evaluation, the design is substantially strengthened and is the preferred design for the evaluation of character education programs (Cline and Feldmesser, 1983).

EVALUATION OF CHARACTER EDUCATION IN THE BLUE RIBBON SCHOOL APPLICATIONS

The final step in the Tyler model of evaluation is to "compare performance data with behaviorally stated objectives." Many of the Blue Ribbon Schools looked at records to gather quantitative data and reported it in their application to support their case. For instance, the Belmont School, one of the five Blue Ribbon Schools with special honors in character education, reports that "discipline referrals dropped by almost 50 percent in two years." The Daisy Ingraham School includes a section on their report card on work habits that rates the students in the following areas: Concern for quality and accuracy in school work; positive response to guidance; responsibility for belongings; responsibility for actions; practice of self-discipline and control; respect for peers and adults; observation of the rules of school and classroom. Some of the Blue Ribbon Schools used the various evaluation instruments mentioned above to gather quantitative data.

The Blue Ribbon Schools, in their applications, also provided a large amount of qualitative data to show they were meeting the objective to foster "the development of sound character, democratic values, ethical judgment and the ability to work in a self-disciplined and purposeful manner." Evaluation of the effectiveness of character education programs was sometimes mentioned in the actual school's application. For example, Dr. Cherry Flanders, the principal at the Flanders Elementary School in Connecticut, explains how her school evaluates its effectiveness:

> We measure our effectiveness in motivating students to learn through their observable excitement and enthusiasm. They show themselves willing to take risks and

participate in class. Former students return and reminisce about our programs. Because of the experience we have provided them in science and computers here, our students have become instrumental in establishing a telecommunications program at the middle school. They run the middle school newspaper, showing off their writing and computer skills. A high percentage of them make the honor roll.

The Burrus Elementary School, a large integrated school in Burris, Georgia, almost one-fourth African Americans, reports on how it evaluates the success of its total school character education program:

> Effectiveness indicators are positive parental feedback, the very small number of disciplinary infractions, and the high degree of on-task engaged student performance. Excellent test scores are another measure of effectiveness. The school climate is very positive and reflects student interest in learning. There are many visitors to the school and their comments almost always refer to busy children who are on task and show excellent behavior as well as a cheerful attitude.

West View Elementary School in Spartanburg, South Carolina, one of the five Blue Ribbon Schools with special honors in character education, is also committed to evaluation of its program.

> Ongoing assessment maintains the effectiveness of our character education program. We have surveyed students on their use of the skills being taught and on the roles played by their teachers in issues of character, decision-making, and conflict management. Overall our students seem to understand the core values of good character, view their teachers as good role models who care about their well-being, and have confidence in their own abilities to act in responsible ways. Assessment, both formal and informal, indicates that our Character Education Program has a tremendous positive impact on students

Evaluation of Character Education by U.S. Department of Education Site Visitors

Most often the site visitor's report was the largest source of documentation regarding the success of the character education efforts in the Blue Ribbon Schools. Under the section on "Student Environment," the site visitors made comments pointing to evidence of the character education outcomes the school was seeking. In their comments, they reported on observed student behaviors and overall school climate as a reflection of good character.

Student Behaviors Showing Character

Here are some examples of observations from site visitors regarding student behavior: At the Gesu School, a large K–8 school with an integrated student body in University Heights, Ohio, a site visitor reported that "Students help in the lunch room, the office, and the library without being paid."

Parent volunteers at Coronado Elementary School in Coronado, California, reported to the visitor, that "Students greet you as they pass you in the hallways, they ask if they can help you find a certain room, they are anxious to talk to us (volunteers) and really value our help. Respect and courtesy for everyone is taught here and I've experienced this personally from all of the children I've met." Teachers at Coronado are also pleased with the students: "I can teach here. I'm teaching almost 100 percent of the time. I don't need to discipline students. They get embarrassed if they mess up. They know what good character is and what it looks like."

"Students pick up papers in the hall even if they did not put them there themselves" at Green Trails School, a large well-integrated school in Chesterfield, Missouri.

The site visitor to the Yakutat Elementary School in Arkansas reported: "Students can be in the library without adult supervision." Yakutat is a rural K–6 school with 55 percent African American students and 30% of the student body from families with low income.

At the Marion Street Elementary School in New York, a suburban school with a homogenous student body, the site visitor's report notes that "Students are given real responsibilities in the school; they operate a school store."

"Students pick up after themselves on the playground" at the Taper Avenue Elementary School, in California, a very large school of over one thousand very diverse students who are 16 percent Hispanic, 17 percent Asian, and 32 percent from lower-income families.

"Lost articles are returned" at the South Valley School, a small K–4 school in Moorestown, New Jersey, with a heterogeneous student body.

The site visitor to the Robert Johnson Elementary School in Kentucky reported that "students stated that they had no money stolen or lost. A teacher said that three dollars stayed on her desk for two weeks, never being disturbed. This school has moral students." Robert Johnson is a large K–6 school with a homogeneous student body in Ft. Thomas, a large central city in Kentucky.

The site visitor to the Gulliver Academy, in Coral Cables, Florida, reported: "The teachers, administrators, and other staff all felt the students were exceptionally well-behaved. They cared about and were of good character. They felt that this was due to a large extent to the emphasis placed on these characteristics at Gulliver." Gulliver Academy is a unique school, it is a for-profit independent K–8 school with a diverse student body of over one thousand students, 30 percent of whom are Hispanic, 3 percent are African American, and 10 percent from lower-income families.

The visitor to the Lewis Powell Magnet School in North Carolina noted these manifestations of good character:

> Students are polite to adults and each other. They hold doors for one another, they address adults with respect and you constantly hear "Thank you." Character-building is integrated into the total school effort. A special education student found $2.00 and immediately turned it into the office saying, "It may be someone's lunch money."

School Climate

School climate is a major factor affecting character education because it must promote the values central to the program (such as caring and respect) or it can negate the effects of any formal program (DeRoche and Williams, 1998). The site visitor to Ponds Spring Elementary found the climate to be the proof of the school's Blue Ribbon status:

> The climate within the school is positive and caring. Adults who work with the children are approachable, concerned, and kind individuals. The learning environment at Ponds Springs is active and orderly. Students treat each other with respect. Teachers treat students with positive respect. They are interested in their students. As a result, the children respect one another and other adults.

One site visitor spoke to a third grade student at the Kathryn Markely School in Malvern, Pennsylvania, about the learning disabled children in the school and received the following response: "We don't treat people differently because they don't learn the same way; we treat them according to the way they act towards others." Kathryn Markely has a large homogeneous student body but also serves students with special educational needs.

The visitor to the Governor Bent School in New Mexico reported that at this school, "caring is the umbrella that supports students in their character and academic development."

A student told the visitor to the Ormand Beach Elementary School in Florida, "my teacher is understanding, honest, and she listens." Ormand Beach is a PreK–5 integrated school that serves a student population that is 24 percent African American, almost 50 percent from lower-income families, and 66 percent special education, as the school serves as the site for the exceptional student population of the eastern part of the Volusia County. The teachers at Ormand Beach continually try to recognize those students who exemplify good behavior and human kindness. They work together with the students to maintain a spirit of cooperation and mutual respect. The students feel that their teachers are doing a very good job at reaching this goal.

SELECTING BLUE RIBBON SCHOOLS FOR SPECIAL HONORS IN CHARACTER EDUCATION

Five of the fifty Blue Ribbon Schools that applied for special recognition in character education were selected for special honors in this area. How were they chosen? They had to meet the following criteria:

1. Program Implementation and Philosophy: Demonstrates a strong philosophy shared among school stakeholders that core ethical values such as caring, honesty, fairness, responsibility, and respect for self and others form the

basis of good character. Integrates core values into all phases of school life. Provides opportunities for moral action to help students develop good character and a strong commitment to uphold the core values.

2. Partnerships: Identifies families as the most important moral educators and involves them in program decision making and planning activities. Communicates character development goals and activities to the families. Demonstrates strong and vital partnership with families and community organizations to promote the core values.

3. Professional Development: Involves all school staff in modeling and promoting the core values. Ongoing professional development affords school staff opportunities to work collaboratively to integrate the core ethical values into school activities. Time is allotted for school staff to reflect on moral matters that are affecting the school.

4. Assessment: Assists the school in promoting a more caring environment. Evaluates the development of school staff as character educators. Appropriately assesses students' understanding of, commitment to, and action upon core values (U.S. Department of Education, 1999).

The five schools chosen were considered by the outside reviewing team from the Character Education Partnership to be model schools that exhibit best practices in character education. These five schools are: Belmont Elementary School in Belmont, Michigan; McCoy Elementary School in Carrolton, Texas; Patterson Road School in Santa Maria, California; Walnut Hill Elementary School in Dallas, Texas; and West View Elementary School in Spartanburg, South Carolina. I have visited each of these five schools in preparing this second edition. As mentioned above, these schools are models of what a comprehensive approach to character education is all about. At these schools, the administration, faculty, staff, parents, and students are working together to promote character. All school activities, classes, and events are opportunities for learning about, caring for and demonstrating good character.

EVALUATIONS OF CHARACTER EDUCATION PROGRAMS

Any district, school, or teacher that is serious about implementing a program of character education will want to evaluate the results of the program (Kirschenbaum, 1995). There are two kinds of evaluation which they will want to use: formative and summative (Bloom, 1971; Scriven, 1973). Formative evaluation is conducted during the operation of the program; it allows the evaluator to gather information (from participants, that is, the students and teachers and from observers—the parents) useful in improving a program that is underway. Formative evaluation is particularly helpful in determining whether or not teachers are implementing a particular character education curriculum effectively. Formative evaluation helps to improve the program by indicating areas that need to be modified, revised, or developed further.

Summative evaluations are conducted at the end of a program in order to assess the program's worth or merit—its overall impact. The data (qualitatively gathered from interviews or surveys, or quantitatively gathered from a formal research design) help the implementers of the program learn if they are accomplishing their stated goals, and can support a rationale for the continuance of the program (Kirschenbaum, 1995). Both formative and summative evaluation techniques should be used as schools seek to implement some of the programs mentioned in this book.

B. David Brooks and Mark Kahn (1993) state that the implementation of a character education program must include a pre-assessment of goals that involves articulating expectations and explicitly detailing the various objectives to be accomplished. During the program implementation, periodic meetings among teachers will help them to keep the goals in mind and to adapt classroom lessons accordingly. Finally, the program should have an assessment of the outcomes based on a post-evaluation of the results obtained from anecdotal reports from teachers and appropriate data on measurable changes in key variables.

Huffman (1994) concurs and suggests the following steps be followed in setting up a character education program evaluation:

1. Design the evaluation component during the initial planning process. Identify the baseline data to use.
2. Review the character education evaluation literature early to get design ideas.
3. Include an implementation assessment in the evaluation design. (As noted in some of the research cited in previous chapters, implementation, specifically poor implementation of a curriculum, is frequently the cause of disappointing results).
4. Be prepared to answer questions about evaluating students.
5. Involve parents, students, and all staff in developing the evaluation component.
6. Conduct the program evaluation.
7. Establish evaluation partnerships with colleges and universities.

Perhaps the most important thing that a school can do before it implements a particular character education program is to gather some baseline data regarding student behavior, to which it later can compare data gathered after program intervention. If at all possible, it would be very valuable to choose randomly the groups of students (classes or schools) that will use the new character education program and the groups of students (different classes or different schools) that will not use it. These conditions, if they can be administratively actualized, will provide the school with a formal structure for evaluation. An evaluation conducted with an experimental or a quasi-experimental design can be added to the very small but growing research base on character education and provide a much needed resource for schools just beginning their character education program.

EVALUATIONS OF BLUE RIBBON SCHOOLS' CHARACTER DEVELOPMENT PROGRAMS

Six of the character education programs found in the Blue Ribbon Schools have been evaluated, either "formally" or "informally." The evaluations used experimental and quasi-experimental or qualitative evaluation designs and were based on either quantitative or qualitative data. We will briefly report on these evaluations so that they may serve as a model for other schools that seek to implement and evaluate character education programs.

Character Education Institute Evaluation

The Character Education Curriculum from the American Institute of Character Education in San Antonio, Texas, has produced character education curriculum materials for grades K–6 for over twenty-five years. The curriculum is in over 18,000 classrooms in forty-four states. The Institute evaluates the effectiveness of its curriculum using survey data and anecdotal comments from persons interviewed who use the curriculum. It reports that a survey of a random sample of 269 elementary school teachers from across the nation showed that 96 percent noted improvement in their students' self-concept, 87 percent in students' oral language skills, 85 percent student behavior in the classroom, 71 percent in behavior in the lunchroom, and 69 percent in behavior on the playground. A survey of 57 elementary school principals from across the nation revealed that 84 percent reported improvement in the relationships between teachers and students; 77 percent, a decrease in discipline problems; 64 percent, a decrease in vandalism; and 68 percent, an increase in attendance.

Two formal evaluations have been conducted of the curriculum. The San Antonio Independent School District administered pre-tests of the Piers-Harris Children's Self-Concept Scale to three schools using the Character Education Curriculum, and three control schools not using the curriculum. A total of 507 students participated in the study. Four months later, a post-test was administered in the same schools and significant changes favoring the experimental schools were noted in many areas of self-concept.

Finally, a five-year evaluation (1991–1995) of the fifteen schools in Spartanburg, South Carolina, using the Character Education Curriculum found that the faculty liked and supported teaching the curriculum. The students thought the topics discussed were important, felt that they learned something new, enjoyed the classes, and said they would like character education to be taught twice a week rather than just once a week (Character Education Institute, 1996).

Child Development Project Longitudinal Evaluation

One of the best evaluations of a character education program is that done of the Child Development Project (CDP) in San Ramon, California (see chapter 3 for a description of the project). Originally funded by the William and Flora Hewlett Foundation, the CDP had from its inception a clear focus on formal evaluation of results. The program was begun in 1982 in the San Ramon Valley Unified School District, a suburban middle-class community thirty miles east of San Francisco. The staff carefully matched two sets of three elementary schools in the district for size, socioeconomic status, and degree of faculty and family interest in the program. Then one school in each group was randomly chosen to receive the program. A cross-sectional pre-program assessment of a large random sample of students from program and comparison schools revealed no large or consistent differences between these two groups with respect to a variety of social attitudes, values, skills, and behaviors (Watson et al., 1989).

The basic design of the program intervention and evaluation was longitudinal; it began with groups of kindergarten students and followed these cohorts as they progressed through to the sixth grade. The evaluation involved both formative studies on teachers' implementation of the various program components—that is, cooperative learning, developmental discipline, teaching prosocial values through literature, and teaching caring through opportunities to help schoolmates and family—and summative evaluation of the program effects on students both during the elementary school years when the program was in effect and in junior high school after it was over. The summative evaluation involved collecting data on students' interpersonal behavior, attitudes, academic, and interpersonal motivation, moral reasoning, and academic performance, using a variety of procedures, such as classroom observation, experimental small-group activities, teacher and student questionnaires, interviews, and achievement tests.

The study showed that CDP students scored significantly higher on measures of sensitivity, consideration of others needs, problem-solving skills, and use of conflict resolution strategies that were more prosocial. With regard to student behavior, the results were mixed depending upon grade level. No difference was detected between the comparison school and CDP school with regard to the incidence of negative behaviors. On the other behavior measures, a significant difference was detected favoring the CDP schools when the combined data was analyzed; however the results were not as strong when analyzed by grade level. What the evaluation did show is that it was possible to teach prosocial behaviors to students and make some difference in their behavior outside of the classroom (Solomon, et.al., 2000).

The evaluation of the CDP is one of the best examples of a formal evaluation study and as such makes a significant contribution to the area of character education evaluation. It was rigorous in its research design, using random assignment of subjects to groups; it used control and test groups, gathered data using multiple measures both qualitative and quantitative, and was longitudinal in its scope. The design had both formative and summative evaluation components. The project and its evaluation have been replicated in various settings and the results have been significantly positive at each site. The program has continued this longitudinal evaluation. For the latest results the reader is referred to their internet homepage: www.devstud.org/CDP-MS-Followup.html.

The Fort Washington Elementary School Evaluation

The character development program at the Fort Washington Elementary School in Clovis, California, has been described in previous chapters. Here we will report on its evaluation of the effectiveness of this award program. There are three major components of the Fort Washington character education program: (1) the co-curricular program; (2) the Exemplary Patriot Award Program; and (3) the Patriotic Classroom Award. The effectiveness of the Fort Washington character development program was evaluated after five years of implementation. Base-line data were gathered on a number of key measures. The administration and faculty sought to examine the cause-and-effect relationship between the instructional program and its impact on student behaviors.

The total character development program was found to be effective in developing a positive, purposeful school climate; several key outcome variables were observed by evaluators. Specifically, scores on achievement tests improved and the number of students on the honor roll grew; daily attendance to school improved and incidence of school vandalism became none existent; and the number of students who participated in school extracurricular activities increased greatly (Sparks, 1991).

Fort Washington found that the award program is instrumental in creating an effective and positive school climate for students as well as staff members and parents. More importantly, Fort Washington reported that the impact of this approach to character development appears to substantiate findings from ongoing "effective schools research" showing that quality schools are achieved when there is: (1) a strong sense of mission; (2) high standards for all; (3) a high level of participation by staff, students and parents; and (4) a well-planned student recognition structure that reinforces the behaviors desired and valued by the school and community.

Evaluation of the Heartwood Institute's Curriculum

James Leming and associates conducted an evaluation of the Heartwood Institute's "Ethics Curriculum for Children" during the 1995–1996 school year. As described in chapter 3, the Heartwood curriculum is a character education program that places the primary focus on children's literature as the vehicle for instruction in values and ethics.

The study was conducted in two school districts; one located in western Pennsylvania, and the other in southern Illinois. A total of 26 teachers in four schools along with their 541 students participated in the study. In each district, there were two other schools similar in size and economic make-up, which agreed to be the comparison group (424 students). The Heartwood curriculum was implemented in a total of twenty classrooms. The program consists of fourteen different lessons, each lasting 30 to 45 minutes on seven different ethical attributes. The intention of the curriculum is to influence childrens' character development in three general areas: cognitive, affective, and behavioral.

This formal evaluation employed the quasi-experimental design advocated by Cline and Feldmesser (1983). There were comparison groups and pre-and post-tests; however assignment to groups were not random but by volunteering. Instruments were developed to measure: (1) the students' understanding of the vocabulary of the character traits taught by the Heartwood curriculum—*ethical understanding*; (2) the extent to which students expressed a preference for actions that exemplify the character attributes that serve as the objectives of the Heartwood curriculum—*ethical sensibility*; and (3) students' character-related behavior—*ethical conduct*. In addition to the pre- and post-tests, interviews were conducted with teachers and students at the end of the academic year, and classroom observations were conducted at random intervals throughout the year. These instruments were administered in both the classrooms using the Heartwood curriculum and the comparison classrooms not using the curriculum.

It was found that program students at all grades demonstrated higher levels of ethical understanding of these attributes than did comparison students. Improved student conduct was also noted by teachers of students in the program as compared to the reports given by teachers in the comparison classrooms. Mixed results were found on affective, and behavioral outcomes.

Leming states in his evaluation that "to be meaningful and to advance systematic thinking about knowledge in the field, research findings must be interpreted from some theoretical or conceptual frame of reference" (Leming, 2000). Leming identifies four discernible perspectives in moral development: Aristotle's virtues and moral sentiments, Kohlberg's moral development, Vitz's narrative thought, and Bandura's social learning theory. Given the implicit teaching/learning model of the Heartwood curriculum, he feels that the social learning theory of Albert Bandura (1977) provides a coherent perspective as to how children's literature might facilitate moral growth in children by providing them with an opportunity for observational learning. Ideally, character education programs should be developed and evaluated from clear perspectives regarding the nature of character and how it is learned (Leming, 1997).

The Quest Evaluation Kit

One of the most significant and valuable contributions to the evaluation of character programs is being made by Quest International. Its Evaluation Kit is designed for schools using positive youth development programs like Quest in such areas as health education, prevention of at-risk behaviors, and family studies. The kit teaches the user how to implement tested evaluation methodologies such as a needs assessment, and pre- and post-test measures, how to evaluate the data, and how to report the results to interested publics. The kit includes inventories, surveys, logs, observational checklists, data collection forms, and interview questions that can be used in conducting an evaluation. Of particular value are the Behavior Rating Tools that include "Observational Checklists for Pro-social Behaviors" and the "Attitude and Projected Behavior Surveys." The Quest International Evaluation Kit can be obtained from Quest International, 537 Jones Road, P.O. Box 566, Granville, OH 43023–0566, Telephone (800) 837–2801.

Quest has gathered a large amount of data regarding the effectiveness of its own programs on student performance in school settings. It has gathered its own surveys of participants in the Quest programs, and it has also used independent research agencies for more formal studies. For example, in 1991, Quest International conducted a study on the effects of the Skills for Adolescence curriculum as measured by attendance, school grades, California Achievement Test scores, and school attitude. A total of 497 students in grades 6 through 8 were selected for the study. A nonrandom assignment, pre-test post-test design was used where students from existing, intact classrooms were designated as either experimental or comparison groups. All students were pre- and post-tested with two instruments: the School Attitude Measure (SAM), a nationally normed measure of students' feelings and attitudes toward self and schools, and the California Achievement Test (CAT) for reading and mathematics. In addition to these two measures, student records were examined to compare school grade point average (GPA), subject area grades, school attendance, and citizenship marks. The School Attitude measure revealed a slight but significant positive effect for students who received the Skills for Adolescence (SFA) program; language arts and mathematics grades were significantly higher for the SFA group; and the SFA group had significantly fewer days absent than the comparison group. However, California achievement test scores showed no difference between SFA and comparison groups. One can conclude that the SFA curriculum does help to increase student performance on some measures of school attitude, attendance, and academic knowledge (Quest, 1991).

The Success Through Accepting Responsibility (STAR) Program

The Jefferson Center for Character Education was founded in 1963 and has had its STAR program, (Success Through Accepting Responsibility), implemented in approximately six thousand schools in virtually every state, in most major cities in the U.S. and in Canada. The STAR curriculum includes short and easy-to-follow weekly lessons that can be infused into the regular curriculum, as well as monthly character themes that are also featured on classroom posters. The key elements of the program include both content and process: (1) direct instruction in the teaching of character values; (2) a language-based curriculum using literature that exemplify the core character concepts in their characters; (3) positive language; (4) a *process* for making good character decisions, (i.e., Stop, Think, Act, Review); (5) a school climate approach; (6) teacher-friendly materials which allow for flexibility and creativity; (7) student participation; and (8) parental involvement.

An informal evaluation of the STAR character education program's implementation in the Los Angeles elementary schools was conducted in the spring of 1991. Data were gathered by interviewing twenty-five administrators in schools where the program was implemented. Combining the data for all schools, it was found that after one year with the curriculum, all forms of discipline problems decreased (major discipline problems decreased by 25 percent, suspensions declined by 16 percent, the number of tardy students dropped by 40 percent, and unexcused absences fell by 18 percent). The median level of student participation in extracurricular activities increased slightly as did the median number of students on the Principals' Honor Rolls; there was also an increase in student morale and an increase in parental involvement in their children's education. The administrators said that the program achieved more than they anticipated: better student self-discipline, an opportunity to teach values in the classroom, and a common reference point to solve conflicts (Brooks and Goble, 1997; Franklin, 1996). The strengths of this evaluation include its pre- and post-comparisons on a number of measures, but its limitations were lack of control groups, and independent observers.

COMPONENTS OF EFFECTIVE
CHARACTER EDUCATION SCHOOLS

What, in conclusion, emerges as the profile of character education in the Blue Ribbon Schools? Our analysis of over 150 character education programs found in various Blue Ribbon Schools suggests that an effective character education program includes:

1. A strong school mission committed to developing a student's sense of morals, character, and good citizenship.
2. A high level of participation by the entire community (teacher, principals, staff, students, and parents) in the decision-making process by which they determine the desired character qualities and the subsequent activities which the school will use to foster good citizenship.
3. High standards for student academic performance that are realized throughout the curriculum by teaching methodologies that promote character, such as highlighting key character qualities in thematic, literature-based and interdisciplinary units and by teaching strategies, such as cooperative learning, learning styles instruction and authentic assessment.

4. High standards for student behavior that are positively stated, and understood by teachers, students, and community. All are involved in creating a caring school that is safe, nurturing, drug-free, and involved in community and global affairs.

5. A well-planned student recognition program that serves to communicate, encourage, and reinforce the character qualities, attitudes, and behaviors that are valued by the school and community.

6. A commitment to character education that is comprehensive, i.e. all faculty, staff, administrators and students are committed to good character. All teachers are involved in integrating character education into the various subjects they teach (math, science, social studies, literature, health, etc.) and all staff members (counselors, cafeteria and playground aides, secretaries, etc.) reinforce the living of these good character traits. In addition, the community makes a commitment to reinforcing good character through the media, the news, and in the neighborhood.

7. A schoolwide evaluation program that includes character objectives in the curriculum that are assessed, character traits that are evaluated on a school report card, and institutional data that measures character growth in all three domains (cognitive, affective, and behavioral.)

SUMMARY

Before being recognized for the Blue Ribbon Award, schools showed on their application and during site visits that they did indeed foster the development of good character in their students. Ideas have been given on how each of the components of good character—moral knowing, moral feeling and moral action—can be evaluated. A framework has been given for setting up a formal evaluation of a character education program. Finally, six character education program evaluations of varying breadth and rigor have been reviewed. The chapter concludes with a list of seven recurring components of character education in Blue Ribbon Schools. Given the facts that: (1) these components are repeatedly found in schools judged worthy of the highest national recognition; (2) some evaluations (such as that of the Child Development project) have experimentally demonstrated the effectiveness of at least some of these components; and (3) such components match the school qualities revealed by effective schools research, it seems reasonable to hypothesize that these seven factors contribute to effective character education. However, questions remain: Are all of these factors equally important? Are any of them dispensable? Are their effects interactive? Are they equally effective at all grade levels? Do the effects of these components on student character generalize beyond school and endure over time? These and similar questions must be answered by future research.

Appendix

The Blue Ribbon Award Program

HISTORY OF THE ELEMENTARY
SCHOOL RECOGNITION PROGRAM

William Bennett, when he was the Secretary of Education, proclaimed 1985–1986 as the "Year of the Elementary School" and, as part of that observance, began the Elementary School Recognition Program, also know as the "Blue Ribbon Award Program." The program was modeled after its successful predecessor, the Secondary School Recognition Program, which began three years before as a positive response to the criticisms made in the report *A Nation at Risk*. The purpose of the Blue Ribbon Award Program was to identify and give public recognition to outstanding public and private elementary schools across the United States. National attention was thus focused on schools that were doing an exceptional job with all of their students in developing a solid foundation of basic skills and knowledge of subject matter and fostering the development of character, moral values, and ethical judgment.

Blue Ribbon Schools are identified on the basis of their effectiveness in meeting their particular goals, as well as the standards of quality applicable to elementary schools generally. An important consideration for recognition is the school's success in furthering the intellectual, social, and moral growth of all its students. In seeking successful schools, the program looks for both schools with an established record of sustained high achievement and schools that have overcome obstacles and problems and are continuing to concentrate on improvement.

According to the criteria set up by the program, "for a school to be recognized, there must be clear evidence that its students are developing a solid foundation of skills in reading, writing, and mathematics. In addition, there must be evidence that school policies, programs, and practices are organized to foster the development of sound character, a sense of self-worth, democratic values, ethical judgment, and self-discipline. Instructional programs should be organized to provide individual students with high-quality instruction appropriate to their age and grade in literature, history, geography, science, economics, the arts, and other subjects that the State, school system, or school deems important" (Department of Education, 1993).

In 1985–1986, special emphasis was given to schools which fostered the development of character, values and ethical judgment in students while developing a solid foundation of basic skills and knowledge of subject matter. In 1987–1988, emphasis was given to schools with unusually effective strategies for teaching math and science to their students; and in 1989–1990, emphasis was given to schools with effective strategies for teaching geography to their students as well as to schools that had serious, content-rich programs in the visual and performing arts. The National Goals for Education were released in February of 1990 and thus became an important component in the National Recognition Program. In 1991–1992, special attention was placed on schools with effective programs meeting the National Goals in history and math; and in 1993–1994, the special emphasis was on schools with effective programs meeting the National Goals in science and, once again, mathematics. In 1996–1997, schools could apply for special honors in school safety, discipline and drug prevention; in professional development or in technology. In 1998–1999, the special honors were in character education or arts education. Finally, in 2000–2001, special honors were in special education or technology.

The Blue Ribbon criteria state: "For any school to be judged deserving of recognition, there should be strong leadership and an effective working relationship among the school, the parents, and others in its community. The school should have an atmosphere that is orderly, purposeful, and conducive to learning and good character. The school should attend to the quality of instruction and the professionalism of its teachers. There must be a strong commitment to educational excellence for all students and a record of progress in sustaining the school's best features and solving its problems (Department of Education, 1994)."

In addition, in order to be eligible for nomination, schools had to meet "eligibility criteria," that included:

1. The school had to be an elementary school (including some combination of grades from K–8) with its own administrator.
2. Private schools must have been in operation for at least five years.
3. The Office for Civil Rights must not have issued a letter of findings to the school district concluding that the nominated school has violated one or more of the civil rights statutes or that there is a district-wide violation that

may affect the nominated school. The Department of Justice must not have a pending suit against a school district alleging that the nominated school has violated one or more of the civil rights statutes or the Constitution's equal protection clause.

4. The school must also meet at least one of the following criteria with regard to student achievement during the last three years:

   a. Seventy-five percent or more of the students must have achieved at or above grade level in mathematics and reading.

   b. The number of students who achieved at or above grade level in mathematics and reading must have increased an average of at least 5 percent annually; and in the last year, 50 percent or more of the students must have achieved at or above grade level in both areas.

   c. The school must demonstrate exemplary progress and growth of students in math and reading individually or as a group as determined by a carefully worked out and fully documented system of evaluation.

THE BLUE RIBBON APPLICATION PROCESS

Once eligibility to apply is determined, a school that desires national recognition must complete an application form documenting how the school addresses the areas of:

Mission and Goals
Organizational Vitality
Leadership
Teaching Environment
Curriculum and Instruction
Student Environment
Parent and Community Support
Indicators of Success

All applications are initially sent to the Chief State School Officers who nominate schools for consideration at the national level. Their applications are then reviewed by a National Review Panel, which selects schools to recommend for site visits based on the quality of information in the nomination form. Two day visits are conducted to each school so nominated. The site visit reports are forwarded to the Review Panel, which meets a second time to review all of the schools that received site visits. The panel recommends the final group of schools for recognition by the Secretary of Education. Representatives from each of the school are invited to Washington, D.C., for a recognition ceremony.

For the most complete history of the Blue Ribbon Recognition Program the reader is referred to its homepage at www.ed.gov/offices/OERI/BlueRibbonSchools/. A sample application form can be found here as well as a list of all the schools that have been recognized. Readers can locate the address and phone number of all the Blue Ribbon Schools at this internet address: www.ed.gov/offices/OERI/ BlueRibbonSchools/sch_honor82.html. A copy of each of the schools cited in this book, the principal, address, and phone number can also be obtained from the author by e-mailing her at mmurphy@stfrancis.edu and requesting a copy of the second edition of *Blue Ribbon Schools*.

References

Adair, J. 2000. "Tackling Teens' No. 1 Problem." *Educational Leadership* 57(6): 44–47.

"A Different Look at DARE." [On-line] Available URL: http://www.drcnet.org/DARE/

Albert, L. 1990. *Cooperative Discipline: Classroom Management that Promotes Self-Esteem: Teacher's Manual.* MN: American Guidance Service.

Alderman, M. K. 1990. "Motivation for At-Risk Students," *Educational Leadership* 48(1): 27–30

Allred, C. G. 1994. *Positive Action 1994–95 Catalog.* Twin Cities, ID: Positive Action Company.

Armstrong, T. 1994. *Multiple Intelligences in the Classroom.* Alexandria, VA: ASCD.

ASCD Panel on Moral Education. 1988a. "Moral Education in the Life of the School," *Educational Leadership* 45(8): 4–8.

ASCD Panel on Moral Education. 1988b. *Moral Education in the Life of the School.* VA: Association for Supervision and Curriculum Development.

"Aspen Declaration on Character Education." 1992. *Ethics in Action.* Marina del Rey, CA: Joseph & Edna Josephson Institute of Ethics.

Ban, J. 1994. "A Lesson Plan Approach for Dealing with School Discipline," *The Clearing House* 67(5): 257–261.

Bandura, A., 1977. *Social Learning Theory.* Englewood Cliffs, NJ: Prentice Hall.

Bangert-Drowns, Robert. 1988. "The Effects of School-Based Substance Abuse Education — A Meta-Analysis," *Journal of Drug Education* 18(3): 243–264.

Baniewicz, J. 1995. "A Parent's Case for Character Education." An Open Letter to the Fairport, NY, Education Community, May 21, 1995.

Beane, J. 1986. "The Continuing Controversy Over Affective Education," *Educational Leadership* 43(4): 26–31.

Beane, J. 1991. "Sorting Out the Self-Esteem Controversy," *Educational Leadership* 49(1):25–30.

Bennett, W. 1988. *First Lessons: A Report on Elementary Education in America.* Washington, DC: U.S. Government Printing Office.

Bennett, W. 1991. "Moral Literacy and the Formation of Character," in *Moral, Character, and Civic Education.* J. S. Benninga, ed. New York: Teachers College Press.

Benninga, J.S., ed. 1991. *Moral, Character, and Civic Education.* New York: Teachers College Press.

Berkowitz, M. 1998. *A Primer for Evaluating a Character Education Initiative.* Character Education Partnership, Washington, DC

Berman, S. 1990. "Education for Social Responsibility," *Educational Leadership* 48(3): 75–80.

Berreth, D., and S. Berman. 1997. "The Moral Dimensions of School." *Educational Leadership* 54(8): 24–27.

Bessell, H. 1972. *The Magic Circle: Methods in Human Development Theory Manual.* Human Development Training Institute: San Diego, CA.

Biehler, R.F., and J. Snowman. 1990. *Psychology Applied to Teaching.* 6th ed. Boston: Houghton Mifflin.

Billig, S. 2000. "Research on K–12 School-Based Service-Learning: The Evidence Builds." *Phi Delta Kappan* 81(9): 658–664.

Bloom, B., J.T. Hasting, and G. Madaus. 1971. *Handbook on Formative and Summative Evaluation of Student Learning.* New York: McGraw-Hill.

Bloom, B.S. 1977. "Affective Outcomes of School Learning," *Phi Delta Kappan* 59(3): 193–98.

Bosworth, K. 1995. "Caring for Others and Being Cared For." *Phi Delta Kappan* 76(9): 686–693.

Botvin, G.J., E. Bake, L. Dysenbury, S. Tortu, and E. Botvin. 1990. "Preventing Adolescent Drug Abuse through a Multimodal Cognitive Behavioral Approach: Results of a 3-Year Study." *Journal of Consulting and Clinical Psychology* 58(4): 437–447.

Boyd, D. 1989. "The Character of Moral Development," in *Moral Development and Character Education.* L. Nucci, ed. CA: McCutchan Publishing Corporation.

Boyer, E. 1990. "Civic Education for Responsible Citizens," *Educational Leadership* 48(3): 4–6.

Braun, J. 1989. "The Empathy Lab: A Strategy for Promoting Perspective Taking and Self-Esteem." A paper presented to the Association for Humanistic Education, Denver, CO. April 28, 1989.

Brooks, B. David, and M. Kahn. 1993. "What Makes Character Education Programs Work?" *Educational Leadership* 51(3): 19–21.

Brooks, B.D., and F. Goble. 1997. *The Case for Character Education: The Role of the School in Teaching Values and Virtue.* Northridge, CA: Studio 4 Publications.

Buie, J. 1987. "Teen Pregnancy: It's Time for the Schools to Tackle the Problem," *Phi Delta Kappan* 68(10): 737–739.

Bush, G. 2001. "State of the Union Address." [On line] Available URL: www.whitehouse.gov/WH/news/other/sotu.html

Butts, R.F. 1991. "Preface" *Civitas: A Framework for Civic Education*. Quigley, C. and C. Bahmueller, eds. Calabasas, CA: National Center for Civic Education, xxi.

Calsyn, R.J., and D.A. Kenny. 1977. "Self-Concept of Ability and Perceived Evaluation of Others: Cause or Effect of Academic Achievement," *Journal of Educational Psychology* 69(2): 136–45.

Cambell, D., and Stanley, J. 1966. *Experimental and Quasi-Experimental Designs for Research*. Chicago: Rand-McNally.

Canfield, J. 1990. "Improving Students' Self-Esteem," *Educational Leadership* 48(1): 48–50.

Canter, L., and M. Canter. 1976. *Assertive Discipline*. Los Angeles: Lee Canter & Associates.

Carlin, D. 1981. "Is Kohlberg a Disciple of Dewey?" *Educational Theory,* summer/fall 1981: 31(3/4), 251–257.

Chance, P. 1992. "The Rewards of Learning, *Phi Delta Kappan* 74(3): 200–207.

"Character Counts Coalition." 1993. *Ethics in Action*. Marina del Rey, CA: Joseph & Edna Josephson Institute of Ethics, May/June, 1993.

Character Education Institute, 1996. *The Character Education Curriculum: Developing Responsible Citizens*. San Antonio, TX.

Character Education Partnership. 1996. *Character-Based Sex Education in Public Schools: A Position Statement*. Arlington, VA: Character Education Partnership.

Character Education Partnership. 1996. *Character Education in U.S. Schools: The New Consensus*. VA: The Character Education Partnership, Inc.

Chaskin, R., and D.M. Rauner. (1995) "Youth and Caring: An Introduction" *Phi Delta Kappan* 76(9): 667–674.

Clifford, M. 1990. "Students Need Challenge: Not Easy Success." *Educational Leadership* 48(1): 22–25.

Cline, H. and R. Feldmesser. 1983. *Program Evaluation in Moral Education*. Princeton, NJ: Educational Testing Service.

Clinton, W. 1997. "State of the Union Address." [On line] Available URL: /www1.whitehouse.gov/WH/news/other/sotu.html

Clinton, W. 1996. "State of the Union Address." [On line] Available URL: www1.whitehouse.gov/WH/news/other/sotu.html

Clinton, W. 1993. "Awards Ceremony." May 13–14, 1993. Washington, DC.

Cobb, C., and J. Mayer. 2000. "Emotional Intelligence: What the Research Says." *Educational Leadership* 58(3): 14–18.

Cohen, E. 1998. "Making Cooperative Learning Equitable." *Educational Leadership* 56(1): 18–21

Communitarian Network. 1996. "The Role of Civic Education." Washington, DC: Communitarian Network, pp. 1–15.

Covey, S. 1998. *7 Habits of Highly Effective Teens*. New York: Simon and Schuster.

Covey, S. 1990. *7 Habits of Highly Effective People*. New York: Simon and Schuster.

Cunningham, C.A. "A Review of Character Education in America's Blue Ribbon Schools: Best Practices for Meeting the Challenge," in *Choice*, May 1999, 1670.

Curwin, R., and A. Mendler. 1988. "We Repeat, Let the Buyer Beware: A Response to Canter," *Educational Leadership* 46(2): 68–71.

Curwin, R. 1995. "A Human Approach to Reducing Violence in Schools," *Educational Leadership* 52(5): 72–75.

Dawson, D. 1986. "The Effects of Sex Education on Adolescent Behavior," *Family Planning Perspectives* 18(4): 162–170.

DeJong, W. 1987. "A Short Term Evaluation of Project DARE (Drug Abuse Resistance Education): Preliminary Indications of Effectiveness." *Journal of Drug Education* 17: 279–294.

DeRoche and Williams. 1998. Educating Hearts and Minds: *A Comprehensive Character Education Framework.* Thousand Oaks, CA: Corwin Press, Inc. Sage Publications, p. 24.

Developmental Studies Center. 1994. "The Child Development Project: Summary of Findings in Two Initial Districts and the First Phase of an Expansion to Six Additional Districts Nationally." Oakland, CA: Developmental Studies Center, pp. 3–4.

Developmental Studies Center. 1991. "Evaluation of The Child Development Project: Summary of Findings To Date." Oakland, CA: Developmental Studies Center, pp. 1–9.

Devine, et al. 2000. *Cultivating Heart and Character: Educating for Life's Most Essential Goals.* Chapel Hill: Character Development Publishing, p. 39.

Dewey, J. 1891. *Outlines of a Critical Theory of Ethics*, Ann Arbor: University of Michigan, p. 3 as cited by Copelston, F. *A History of Philosophy.* Vol. 8. New York: Image Books.

Dewey, J. 1909. *Moral Principles in Education.* Carbondale, IL: Southern Illinois University Press.

Dewey, J. 1916. *Democracy and Education.* New York: Macmillan.

Dewey, J. 1929. *The Quest for Certainty.* New York: Macmillan.

DiGiacomo, James. 2000. *Teaching Right from Wrong: The Moral Education of Today's Youth.* Washington, DC: National Catholic Education Association.

Dolenga, J. 1990. "The Civic Achievement Award Program," *Educational Leadership* 48(3): 89.

Durkheim, E. 1973. *Moral Education: A Study in the Theory and Application of the Sociology of Education.* New York: The Free Press.

Dunn, R., J. Beaudry and A. Kavis. 1989. "Survey of Research on Learning Styles," *Educational Leadership* 46(6): 50–58.

Eldrigde, M., Barcikowsk, R., and Witmer, J. 1973. "Effects of DUSO on the Self-Concepts of Second-Grade Students." *Elementary School Guidance and Counseling* 7(4): 256–260.

Eliam, S., L. Rose, and A. Gallup. 1993. "The 25th Annual Phi Delta Kappa/Gallup Poll of the Public's Attitudes Toward the Public Schools," *Phi Delta Kappan* 75(2): 137–152.

Eliam, S., L. Rose, and A. Gallup. 1994. "The 26th Annual Phi Delta Kappa/Gallup Poll of the Public's Attitudes Toward the Public Schools," *Phi Delta Kappan* 76(1): 41–56.

Eliam, S., L. Rose and A. Gallup. 1996. "The 28th Annual Phi Delta Kappa/Gallup Poll of the Public's Attitudes Toward the Public Schools," *Phi Delta Kappan* 78(1): 40–55.

Ennett, S., N. Tobler, C. Ringqalt and R. Fewelling. 1994. "How Effective is Drug Abuse Resistance Education? A Meta-analysis of Project DARE Outcome Evaluations," *American Journal of Public Health* 84(9): 1394–1401.

Escriva de Balaguer, J.M. 1973. *Human Virtues* New York: Scepter Press.

Escriva de Balaguer, J.M. 1973. "Working for God," in *Friends of God*. New York: Scepter, p. 62.

Estes, T., and D. Vasquez-Levy. 2001. "Literature as a Source of Information and Values." *Phi Delta Kappan* 82(7): 507–512.

Fay, J., and D. Funk. 1995. *Teaching with Love and Logic*. Golden, CA: The Love and Logic Press.

Fernstermacher, G. 1990. "Some Moral Considerations on Teaching as a Profession," in *The Moral Dimensions of Teaching*. J. Goodland, R. Soder, and K. Sirotnik, eds. CA: Jossey Bass.

Franklin, Z. 1996. "Jefferson Center for Character Education." [On line] available URL: www.netspce.org/~zaqix/jefferson.html

Froschl, M., and N. Gropper. 1999. Fostering Friendships, Curbing Bullying. *Educational Leadership* 56(8): 72–75.

Frymier, J. 1974. *Motivation and Learning in School*. Bloomington, Indiana: Phi Delta Kappa Educational Foundation.

Frymier, J., L. Cunningham, W. Duckett, B. Gansneder, F. Link, J. Rimmer, and J. Scholz. 1995. *Values on Which We Agree*. IN: Phi Delta Kappa.

Gage, N.L., and D. Berliner. (1991). *Educational Psychology*. 5th ed. Geneva, IL: Houghton Mifflin Co.

Galina, B. 1973. Testing the Stated Objectives of *Developing Understanding of Self and Others* curriculum (Doctoral dissertation, Georgia State University, Atlanta 1972). *Dissertation Abstracts International*, 33, 4056A.

Gardner, H. 1983. *Frames of Mind: The Theory of Multiple Intelligences*. New York: Basic Books.

Gardner, H. 1995. "Reflections on Multiple Intelligences: Myths and Messages." *Phi Delta Kappan* 77(3): 200–209.

Gathercoal, F. 1990. *Judicious Discipline*. Ann Arbor, MI: Caddo Gap Press.

Glasser, W. 1986. *Control Theory in the Classroom*. New York: Harper & Row Publishers.

Glasser, W. 1990. *The Quality School*. Perennial Library. New York: Harper & Row Publishers.

Goleman, D. 1995. *Emotional Intelligence: Why It Can Matter More than IQ*. New York: Bantam Books.

Goodland, J., R. Soder and K. Sirotnik, eds. 1990. *The Moral Dimensions of Teaching*. CA: Jossey Bass.

Grenadier, A. 2001. *State Education Legislative Activity*. Character Education Partnership Report, Washington, DC.

Gutek, G. 1970. *An Historical Introduction to American Education*. New York: Thomas Crowell Company.

Gutek, G. 1988. *Philosophical and Ideological Perspectives on Education*. Boston: Allan & Bacon, pp. 97–98.

Harmin, M. 1988. "Value clarity, high morality—Let's go for both." *Educational Leadership* 45(8): 24–30.

Harmin, M. 1990. "The Workshop Way to Student Success," *Educational Leadership* 48(1): 43–47.

Harrison, G. 1980. "Values Clarification and the Construction of the Good." *Educational Theory* 30(3): 185–191.

Hawley, R. 1987. "School Children and Drugs: The Fancy that Has Not Passed." *Phi Delta Kappan* 68(9): K1–K8.

Herman, J., P. Aschbacher, L. Winters. 1992. *A Practical Guide to Alternative Assessment.* Alexandria, VA.: Association for Supervision and Curriculum Development.

Hiebert, E. and C. Fisher. 1990 "Whole Language: Three Themes for the Future," *Educational Leadership* 47(6): 62–63.

Hill, David. 1990. "Order in the Classroom." *Teacher's Magazine*, April 1990, 70–77.

Hopkins, R.A., A. L. Mauss, K. Kearney, and A. Weisheit. 1988. "Comprehensive Evaluation of a Model Alcohol Education Curriculum," *Journal of Studies on Alcohol* 49: 1, 38–50.

Huffman, H. 1994. *Developing A Character Education Program: One School District's Experience*. Alexandria, VA: ASCD.

Isaac, S., and W. Michael. 1984. *Handbook in Research and Evaluation.* San Diego, CA: Edits Publishing.

Johnson, D., and Johnson, R. 1986a. *Circles of Learning: Cooperation in the Classroom, revised edition*. Edina, MN, Interaction Book Co., p. 1:23.

Johnson, D., and Johnson, R. 1986b. *Learning Together and Alone*. 2nd Ed. Englewood Cliffs, NJ: Prentice-Hall.

Johnson, D., and R. Johnson. 1995a. *Teaching Students to Be Peacemakers*. Edina, MN: Interaction Book Co.

Johnson, D., and R. Johnson. 1995b. *Reducing School Violence through Conflict Resolution*. Alexandria, VA: Association for Supervision and Curriculum Development.

Johnson, D., R. Johnson, B. Dudley, and R. Burnett. 1992. "Teaching Students to Be Peer Mediators." *Educational Leadership* 50(1): 10–13.

Johnson, S. and Blanchard, K. 1982. *The One Minute Manager*. New York: Morrow.

Josephson Institute. 1993. "Character Counts Coalition." *Ethics in Action*. Marina del Rey, CA: Joseph & Edna Josephson Institute of Ethics, May/June, 1993.

Kenney, Asta. 1987. "Teen Pregnancy: An Issue for Schools." *Phi Delta Kappa* 68(10) Special Report: 728–736.

Kielsmeier, J. 2000. "A Time to Serve, A Time to Learn: Service Learning and the Promise of Democracy." *Phi Delta Kappan* 81(9): 652–657

Kilpatrick, W. 1992. *Why Johnny Can't Tell Right from Wrong*. New York: Simon and Schuster.

Kim, S. 1987. "A Short-and Long-Term Evaluation of Here's Looking at You Alcohol Education Program," *International Journal of Health Services* 17(1): 235–242.

Kirschenbaum, H. 1995. *100 Ways to Enhance Values and Morality in Schools and Youth Settings*. Boston, MA: Allan & Bacon.

Kletzien, S. 1993. "Reading Programs in Nationally Recognized Elementary Schools." *National Reading Conference*, Charleston, SC.

Kletzien, S., Bas-Isaac, E., Brown, R., Carter, D. Gilbert, A., McGree, K., Murphy, M., and Russo, R. 1992. "Models of Excellent Practices in the U.S. Department of Education Blue Ribbon Schools*." American Educational Research Association Annual Conference*. San Francisco, CA.

Kohlberg, L. 1975. "Moral Education for a Society in Moral Transition." *Educational Leadership* 33(2): 46–54.

Kohlberg, L. 1978. "The Cognitive-Developmental Approach to Moral Education." in Peter Scharf, ed. *Readings in Moral Education*. MN: Winston Press.

Kohlberg, L. 1984. *Essays on Moral Development, Vol. 2.: The Psychology of Moral Development.* San Francisoco, CA: Harper and Row.

Kohn, A. 1990. "The ABC's of Caring." *Teacher Magazine*. January, 1990: 52–58.

Kohn, A. 1991. "Caring Kids: The Role of Schools." *Phi Delta Kappan* 72(7): 496–506.

Kohn, A. 1993. *Punished by Rewards.* Boston, MA.: Houghton-Mifflin, p. 194, 270, 174.

Kohn, A. 1994. "The Truth about Self-Esteem," *Phi Delta Kappan* 76(4): 272–282.

Kohn, A. 1996. *Beyond Discipline: From Compliance to Community.* Alexandria: Association for Supervision and Curriculum Development.

Laird, M. 1993. *Quest International Evaluation Kit.* Ohio: Quest International.

LeGette. 1999. *Parents, Kids and Character.* Chapel Hill: Character Development Publishing.

Leming, J. 1993a. "Synthesis of Research: In Search of Effective Character Education," *Educational Leadership* 51(3): 63–71.

Leming, J. 1993b. *Character Education: Lessons from the Past, Models for the Future.* Camden, Maine: Institute for Global Ethics.

Leming J. 1997. Research and Practice in Character Education: A Historical Perspective. In *The Construction of Children's Character: Ninety-sixth Yearbook of the National Society for the Study of Education*, edited by A. Molnar. Chicago: University of Chicago Press.

Leming, J. 2000. "Tell Me a Story: an Evaluation of a Literature-based Character Education Programme." *Journal of Moral Education* 29(4): 413–427.

Leming, J., A. Hendricks-Smith and J. Antis. 1997. "An Evaluation of the Heartwood Institute's "An Ethics Curriculum for Children." *American Educational Research Association*. Chicago, IL.

Leo, J. 1990. "The Trouble with Self-Esteem." *U.S. News & World Report*, April 2, 1990:16.

Letwin, A. 1991. "Promoting Civic Understanding and Civic Skills through Conceptually Based Curricula," in *Moral, Character, and Civic Education in the Elementary School*. J. Benninga, ed. New York: Teachers College Press.

Lickona, T. 1991. *Educating for Character: Teaching Respect and Responsibility in the Schools.* New York: Bantam, pp.3–5, 20–22, 53, 67–70.

Lickona, T. 1993a. "The Return of Character Education," *Educational Leadership* 5(3): 6–11.

Lickona, T. 1993b. "Where Sex Education Went Wrong," *Educational Leadership* 51(3): 84–89.

Lickona, T. 1994. "Directive Sex Education is Our Best Hope," *Educational Leadership* 52(2): 76–78.

Lickona, T. 1998. "Character Education: Seven Crucial Issues." *Action in Teacher Education Journal of the Association of Teacher Educators* 20(4): 77–84.

Lickona, Thomas. 2000. "Character-Based Sexuality Education: Bringing Parents into the Picture." *Educational Leadership* 58(2): 60–64.

London, J. 1987. "Character Education and Clinical Intervention: A Paradigm Shift for U.S. Schools," *Phi Delta Kappan* 68(9): 667–673

MacIntyre, A. 1981. *After Virtue.* Notre Dame: Univ. of Notre Dame Press.

McCarthy, B. 1983. *4-MAT in Action* Oak Brook, IL: EXCEL, Inc.

McClellan, B.E. 1992. *Schools and the Shaping of Character: Moral Education in America, 1607–Present.* Bloomington, IN: ERIC Clearinghouse for Social Studies.

McClellan, M. C. 1987. "Teenage pregnancy." *Phi Delta Kappan* 68(10): 789–792.

McDaniel, T. 1989. "The Discipline Debate: A Road Through the Thicket," *Educational Leadership*, March, 1989: 81–82.

McDonnell. 1999. Foreword in *Building Character in Schools: Practical Ways to Bring Moral Instruction to Life.* San Francisco: Jossey-Bass Publisher.

McKeon, R. 1941. *The Basic Works of Aristotle.* New York: Random House.

McKown, Harry. 1935. *Character Education.* New York: McGraw-Hill.

Males, M. 1993. "Schools, Society and 'Teen' Pregnancy," *Phi Delta Kappan* 74(7): 566–568.

Medical Institute for Sexual Health. 1996. *National Guidelines for Sexuality and Character Education.* Austin, TX: MISH.

Mendler, A. 1988. *Discipline with Dignity* Alexandria, VA: ASCD.

Mendler, A. 1992. *What Do I Do When.. How to Achieve Discipline with Dignity in the Classroom.* Bloomington, IN: National Educational Service.

Mendler, A. 1993. "Discipline with Dignity in the Classroom: Seven Principles," *The Educational Digest* 58(7): 4–10.

Milson, Andrew. 2000. Creating a Curriculum for Character Development: A Case Study. *The Clearing House* 74(2): 89–95.

Molnar, A. 1990. "Judging the Ethics of Ethics Education," *Educational Leadership* 48(3): 73–74.

Murphy, M. 1991. "Models of Moral Education That Work: Values Education Programs in the U.S. Department of Education Award Winning Schools" *Association of Moral Education Annual Conference*, Atlanta, GA.

Murphy, M. 1995a. "Character Education Programs in the U.S. Department of Education Blue Ribbon Schools." *Character Education Partnership 2nd Annual Forum.* Washington, DC.

Murphy, M. 1995b. "Character Education Programs in the U.S. Department of Education Blue Ribbon Schools." *Character Educator* 1(3): 1–7.

Murphy, M. 1995c. "Good Discipline Programs Create Safe Schools and Help Develop Character." *Illinois School Research and Development Journal* 32(1): 3–6.

Murphy, M. 1996. "Character Education Programs in the U.S. Blue Ribbon Schools." *National Character Education Conference*. St. Louis, MO.

Murphy, M. 1998a. "Character Education in America's Blue Ribbon Schools." *Philosophy of Education Annual Meeting*. Boston, MA.

Murphy, M. 1998b. "Six Components of Effective Character Education Schools as found in the Blue Ribbon Schools." *Character Education Partnership Annual Forum*. Denver, CO.

Murphy, M. 1998c. "Character Education Ideas from America's Blue Ribbon Schools." *Summer Institute in Character Education,* SUNY Cortland, New York.

Murphy, M. 2001. "Three Essential Components of Character Development" in *Una voz diferente de educacion moral*, Naval, C. ed. EUNSA, Pamplona, Spain.

National Association of Christian Educators/Citizens for Excellence in Education. 1996a. *Duso & Pumsy*. Special Report #19. Costa Mesa, CA: NACE/CEE.

National Association of Christian Educators/Citizens for Excellence in Education. 1996b. *Affective Education* Special Report #18. Costa Mesa, CA: NACE/CEE.

National Association of Christian Educators/Citizens for Excellence in Education. 1996c. "Creating Healthy Self-Esteem in Children." Costa Mesa, CA: NACE/CEE.

National Association of Elementary School Principals. 1994. *Best Ideas from America's Blue Ribbon Schools*. Thousand Oaks, CA: Corwin Press.

National Association of Elementary School Principals. 1995 *Best Ideas from America's Blue Ribbon Schools*. Vol. 2. Thousand Oaks, CA: Corwin Press.

National Commission on Excellence in Education. 1983. *A Nation at Risk: The Imperative for Educational Reform*. Washington, DC.: U.S. Government Printing Office. April, 1983.

National Diffusion Network. 1993. *Educational Programs That Work* Colorado: Sopris West, Inc.

National Education Association 1895. *The Report of the National Education Association Committee of Fifteen.* As cited in W. Bennett. *First Lessons: A Report on Elementary Education in America.* 1996. Washington, DC.: U.S. Government Printing Office, p. 56.

Nielsen, Lynn. 1998. New Study Shows States Returning to Character Education. *Character Educator* 6(3):1–3.

Nielsen Jones, E., K. Ryan, et al. 1998. "Character Education and Teacher Education." *Action in Teacher Education: Journal of the Association of Teacher Educators* 20(4): 11–28

Nelsen, J. 1987. *Positive Discipline*. New York: Ballantine Books.

Noblit, G., D. Rogers, and B. McCadden. 1995. "In the Meantime The Possibilities of Caring." *Phi Delta Kappan* 76(9): 680–685.

Nucci, L. 1987. "Synthesis of Research on Moral Development." *Educational Leadership* 44(5): 86–92.

Nucci, L. 1989. "Challenging Conventional Wisdom About Morality: The Domain Approach to Values Education," in *Moral Development and Character Education: A Dialogue*. Berkeley, CA: McCutchan Publishing Corp.

Nucci, L., ed. 1989. *Moral Development and Character Education: A Dialogue*. Berkeley, CA: McCutchan Publishing Corp.

Nucci, L. 1991. "Doing Justice to Morality in Contemporary Values Education." In J. Benninga, ed. *Moral, Character and Civic Education in the Elementary School*. New York: Teachers College Press.

Nucci, L. 2001. *Education in the Moral Domain*. Cambridge: Cambridge University Press.

Ogden, E., and V. Germinarion. 1994. *The Nation's Best Schools: Blueprints for Excellence, Volume 1: Elementary and Middle Schools* Lancaster, PA: Technomics.

Ornstein, A., and F. Hunkins. 1988. *Curriculum: Foundations, Principles, and Issues*. NJ: Prentice Hall, p 6–8, 305–311.

Paul, R.W. 1990. *Critical Thinking*. Rohnert Park, CA: Sonoma State University, Center for Critical Thinking and Moral Critique.

Pereira, C. 1988. "Educating for Citizenship in the Elementary Grades." *Phi Delta Kappan* 69(5): 429–431.

Pereira, C. 1991. "Educating for Citizenship in the Early Grades." In *Moral, Character, and Civic Education in the Elementary School*. J. Benninga, ed. New York: Teachers College Press.

Pietig, J. 1977. "John Dewey and Character Education." *Journal of Moral Education* 6(3): 170–180.

Pilon, G. 1988. *Workshop Way*. New Orleans: The Workshop Way, Inc.

Plato. 1949. *Meno*. Translated by Benjamin Jowett. New York: Macmillan Publishing Co.

Power, C., A. Higgins, and L. Kohlberg. 1989. "The Habit of the Common Life: Building Character Through Democratic Community Schools" In *Moral Development and Character Education*. L. Nucci, ed. CA: McCutchan Publishing Corporation.

Quain, P., Jr. 1977. "Affective Education, Teacher Training for Affective Education: Change in Self-Concept and Affectivity in Kindergarten Children (Doctoral dissertation, St. Louis University, 1976.) *Dissertation Abstracts International* 37, 7604A.

Quest International. 1991. "Analysis of Lions-Quest's Skills for Adolescence Program in Detroit Schools Using School Records, School Attitude Measures, and California Achievement Test Data." Quest International Research and Evaluation Department.

Quigley, C., and C. Bahmueller, eds. 1991. *Civitas: A Framework for Civic Education*. Calabasas, CA: National Center for Civic Education.

Quigley, C. 1996. Cited in "The Role of Civic Education." Washington, D.C.: The Communitarian Network.

Raths, L., M. Harmin, and S. Simon. 1966. *Values and Teaching*. Ohio: Charles Merrill Publishing Co.

Reimer, J., D.P. Paolitto, and R.H. Hersh. 1983. *Promoting Moral Growth: From Piaget to Kohlberg*. Prospect Heights, IL: Waveland Press.

Reische, D. 1987. *Citizenship Goal of Education*. Arlington, VA: American Association of School Administrators.

Render, G., J. Padilla, and M. Krank. 1989. "Assertive Discipline: A Critical Review and Analysis." *Teachers College Record* 90(4): 607–627.

Rich, D. 1991. "Parents Can Teach MegaSkills to their Children." *Educational Leadership* 49(1): 42.

Riley, R. 1995. Forward to *Best Ideas from Americans Blue Ribbon Schools,* Vol. 2, by National Association of Elementary School Principals. CA: Corwin Press.

Robbins, P. 1990. "Implementing Whole Language, *Educational Leadership*, 47(60): 50–51.

Rose, L., A. Gallup, and S. Elam. 1997. "The 29th Annual Phi Delta Kappa/Gallup Poll of the Public's Attitudes Toward the Public Schools" *Phi Delta Kappan* 79(1): 41–56.

Rose, L., and A. Gallup. 1998. "The 30th Annual Phi Delta Kappa/Gallup Poll of the Public's Attitudes Toward the Public Schools" *Phi Delta Kappan* 80(1): 41–58.

Rose, L., and A. Gallup. 1999. "The 31st Annual Phi Delta Kappa/Gallup Poll of the Public's Attitudes Toward the Public Schools." *Phi Delta Kappan* 81(1): 41–56.

Rose, L., and A. Gallup. 2000. "The 32nd Annual Phi Delta Kappa/Gallup Poll of the Public's Attitudes Toward the Public Schools." *Phi Delta Kappan* 82(1): 41–58.

Rose, L., and A. Gallup. 2001. "The 33rd Annual Phi Delta Kappa/Gallup Poll of the Public's Attitudes Toward the Public Schools." *Phi Delta Kappan* 82(1): 41–58

Rosenbaum, Dennis, and Gordon Hanson. 1998. "Assessing the Effects of School-Based Drug Education A Six-Year Multilevel Analysis of Project D.A.R.E." *Journal of Reserach in Crime and Delinquency* 35(4): 381–412.

Rosenblatt, R. 1995. "Who'll Teach Kids Right from Wrong?" *New York Times Magazine*, April 30, 1995: 36–65.

Rowe, J. 1990. "To Develop Thinking Citizens." *Educational Leadership* 48(3): 43–45.

Rushton. J., C. Brainerd, and M. Pressley. 1983. "Behavioral Development and Construct Validity: The Principle of Aggregation." *Psychological Bulletin* 94(1): 18–38.

Ryan, K. 1981. *Questions and Answers on Moral Education*. PDK Fastback 153, Bloomington IN: Phi Delta Kappa.

Ryan, K. 1993. "Mining the Values in the Curriculum." *Educational Leadership*, November 1993.

Ryan, and Bohlin. 1999. *Building Character in Schools: Practical Ways to Bring Moral Instruction to Life*. San Francisco: Jossey-Bass Publisher.

Sadowsky, E. 1991. "Democracy in the Elementary School: Learn by Doing." In *Civitas: A Framework for Civic Education*. Charles F. Bahmueller, ed. Calabasas, CA: National Center for Civic Education.

Saterlie, M.E. 1988. "Developing a Community Consensus for Teaching Values." *Educational Leadership* 45(8): 44–47.

Schlaflly, P. 1984. *Child Abuse in the Classroom*. Westchester, IL: Crossroads Publisher.

Schaps, E., V. Battistich, et al. 1997. "School as a caring Community: A Key to Character Education." In *The Construction of Children's Character: Ninety-sixth Yearbook of the National Society for the Study of Education*. A. Molnar, ed. Chicago, University of Chicago Press. IL: 127–139.

Schubert, W. 1986. *Curriculum: Perspective, Paradigm, and Possibility*. New York: Macmillian.

Schultz, F., ed. 1995. "Managing Life in Classroom." In *Education: Annual Editions 95/96*. Guildord, CT: Duskin.

Scriven, M. 1973. "The Methodology of Evaluation." In *Educational Evaluation: Theory and Practice*. B.R. Worthen & J.R. Sanders, ed. Belmont, CA: Wadsworth.

Slavin, R. 1990. *Cooperative Learning: Theory, Research, and Practice.* Boston, MA: Allyn and Bacon.

Slavin, R. 1991. "Synthesis of Research on Cooperative Learning." *Educational Leadership* 48(5): 71–82.

Smith, D., L. McCormick, A. Steckler, and K. McLeroy. 1993. "Teachers' Use of Health Curricula: Implementation of Growing Healthy, Project SMART and the Teenage Health Teaching Modules." *Journal of School Health* 63(8): 349–354.

Snart, F., and T. Maguire. 1987. "Effectiveness of the Kids on the Block Puppets: An Examination." *B.C. Journal of Special Education* 11(1): 9–16.

Solomon, D., Battistich, V., Watson, M., Schaps, E., and Lewis, C. 2000. "A Six-District Study of Educational Change: Direct and Mediated Effects of the Child Development Project." *Social Psychology of Education* 4: 3–51.

Sparks, R. 1991. "Character Development at Fort Washington Elementary School." In *Moral, Character, and Civic Education.* J.S. Benninga, ed. New York: Teachers College Press.

Stacey, S., and J.O. Rust. 1985. "Evaluating the Effectiveness of the DUSO-1 (Revised) Program." *Elementary School Guidance and Counseling* 20: 84–90.

Stomfay-Stitz, A. 1993. *Peace Education in America 1828–1990.* Metuchen, NH: Scarecrow Press.

Stomfay-Stitz, A. 1994. "Conflict Resolution and Peer Mediation Pathways to Safer Schools." *Childhood Education* 70(5): 279–282.

Sylvester, R. 1994. "How Emotions Affect Learning." *Educational Leadership* 52(2): 60–65.

Texeira, E. 1995. "Study Assails School-Based Drug Programs." *Los Angeles Times*, Oct. 21, 1995 [On-line] Available URL: turnpike.net/~jnr/dareinef.htm

Tom, A. R. 1984. *Teaching as a Moral Craft.* New York: Longman.

Traiger, J. 1995. "The Time is Now: Reflections on Moral Education," *Education* 115(3): 432–434.

Travis, M.P. 1985. *Student Moral Development in the Catholic Schools.* Washington, DC.: National Catholic Educational Association.

Tyler, R., 1949. *Basic Principles of Curriculum and Evaluation.* Chicago, IL: University of Chicago Press.

Ullman, Jodie, Judith Stein, and Richard Dukes. 2000. "Evaluation of D.A.R.E. (Drug Abuse Resistance Education) With Latent Variables in the Context of a Solomon Four Group Testing." In *Multivariate Applications in Substance Use Research: New Methods for New Questions*, J. Rose, and L. Chassin, eds. Mahwah, NJ: Lawrence Erlbaum.

U.S. Department of Education. 1996. "Partnerships in Character Education Pilot Project" *Elementary and Secondary Education Act: Section 10103* [On-line]: URL: www.ed.gov/offices/OERI/charactr.html.

United States Department of Education. 1987. *What Works: Research About Teaching and Learning.* 2nd ed. Pueblo, CO: USDE.

U.S. Department of Education. 1988. *Drug Prevention Curricula: A Guide to Selection and Implementation.* Washington, DC.

U.S. Department of Education. 1989. *What Works: Schools Without Drugs.* Washington, DC.

U.S. Department of Education. 1991. *America 2000 An Education Strategy: Sourcebook.* Washington, DC.

U.S. Department of Education. 1993. *Application for 1993–94 Elementary Blue Ribbon Schools Program.* Washington, DC.

U.S. Department of Education. 1993. *Reaching the Goals. Goal 6: Safe, Disciplined and Drug Free Schools.* Washington, DC: Office of Educational Research and Improvement.

U.S. Department of Education. 1994. *Application for Elementary School Recognition Program.* Washington, DC: U.S. Department of Education.

U.S. Department of Education, 1999. *Blue Ribbon Schools—Character Education.* Web site: www.ed.gov/offices/OERI/BlueRibbonSchools/frames/charactered.html.

U.S. Department of Education, 1999. *Making the Grade: A Guide to School Drug Prevention Programs.* Washington, DC.

U.S. Department of Health and Human Services. 1990. *Third Triennial Report to Congress: Drug Abuse and Drug Abuse Research.* Washington, DC.: Department of Health and Human Services.

Vail, H. 1909. *McGuffey's Eclectic Primer, Revised Edition.* New York: Van Nostrand Reinhold.

Valett, R. 1991. "Teaching Peace and Conflict Resolution." In *Moral, Character, and Civic Education in the Elementary School.* J. Benninga, ed. New York: Teachers College Press.

Van Ness, R. 1995. *Raising Self-Esteem of Learners.* Bloomington, IN: Phi Delta Kappa Education Foundation.

Vessels, Gordon G. 1998. *Character and Community Development: A School Planning and Teacher Training Handbook.* Westport, CT: Praeger Publishers.

Vincent, P.F. 1994. *A Primer: Developing Character in Students.* Chapel Hill, NC: New View Publications.

Wakefield, D.V. 1996. "Moral Education Methods Survey Results." Baylor University, March 16, 1996: 1–4.

Walberg, H., and E. Wynne. 1989. "Character Education: Toward a Preliminary Consensus." In *Moral Development and Character Education: A Dialogue.* L. Nucci, ed. Berkeley, CA: McCutchan Publishing.

Walsh, T. 1993. "Drug Abuse Education Information and Research: Review of Existing DARE Evaluations." [On-line] Available URL: hyperreal.com/drug/politics/dare/dare.evaluations.

Watchman Expositor. 1996. "New Age Drug Education Programs." [On-line] Available URL: rampages.onramp.net/~watchma/drugs.htm

Watson, M., D. Solomon, V. Battistich, E. Schaps, and J. Solomon. 1989. "The Child Development Projects: Combining Traditional and Developmental Approaches to Values Education" *In Moral Development and Character Education.* L. Nucci, ed. Richmond, CA: McCutchan Publishing.

Wheelock, A. 1999. "Junior Great Books: Reading for Meaning in Urban Schools." *Educational Leadership* 57(2): 47–50.

Wiley, Lori Sanford. 1998. *Comprehensive Character-Building Classroom: A Handbook for Teachers*. De Bary, FL: Longwood Communications.

Wood, G. 1990. "Teaching for Democracy," *Educational Leadership* 4(3): 32–37.

Worthen, B., and J. R. Sanders. 1987. *Educational Evaluation*. New York: Longman.

Wynne, E., and Walberg, H. 1985. "The Complimentary Goals of Character Development and Academic Excellence." *Educational Leadership* 43(4): 15–18.

Wynne, E. and H. Walberg, eds. 1989. "Character Education: Toward a Preliminary Consensus" in *Moral Development and Character Education: A Dialogue*. Berkeley, CA: McCutchan Publishing Corp.

Wynne, E. 1989. "Transmitting Traditional Values in Contemporary Society." In *Moral Development and Character Education: A Dialogue*. L. Nucci, ed. Berkeley, CA: McCuthan.

Wynne, E., and K. Ryan. 1993. *Reclaiming Our Schools*. New York: Macmillan.

Index

About the Author

Dr. Madonna Murphy is Professor of Education at the University of St. Francis. She teaches history and philosophy of education, and character education for teachers to both graduate and undergraduate students. She published the first edition of this book *Character Education in America's Blue Ribbon Schools* in 1998. She is director of the Center for Character Education at the University of St. Francis. She serves as the character education consultant for a series of character education books for elementary school children published by Capstone Press. Professor Murphy has presented her research on the Blue Ribbon Schools at the American Educational Research Association, the Character Education Partnership Forum, the Association for Moral Education's Annual meeting, the National Character Education Conference, and at the Summer Institute on Character Education in Cortland, New York. She has conducted several in-services at schools interested in beginning character education programs.

Dr. Murphy received her Ph.D. in education and M.Ed. from Loyola University, Chicago, and her B.A. in philosophy from the University of Chicago. She has taught at the elementary, high school, and college level. For the past twenty years, she has taught philosophy, ethics, and character education to college students. She is a member of the Character Education Partnership, the Association of Moral Educators, Association for Supervision and Curriculum Development, and Phi Delta Kappa. She has served on a national committee recognizing K–12 schools for their character education and a national committee for promoting character education in teacher education institutions.